◆**ALTERNATIVES** *is a series under the general editorship of* Eric S. Rabkin, Martin H. Greenberg, and Joseph D. Olander *which has been established to serve the growing critical audience of science fiction, fantastic fiction, and speculative fiction.*

Other titles from the Eaton Conference are:
Bridges to Science Fiction, edited by George E. Slusser, George R. Guffey, and Mark Rose, 1980
Bridges to Fantasy, edited by George E. Slusser, Eric S. Rabkin, and Robert Scholes, 1982
Coordinates: Placing Science Fiction and Fantasy, edited by George E. Slusser, Eric S. Rabkin, and Robert Scholes, 1983
Shadows of the Magic Lamp: Fantasy and Science Fiction in Film, edited by George E. Slusser and Eric S. Rabkin, 1985
Hard Science Fiction, edited by George E. Slusser and Eric S. Rabkin, 1986
Storm Warnings: Science Fiction Confronts the Future, edited by George E. Slusser, Colin Greenland, and Eric S. Rabkin, 1987

INTERSECTIONS
FANTASY AND SCIENCE
FICTION

Edited by
George E. Slusser
and
Eric S. Rabkin

Southern Illinois University Press
Carbondale and Edwardsville

Copyright © 1987 by the Board of Trustees,
Southern Illinois University
All rights reserved
Printed in the United States of America
Edited by Stephen Kennett
Designed by Quentin Fiore
Production supervised by Natalia Nadraga

90   89   88   87   4   3   2   1

Library of Congress Cataloging-in-Publication Data

Intersections: fantasy and science fiction

(Alternatives)
Essays presented at the Seventh Eaton
Conference, held April 12–14, 1985, at the University
of California, Riverside.
Bibliography: p.
Includes index.
1. Science fiction—Congresses. 2. Fantastic
fiction—Congresses. I. Slusser, George Edgar.
II. Rabkin, Eric S. III. Eaton Conference on Science
Fiction and Fantasy Literature (7th : 1985 : University
of California, Riverside) IV. University of
California, Riverside. V. Series.
PN3433.2.I58   1987   809.3'876   87-9508
ISBN 0-8093-1374-X

Contents

Part 2
Gestations

Part 3
Fields

Introduction: Toward a Theory
of Interaction

As late as 1938, Mikhail Bakhtin could state that "as of today genre theory has added nothing substantial to what Aristotle has already done." Whatever the state of genre theory, the present nature of literary forms reveals a pressing need to go beyond Aristotle. The form we are considering here, fantasy and science fiction, is ample proof of this need. We can attribute to Aristotle three major "modes of imitation," or representation: lyrical, epic and dramatic poetry. What we have today, however, are more modes of presentation: prose fiction, film, comic strips. How do we deal with them? And how do we deal with the compound forms that operate within, and across, these systems of presentation, forms such as fantasy and science fiction? SF is already a compound of two kinds of discourse: science and fiction. And when it is connected with fantasy, a whole group of forms, potential or otherwise, arise from the interaction: the uncanny, marvelous, horror, romance, mystery.

Fantasy and science fiction, then, appear to exist at the center of the generic field today. Our question, however, is this: for this field, is there a whole present before its parts, or do the parts come before a whole? In other words, is field analysis a matter of division into parts, or of the integration of parts to form various wholes? Aristotle believes he knows the whole: literature, poetry. But what if the whole is nothing more than the product of the interaction of various, and varying, parts? This is the subject of this book: seventeen essays that focus on the structural and generic nature of fantasy and science fiction, and beyond that on the question of interaction itself.

In his recent book, *Introduction à l'architexte*, Gérard Genette senses the need for a general theory, not of genres, but of interactions. For what exactly is an "architext"? Is it (pardon the pun) an *architexture*, a structure of interacting forms that goes beyond the grids and triangles and "rose windows" of traditional genre theory to integrate, as stresses and supports, extraliterary or "transcendental" elements as well? Or is it rather some generative structure—*archi-* as "first" or *Ur-* form: an edifice of forms this time gestated out of dynamic interaction between various contexts and the literary system? Or is it something else again? In the first and second types of architext, we preserve a distinction between vertical and horizontal directions. But what of a third type that centers its emphasis on the intersection between these as coordinates, in other words, a field theory of literary interactions, focusing neither on the nature of forms in themselves, nor on their discrimination, but on conjunctions and configurations, on the shaping of architextual space itself?

In the essays in this volume, all three of models have been used. The papers in the first section, "Discriminations," approach the interactive compound fantasy and science fiction in an essentially analytical manner. They seek, to use Robert Scholes's term, to boil down the roses. In the lead essay Scholes examines the nature of that strange-seeming hybrid, science fantasy. Joseph Miller, focusing on the scientific concept of parallel universes, seeks to distinguish the interactive form or forms that might thematically embody it: fantasy or SF. Michael McClintock makes further "discriminations" between fantasy and science fiction, but implies by his qualifier "some" that he cannot exhaust the shapes arising from this interaction. Timothy Bagwell and Michael Collings both seek to broaden the interconnective base of the fantasy and science fiction structure— Bagwell by examining the interaction of these to a third category, realism; Collings by studying their relation to horror. Finally, Roger Zelazny discusses the complex and intimate interrelation of fantasy and SF in his own writing. In doing so, he warns us, tacitly, of the difficulty of erecting these edifices of discrimination.

Essays in the second section, "Gestations," examine the connection between fantasy and science fiction in terms of genesis rather than analysis. Writer-critic Samuel R. Delany describes the gestation of these genres as forms developing from one to the other under pressures of the marketplace and its capacity to mark texts, and thereby connect them to the dynamics of readership. Michael Holquist, in like manner, considers the genesis of SF in the Soviet Union out of a sense of science itself developing in a context he calls literary—a form of utopian fantasy. The papers that follow focus on the genesis of specific forms. Kathleen Spencer traces the rise of the "urban gothic"—still a component of SF—out of the interaction of real and fantastic in Victorian England. Michael Clifton seeks the genesis of what Scholes calls science fantasy in vision-inducing experiments and the rise of computerized technology. David Leiby sees time travel, a common element in fantasy and science fiction, coming from sources in contemporary speculation on the nature of time. And finally, Frank McConnell takes fantasy, science fiction, and fiction itself, back to the archi- or *Ur*-text of the joke. In doing so, he hopes to define the basic frames of the edifice of storytelling in general.

By moving from primary forms to present-day metamorphoses of those forms in comic strips like *Garfield*, McConnell provides the transition from genesis to synthesis, to the series of essays that comprise the third section, "Fields." George Slusser, examining the function of the "and" in fantasy and science fiction and other fantasy compounds, attempts to give a topology of modern forms—the shape of the field. The following essays target more specific examples of synthetic permutations within this field: Celeste Pernicone that of fantasy and horror; Brian Attebery, that of science fantasy and myth; and Kathryn Hume, the extended field of SF, fantasy, and mythology. In the concluding essay, David Clayton argues, in theoretical terms, that traditional genre theory, embracing the interactive field of forms vaguely grouped as SF, itself turns in circles: closed structures instead of the open, interconnective ones it purports to describe. If we are to map the complex configurations of fantasy and science fiction, we will have to break these circles.

All essays in this volume are original, and all were presented at the seventh Eaton Conference, held April 12–14, 1985, at the University of California, Riverside. Guests of honor at this conference were: Robert Scholes, Samuel R. Delany, and Roger Zelazny. The conference organizers wish to thank them for their participation and interest. They also wish to thank all those who helped and supported this conference: Frank McConnell of the University of California, Santa Barbara, for ideas and inspiration; Jean-Pierre Barricelli, the patron saint of the Eaton Conference; Dean David Warren,

Librarian John Tanno, and Peter Briscoe, Collection Development Officer, all of whom have kept the Eaton collection alive in thick and thin. Thanks to all these people, and their firm support over the years, the Eaton is no longer a conference but an institution.

Riverside, California
George E. Slusser
Eric S. Rabkin

Part 1
Discriminations

Boiling Roses: Thoughts on Science Fantasy

Robert Scholes

I say again, if I cannot draw a horse, I will not write THIS IS A HORSE under what I foolishly meant for one. Any key to a work of imagination would be nearly if not quite, as absurd. The tale is there, not to hide, but to show: if it shows nothing at your window, do not open your door to it; leave it out in the cold. To ask me to explain, is to say, "Roses! Boil them, or we won't have them!" My tales may not be roses, but I will not boil them.

—George MacDonald, *A Dish of Orts*

The first version, that of 1926 I believe: a carefully drawn pipe, and underneath it (handwritten in a steady, painstaking, artificial script, a script from the convent, like that found heading the notebooks of schoolboys, or on a blackboard after a lesson on things), this note: "This is not a pipe."
The other version . . . . The same pipe, same statement, same handwriting. But . . . the text and the figure are set within a frame. The frame itself is placed upon an easel, and the latter in turn upon the clearly visible slats of the floor. Above everything, a pipe exactly like the one in the picture but much larger.

—Michel Foucault, *This Is Not a Pipe*

My epigraphs are linked by their employment of a similar concept: a representation, an image, well or ill drawn, with a verbal caption that asserts or denies some linkage between the image and a category of reality. I find it interesting that the Victorian fantasist and the modern surrealist should hit upon the same formula for problematizing the questions of reference and representation. Their differences are also instructive. The fantasist is mainly concerned with how to achieve the power of illusion, to generate authenticity for his illusion. The surrealist, on the other hand, progresses from questioning the

3

status of images as illusions to questioning the status of reality itself. The fantasist, as we shall see, wants to create a second nature, a second culture, while the surrealist wants to deny the first nature, the first culture. In literature the Alice books of Charles Dodgson are dominated by a surrealist impulse. *The Lord of the Rings*, on the other hand, is a work of fantasy. I consider it an error for that admirable theoretician, Eric Rabkin, to have founded a theory of fantasy upon what I would call surrealism, just as I consider it an error for that perhaps even more admirable theoretician, Tzvetan Todorov, to have appropriated the word fantasy for what most of us would call the uncanny. Theoreticians, no matter how admirable, are often wrong, it would seem, but this is not their fault, it is their trade, their *métier*, to be wrong so as to set the rest of us thinking about what might be right.

Having established myself as a non-theoretician, I shall now proceed to theorize, boiling a few roses of my own. It is asserted on all sides that fantasy is flourishing and that a new genre, designated "science fantasy," has begun to dominate that segment of the literary field loosely called SF. There is certainly enough plausibility to these claims to make them worth investigating.

In my tireless quest for truth and beauty—conducted under the strange device of "literary criticism"—I have been willing to go anywhere—even to fly over mountains, to cross the deadly desert, seeking the emerald city of Riverside—to listen to anyone—physicists from Irvine, fantasists from Idaho, even polymorphous polymaths from the Big Apple—and to read anything—even the dust jackets of science fantasy novels. You shudder with horror, no doubt, at my willingness to sink to such depths, but I can say in truth that on countless occasions the perusal of such ephemeral prose has spared me hours of anguish that I should have endured had I ventured beyond the jacket into the chaotic maunderings enclosed therein. In my experience at least half the time one does best to violate all proverbs, sayings, and other repositories of gnomic wisdom. Often one can, should, and does judge a book by its cover.

In this case, however, we are not judging a book but discussing an apparently curious and unnatural phenomenon: an oxymoronic monster named science fantasy. A few lines from the land of blurbs and blushes will serve to launch us on our mission: which is nothing other than an attempt to determine the status—real or imaginary—of this purported creature. Here are the magic words: "a stunning blend of the lyric extravagance of fantasy and the keen edge of science fiction, meeting in a future so distant that it seems like the ancient past" (from the jacket of Gene Wolfe's *Shadow of the Torturer*, 1980). In its stunning blend of confidence and vagueness this blurb might serve as cover for many works of science fantasy. If we don't look at it too closely, it even seems an accurate description of what we may find inside the book itself. These particular words served as a pitch for Gene Wolfe's *Shadow of the Torturer*, the first volume of his *Book of the New Sun*, but they would be no less (and no more) appropriate for Samuel Delany's *Nevèrÿon* books and for many others.

If by "lyric extravagance" we mean language spinning discourse out of itself, words flowing from previous words, sounds echoing sounds, textuality rampant, semiosis unlimited, narrativity unbounded—well then, yes, these works are indeed characterized by "lyric extravagance," or "extra-vagance" as Thoreau liked to think of it. They are in principle interminable, affecting closure rather than effecting it. But what is the "keen edge of science fiction?" Obviously, it is meant to contrast with lyric extravagance on the principle of center and circumference or hard and soft—in some way to suggest by naming the extremes that everything has been included here.

Science fiction is described as hard and sharp—in contrast with the soft and shapeless lyric extravagance of fantasy. Science fantasy, then, is by definition an impossible object, hard and soft, pointed and uncircumscribed: a monstrosity. Yet it is said to exist. The existence of strange objects implies the strangeness of the world in which they exist. "Toto, I don't think we're in Kansas anymore," says Dorothy in the film version of *The Wizard of Oz*, when the door of her hovel swings open upon a gang of Hollywood midgets in technicolor. And she's right. She's in California, the land of magical transportations and transformations.

But we are straying from our text. That blurby quotation concludes by asserting that Wolfe's narrative is set "in a future so distant that it seems like the ancient past." The assumptions behind this phrase are interesting. A whole theory of history is implicated in the syntactic structure governed by two little words: *so* and *that*. So far into the future that it resembles the ancient past. A notion of history as a cyclical pattern of possibilities presides over this utterance. At some point down the linear path of history the scenery and decor will become familiar and humanity will be found organized in ways that are recognizable to us from the period of Western history extending from the Egyptian empire to the later middle ages. Faced with this pattern, which occurs in book after book, we are driven to ask certain questions. One which fascinates me is, "Why not extend the cyclical future just a bit further until we reach the moment that resembles our own present time?" What would a science fantasy set "in a future so distant that it seems like the present" actually be like? *Gravity's Rainbow? The Public Burning?* Such works certainly have their fantastic dimensions, but they present themselves as versions of our world rather than as other worlds. Whereas, I shall be arguing, fantasy became a full fledged modern genre only when it took as its central principle the construction of other worlds than ours. One question that needs to be answered, however, about the genres of fantasy and science fantasy, is why the worlds they present seem always to bear some resemblance to our own ancient past.

This is by no means a simple question, nor can it be answered in a few words, but I would like to offer a hypothesis. Whole worlds inhabited by sentient creatures take dimensions of development that no mind can encompass. No writer can invent a world. Thus, every fictional world must borrow more than can be invented by its author. An understanding of human history enables a writer to think of one facet of a fictional world—say combat with swords—and many other social, economic, and physical situations make themselves available as being culturally compatible with the chosen feature. Habits of information—what Umberto Eco calls our "encyclopedia"—come to the aid of the fictional imagination, which could not function without them.

Thus, the past is always present in the future of fantastic imagining. Why this past is so often a quasi-medieval one is a second question that we should consider. I believe that the medieval past dominates fantasy for a number of reasons. One obvious reason is that it presents a world in which magic fits comfortably, a world in which science had not yet made magic fantastic. A second reason is that fantasy has powerful generic links with both fairy tales and medieval romances. A third reason is ethical. Fantasy, until very recently, has always offered us a Manichean world, in which values are polarized by absolutes of good and evil, a world especially compatible with the mixture of pagan and Christian beliefs prevalent in Europe in the Middle Ages. Fictions grounded in such a matrix regularly present ultimate good and ultimate evil embodied in the fictional characters of the text. It is this feature of modern fantasy more than any other that makes it anachronistic in our time. But we are getting prochronistic ourselves, and must turn to more basic questions of definition. If we are going to talk about science fantasy, we must at least consider the notions of science and fantasy themselves.

I do not believe that there are entities out there for which *fantasy* and *science* are simply the proper names. If we are going to discuss these notions we shall have to begin by looking at the words themselves, rather than by trying to describe any changeless thing that might be named by such words. Let us begin with *fantasy*.

This word has deep roots in ancient Greek culture. All of its modern meanings can be traced to these roots. Our present spelling of the word is based upon its Romanized transliteration. In Greek its initial letter is *phi*. The Greek word *phantasía* is derived from the adjective *phanós* (meaning light or bright), the noun *phanós* (meaning torch), and the verb *phaíno* (which means "bring to light" in the active and "come to light" or "appear" in the passive). The standard term in Greek philosophy for things that appear to the senses is *phainómena*, the neuter plural participial form of the verb *phaíno*. The Greek word *phantasía* is thus very closely related to *phainómena*. A *phainómenon* is a thing insofar as it appears to us. *Phainómena* are the visible or apprehendable aspects of things. A *phantasía*, on the other hand, is a mental image, perhaps our recollection of the appearance of a thing, perhaps drawn from some other source. In Aristotelian thought, the word *phantasía* also names the faculty by which things are imaged or imagined to be present. The word can also refer to a poet's ability to suggest the presence of things through images. Because this word was tied to appearances and imaginings it was frequently used to refer to instances of imagination unaccompanied by presence: for hallucination, for exaggeration, for inauthenticity. If we can imagine the fortunes of this word in Greek history, we must see it as gradually being pushed from its connection with light, in which things may be seen as they actually are, to a more marginal position, pushed out by its opposition (in Aristotelian thought especially) to other words like *doxa, episteme, nous, dianoia*.

Its English cognates are *fancy* and *feign*. The English word *phenomenon* keeps its distance from fantasy by retaining a remnant of Greek spelling, the *phi* that justifies our use of *ph* in place of *f*. In the world of positive science, fantasy is Cinderella. But where is the prince in such a world?

The word *science* has another history altogether. The modern word has a clear pedigree going back to Latin, where it appears as *sciens* (knowing), the past participle of *scire* (to know or know how to). This word and its close relative *sciscere* (to investigate, inquire) with its participle *scitus* (clever) delineate clearly the path that the word science will follow: science as knowledge and science as technique or technology. In the medieval world God's knowledge could be called science. After Bacon and Newton the word came gradually to apply only to knowledge acquired by approved methods within an institutionally guaranteed empirical paradigm. Thus, for a thousand years and more, science has meant the best knowledge, the highest learning, by whatever standards were in place at the time. A lucky word, to have kept what our blurb-writer called its "keen edge." But why has the word no history before Rome? Why did it appear amid the grandeur of empire and technology rather than as a centerpiece in the glories of Greek art and—well—science?

The Greeks had plenty of words for knowledge, one of which, *gnosis*, gave Latin *cognoscere* (to get to know, and in the perfect tense to know, to recognize). The Latin *scire* may be a shortened form of *cognoscere*—though this is mere speculation on my part. But even if it is, it seems to have been attracted to and shaped by another cognate that Webster tells us is "akin" to *scire*. This other word is *scindere: to cut, rend, split; to divide, separate*. The Latin *scindere* does have a pedigree in Greek, deriving from *schízo*: to split, cleave, part, separate, or divide. The word in Greek was used to refer to logs, bodies, minds—anything that could be divided. Birds, whose wings were divided into feathers (unlike bats and beetles), were called *schizopteros* (split-winged). Splinters and chips of wood for kindling were called *schizes*. Everything from a division of opinion to a distinguishing feature of female anatomy could be called a *schisis*.

The linkage between *scindere* and *scire* in Latin justifies the banal metaphor of our contemporary blurb-writer. Science fiction comes by its "keen edge" honestly, for science as knowledge has been intimately linked from its beginning with splitting, dividing, dissecting in order to know. Fantasy which began as knowledge of things from the way they present themselves to the senses as images, forms, appearances, has had to yield its place to science which learns by taking things apart to see how they work. For centuries, the nonviolent knowing of fantasy has been displaced by the violent knowing of science. For centuries we have believed that the power-knowledge called science was real knowledge, and the intuitive knowledge called fantasy was false knowledge. We have believed, in short, that science was science and fantasy was fantasy. Were we wrong? We could do no other than what we did. The interesting question is whether we are changing now. I propose to approach that question by looking at the literary genres that have been associated with science and with fantasy, and finally, at this new hybrid, science fantasy.

The notion that fantasy is a literary genre, a subcategory of fiction like "Gothic" or "picaresque" is an extremely recent arrival in the world of criticism. The many definitions of fantasy in such major tomes as the *Oxford English Dictionary* and *Webster's New International Dictionary*, Second Edition, do *not* include an entry defining fantasy as a fictional genre. Most critical studies of narrative literature produced in this century have no index entry for fantasy. Even the wise and witty E. M. Forster in *Aspects of the Novel* made a hopeless botch of his chapter on fantasy, calling *Tristram Shandy* "the greatest of them" (Harvest edition, p. 111) and insisting that Joyce's *Ulysses* belonged in this category because "the raging of Joyce . . . seems fantastic" (p. 123). These atrocities in a book which was in many ways so astute are quite startling, but they document a state of incomprehension that extended well beyond the confines of Cambridge and Bloomsbury. Fantasy was not perceived as a fictional genre until quite recently. This or that element in a work might be called fantastic, but the concept of a genre, a consistent set of practices that could be called "fantasy," seems to have been almost unthinkable until well into the present century. There are reasons for this that will be worth investigating.

One person who tried to think of fantasy as a unique form of discourse was Sir Herbert Read, a poet, critic, and art historian who produced (in 1935) one fantastic novel himself, *The Green Child*. In his book on *English Prose Style* (first published in 1928 but revised in the late forties and reissued in 1952) Read devoted a chapter to what he called "Fantasy (Fancy)." Throughout this book Read was trying to organize prose styles into eight modes based upon Jung's classification of the four types of psychic function (thinking, feeling, sensation, and intuition) multiplied by the two types of psychic energy (extraversion and introversion). The kindest thing one can say about this effort is not that he was unequal to it, though he was, but that he often managed to ignore its difficulties and the inconsistencies in which he became enmeshed, and to present simply and directly the insights to which it led him. (One should also perhaps note in passing that attempts like this undoubtedly fueled Northrop Frye's far greater achievement in *Anatomy of Criticism*. Read's scheme—p. 85— should be compared to Frye's theory of "continuous forms.")

Read complicated his work further by relying upon the Coleridgean distinction between imagination and fancy to separate a higher form called invention (about which he can find almost nothing to say) from the lower form called fantasy, about which he says some interesting things. Quoting Coleridge, Read observes that "fancy is concerned with fixities and definites. In other words it is an objective faculty. It does not deal with vague entities; it deals with things which are concrete, clearly perceptible, visibly defined" (p. 126). This is excellent, applying equally well to the Grimm Brothers' "Little Briar-Rose" and Roger Zelazny's "A Rose for Ecclesiastes," but without the concepts of invention and imagination. Read can go no further in his search for the pure essence of fantasy. When he comes to the point of naming a literary form in which fancy or fantasy embodies itself he can find only one: the fairy tale.

There is much to be learned from Read's impasse. It is clear that he admired fantasy and knew something about it. He raised the truly interesting questions of how the modern writer could generate a form of fantasy equivalent in power and beauty to folk tales that have been shaped by many mouths over generations of transmission. And he lamented—in speaking of the *Thousand and One Nights*—that the "Western world does not seem to have conceived the necessity of fairy tales for grown-ups" (p. 134). But the literary fantasy he most admired was Robert Southey's story of "The Three Bears," which as he observes, "so perfectly conforms to the requirements of a folk tale that it has actually been adopted as such, and is everywhere and in almost every language reprinted and retold with little consciousness of the fact that it is a deliberate creation of an English writer of the early nineteenth century" (p. 131).

Read had a powerful sense of the human need for fantasy. He suggested, quite astutely, that if writers could free themselves from the domination of Romantic modes of thinking, which allotted fancy (as opposed to imagination) only a subordinate role in cultural activity, then they might "turn to fantasy as a virgin soil, and give to English literature an entertainment comparable to the *Thousand and One Nights*" (p. 135). But he was prevented from reconceiving the possibilities of fantasy himself because his own thought remained, precisely, dominated by Romantic attitudes. Specifically, he insisted that fantasy always "dispenses with all logic and habit, and relies on the force of wonder alone" but he reserved what he called "imagination and invention" for other forms of discourse than the fantastic. Deprived of both logic and invention, fantasy could only be conceived of as a childish form: what Read himself called "fairy tales for adults." Trying to look ahead toward the development of a new fantastic fiction, Read, under the spell of the Romanticism he condemned, could do no more than gaze into the past. On a clear day he might have discerned George MacDonald looking toward and beyond him, for MacDonald could see in both directions.

In 1893, a little more than a decade before he died, MacDonald wrote an introductory essay for an American edition of some of his fairy tales. The essay appeared the same year in England in *A Dish of Orts*, entitled "The Fantastic Imagination." In it MacDonald articulated what seem to me the most fundamental principles of fantasy. Let us listen to him: "The natural world has its laws, and no man must interfere with them in the way of presentment any more than in the way of use; but they themselves may suggest laws of other kinds, and man may, if he pleases, invent a little world of his own, with its own laws" (as reprinted in Boyer and Zahorski, *Fantasists on Fantasy*, p. 15). This is the key to modern fantasy, indicating both the point at which it breaks with the traditional folk tale and with the realistic novel. *An invented world, with laws of other kinds.* For their makers and their audiences, the folk tales were mostly of their actual world, though attending to aspects of it normally hidden, dark, or mysterious. Only the development of positivistic science and its literary handmaiden, realism, made the folk tales fantastic, because they made the world scientific and realistic. The discovery of folk tales by sophisticated courtiers and scholars led almost instantly to the production of pseudofolk tales or fantasies grounded upon the peasant medievalism of the European folk tales that we have come to know. The production of these "fairy tales," *contes des fées* as the French called them, has continued up to the present time.

The sophisticated (or "sentimental," in Schiller's term) imitators of naive folk tellers found a world already made for them. They did not have to invent new worlds with new laws. But MacDonald, in his later years, had begun to frame the problems of fantasy in a new light. He was cautious about using his own fantasies as an example, because as he put it "my long past work in that kind might but poorly instance or illustrate my now matured judgment" (p. 15). Thus the model he developed, however briefly, was a foreshadowing of a genre that had not yet established itself at the time when he wrote, and which Herbert Read could not describe even fifty years later: a genre based upon the fabrication of an invented world with its own laws. This is how MacDonald described such inventions:

> His world once invented, the highest law that comes next into play is, that there shall be harmony between the laws by which the new world has begun to exist; and in the process of his creation, the inventor must hold by those laws. The moment he forgets one of them, he makes the story, by his own postulates, incredible. To be able to live a moment in an imagined world, we must see the laws of its existence obeyed. Those broken, we fall out of it. The imagination in us, whose exercise is essential to the most temporary submission to the imagination of another, immediately, with the disappearance of law, ceases to act (p. 15).

For MacDonald, a world is a world precisely because it has a system of laws: laws that harmonize with one another. This view is compatible, it should be noted, with both Victorian theology and postivistic science, which together formed the matrix from which the full-fledged modern genre of fantasy emerged. And it emerged side by side with another new genre that glorified the transformation of *this* world: science fiction. Moreover, though one can point to relatively pure examples of both science fiction and fantasy, for the most part the two genres were thoroughly entangled from the beginning.

In fact, for the first half of the twentieth century, it is fair to say that fantasy flourished only as a parasite on its more popular cousin, science fiction. Even such pure fantasists as Edgar Rice Burroughs and David Lindsay needed some of the trappings of science fiction to account for the other worlds they wanted to construct. That Lindsay's extraordinary *Voyage to Arcturus* should need its frame of space travel is evidence of the weakness felt by those writers who wanted, in MacDonald's terms, to create little worlds of their own. Even C. S. Lewis, who despised the values that dominated the science fiction of his time, used its machinery in his Space Trilogy and did not publish his first Narnia volume until 1950.

The spectacle of L. Frank Baum struggling to define his own enterprise—and to resist the call to become a major writer of fantasy—is as edifying as the biblical story of Jonah. Baum's attempt to define his project begins in the letter that appeared as an introduction to *The Wizard of Oz* when it was first published in 1900.

> Folklore, legends, myths and fairy tales have followed childhood through the ages, for every healthy youngster has a wholesome and instinctive love for stories fantastic, marvelous and manifestly unreal. The winged fairies of Grimm and Andersen have brought more happiness to childish hearts than all other human creations.
>
> Yet the old-time fairy tale, having served for generations, may now be classed as "historical" in the children's library; for the time has come for a series of newer "wonder tales" in which the stereotyped genie, dwarf and fairy are eliminated, together with all the horrible and blood-curdling incidents devised by their authors to point a fearsome moral to each tale. Modern education includes morality; therefore the modern child seeks only entertainment in its wonder-tales and gladly dispenses with all disagreeable incidents.
>
> Having this thought in mind, the story of "The Wonderful Wizard of Oz" was written solely to please children of today. It aspires to being a modernized fairy tale, in which the wonderment and joy are retained and the heartaches and nightmares are left out.

This introduction provides a plentiful supply of blossoms for those who like to boil roses. Let us put the kettle on and see what we can brew up. First of all, Baum quite clearly takes his point of departure from the traditional or "old-time" fairy tale, as he calls it. He is definitely writing modern fairy tales for children rather than for adults, and his books have remained children's classics, unlike the Alice books, for instance, which have a significant adult audience. Even so, Baum must find his own name for this new enterprise— more evidence that "fantasy" was not yet understood as a literary kind or genre. He called his "newer" mode of writing "wonder tales"—a term which did not stick. He also undertook to purge all the "horrible and blood curdling incidents" from the "old-time" tales to produce a "modernized fairy tale," with the "wonderment and joy" retained and the "heartaches and nightmares" left out. This proved easier said than done, of course, and resulted in such awkward episodes as the attack on Dorothy and her friends by wolves, who have been ordered by the wicked witch of the West to "tear them into small pieces" (p. 121). In the event the Tin Woodman takes charge:

> "This is my fight," said the Woodman; "so get behind me and I will meet them as they come."
> He seized his axe, which he had made very sharp, and as the leader of the wolves came on the Tin Woodman swung his arm and chopped the wolf's head from its body, so that it immediately died. As soon as he could raise his axe another wolf came up, and he also fell under the sharp edge of the Tin Woodman's weapon. There were forty wolves, and forty times a wolf was killed; so that at last they all lay dead in a heap before the Woodman.

Having wolves tear you into small pieces is neither nice nor modern, but having them line up in a row of forty to be decapitated by one person (a tin man with no supernatural powers beyond life and durability) is simply implausible—or unlawful, as MacDonald might have said. It is a blemish and results in a momentary weakening of the book's imaginative power—even over a child. (I should add that I have been waiting almost fifty years to make this criticism to somebody who might care about it.)

The weakness of this episode might be contrasted with such matters as the rusting of the Tin Woodman's body or other instances where the logic of this new world is developed in an inventive way. Even the matter of eliminating the gruesome results in some truly fine moments, such as that of the Cowardly Lion's dinner. After his offer to kill a deer for the party is turned down on the grounds that it would make the Woodman weep and rust his jaws, the Lion takes care of himself: "But the lion went away into the forest and found his own supper, and no one ever knew what it was, for he didn't mention it" (pp. 58–59). Here Baum is able to let his lion be a lion but to keep the "horrible" or unpleasant aspects of this off stage.

In *The Wizard of Oz*, of course, Baum was not a committed fantasist. Not only was he not committed to any ongoing enterprise called "The Oz Books," he was not even totally committed to his own invented world. Peter Beagle once remarked of another fantasist: "Tolkien believes in his world, and in all those who inhabit it." I think it is safe to say that Baum did not feel this kind of commitment to his enterprise. If the Wizard is a humbug in that first book it is because Baum felt himself to be a humbug, too. The Emerald City itself is a kind of fraud, in which everything is green because it is seen through green spectacles. It is only halfway through the second book, *The Land of Oz*, that the spectacles are dropped, with some characters wearing them and others not, as documented in John R. Neill's splendidly faithful illustrations to the ninth chapter. They are dropped in the midst of an invasion by General Jinjur's feminist army, of course, who loot the city of its emeralds by prying them up with their knitting needles, and in this confusion Baum switches from whimsy to fantasy. Henceforth, the Emerald City is really green.

Baum's resistance to continuing the Oz books is worthy of one of his own characters—the Reluctant Fantasist, perhaps. The comic traces of this reluctance can be found in the prefatory letters to each book:

2. *The Land of Oz*. "And now, although pleading guilty to a long delay, I have kept my promise in this book.

3. *Ozma of Oz*. Indeed, could I do all my little friends ask, I should be obliged to write dozens of books to satisfy their demands.

4. *Dorothy and the Wizard of Oz*. "It's no use; no use at all. The children won't let me stop telling tales of the land of Oz. I know lots of other stories, and I hope to tell them, some time or another; but just now my loving tyrants won't allow me. They cry "Oz—Oz! more about Oz, Mr. Baum!" and what can I do but obey their commands?"

5. *The Road to Oz*. " . . . I thought I had written about Oz enough; but . . . I have been fairly deluged with letters from children . . . . I have received some very remarkable news from The Land of Oz . . . . . But it is such a long and exciting story that it must be saved for another book—and perhaps that book will be the last story that will ever be told about the Land of Oz.

6. *The Emerald City of Oz*. There will be no lack of fairy-tale authors in the future, I am sure. My readers have told me what to do with

> Dorothy . . . and I have obeyed their mandates . . . . My readers
> know what they want and I try to please them. The result is very
> satisfactory to the publishers, to me, and (I am quite sure) to the
> children. I hope, my dears, it will be long time before we are obliged
> to dissolve the partnership.

Like Jonah, Baum seems to have struggled against his fate,
thinking each book—or the book after the next—would be the last,
until the sixth, in which he accepted his fate, after being swallowed by
the leviathan of success. There he speaks to his dear little readers of
publishers and partnerships. The man, who perhaps wanted no more
than to be a humbug, has become an institution, a factory which
inputs letters of suggestion and turns out fantasies to order. It is a
cautionary tale, funny and sad, a bittersweet American success story.
The stories themselves, when read today by an adult, have moments
of wit and charm, happily invented scenes and characters, but seem
always to have been powered more by the wishes of their readers
than by the vision of their writer, who never quite understood why his
readers kept demanding "Oz—Oz!"

If I complain, I complain as one who spent hours making maps of
Oz—before they put them in the books as they do now. Given where
he was and who he was, Baum achieved something remarkable in
those books. Among other things he made the great discovery that
another world could be the basis for fictions that were not program-
matically Utopian but simply pleasing in their combination of
strangeness and familiarity. In doing this he made American fantasy
possible for others, a situation hinted at in Samuel Delany's
Neveryóna:

> "Earlier today, Ergi, out on Black Avenue," Madame Keyne
> called down, "I saw a woman try to deliver some very interesting bricks
> to a slug-a-bed not yet up to receive his shipment. These bricks were
> yellow—not your usual red. I want you to find out everything you can
> about them: their manufacture, functionality, durability, cost, mainte-
> nance—everything that contours their value, in any and every direc-
> tion. See if they'd be good for paving. Then report back to me."

"See if they'd be good for paving." I love that. Not only were
they good for paving, those yellow bricks made a road that led
someplace. But they couldn't lead there in Baum's day. He went as
far as he could. He showed how a person could invent "a little world"

which was not the medieval world of the folk tales, but having made it, he never knew quite what to do with it. I would contrast Baum with the creator of Narnia—a much more learned man—who knew only too well what to do with his created world. Both Baum and C. S. Lewis had the gift of invention. What Baum lacked was vision, a world view that would support a world. Lewis suffered from the opposite problem: a vision too thoroughly worked out, so that his fantastic world always threatens to become a mere vehicle for allegorical meanings—and often succumbs. It was J. R. R. Tolkien who put it all together, who produced adult fantasy that has invention and vision, that is more memorable as itself than as the vehicle for any system of beliefs. He began with *The Hobbit* in 1937, of which he wrote to W. H. Auden, "It was unhappily really meant, as far as I was conscious, as a 'children's story,' and as I had not learned sense, then . . . it has some of the sillinesses of manner caught unthinkingly from the kind of stuff I had had served to me . . . I deeply regret them. So do intelligent children" (*F on F*, p. 91). It is Tolkien, in his superb essay "On Fairy-Stories," who claims the name *Fantasy* for the genre in which he himself aspired to work. He knew exactly what he was doing and knew what it should be called. *The Lord of the Rings* is the paradigm of fantasy in our time. If there is such a thing as science fantasy, we will be able to locate it by its resemblance to and difference from Tolkien's great work.

I observed earlier that the genre we have learned to call science fiction has been entangled with its other, its antigenre, fantasy, from the beginning, as Herbert Read noted in his usual blundering but perceptive manner, saying of H. G. Wells that he "comes as near as any modern writer to a sense of pure fantasy. He errs, as in *The Time Machine*, by imparting to his fantasies a pseudo-scientific logicality; it is as though having conceived one arbitrary fantasy he were compelled by the habits of his scientific training to work out the consequences of this fantasy" (pp. 133–34). Here Read stumbled upon one of the better definitions of science fiction, but treated the whole enterprise simply as fantasy gone wrong. Read himself has gone wrong here, of course, by following the pseudoscientific logicality of his own definitions, but I want to suggest that he is also, at a very profound level, right. He is right in seeing science fiction as a branch of fantasy.

Given the positivistic matrix that dominated thought in nineteenth century England and America, continuing well into the twentieth century, works of fiction that sought to present alternate or secondary worlds were forced to align themselves according to the binary polarities offered by positivism: science or magic, extrapolation or escapism, this primary world transformed or a secondary world created: positivism itself or religion, the antagonist of science. Under this dispensation, many fantasists tried to don the mantel of science, and those that did not worked out of an essentially medieval religious position: not just Christianity, but a very Catholic version of it. This positioning essentially pitted the religion of science against the traditional religion of faith and revelation. The one looked forward toward the extension of human powers and happiness through scientific progress. The other mourned for a lost universe permeated by ethical principle. Whenever the fictions of science turned into a struggle between good and evil, the text in question became a fantasy, whatever the furniture or machinery of its alternate world, for such notions as good and evil are grounded in the human past and in theology.

If the expression science fantasy indicates anything beyond the desire of publishers to promote the books they have capitalized, it might simply designate most of what we have been calling science fiction for many decades. On the other hand, this term suggests that we might at last be sufficiently beyond positivism and beyond medieval religion to be confronted, finally, by a new form, that has positioned itself beyond both the truth/fiction opposition of science and the good/evil opposition of religion. I am not sure that science fantasy is the best name for such a genre but we may find that its very oxymoronic structure does indeed convey something important about this new and extremely interesting fictional development. Without pretending to have surveyed the entire field, I should like to conclude by noting that a work like Gene Wolfe's *Book of the New Sun* seems to me at least partly to have gone beyond the old religious and scientific oppositions and that Samuel Delany's *Neveryóna*, *Tales of Nevèrÿon*, *Flight from Nevèrÿon*, and even his earlier *Triton* are exceptionally full and satisfying embodiments of an enterprise that might fairly and hopefully be called "science fantasy."

Parallel Universes:
Fantasy or Science Fiction?

Joseph D. Miller

The question is whether it is possible to distinguish between fantasy and science fiction. I am reminded of the analogy, attributable I believe, to Theodore Sturgeon, of the elf ascending vertically the side of a brickwall. In a science fiction story the knees of the elf would be bent, his center of gravity thrown forward, his stocking cap hanging down his neck, with his feet quite possibly equipped with some form of suction cups. In a fantasy, on the other hand, the elf would simply stride up the wall in a normal walking posture, with his stocking cap standing straight out from his brow. What is the difference between these scenarios? The typical answer is that the science fiction story must play by the implicit rules of the game; in this instance, gravitation. Fantasy, however, need not "tip its hat" to the Law of Universal Gravitation.

But what if, for some specified reason, in the local vicinity of the elf on the wall, the vector of gravitational force just happens to be perpendicular to the side of the wall rather than parallel to it? In this case the behavior of the elf in the fantasy would be in perfect accord with physical law. One might then say that the fantasy is actually science fiction since we have posited a "scientific" explanation for the behavior of the elf.

Of course, this is an entirely unacceptable justification for applying the label science fiction. But what if we posit a very small quantity of condensed matter or neutronium maintained in an incredibly tight magnetic field in the center of the wall? What if we continue from there to give a rationale for the creation and eventual presence of that neutronium in the wall? What if we somehow succeed in explaining away the gravitational tidal effects that should actually reduce the wall to powder and our poor elf to a state of "elflessness"? The point is, if our explanation is sufficiently intricate, we will eventually convince the reader that the basic phenomenon under discussion is technologically "doable" or, at least, not entirely contrary to physical law.

But there is a shortcut to all this. If we like, we may simply state that our story takes place in one of an infinite number of parallel universes, all with slightly differing physical laws. Surely in one of these universes it should be the case that the direction of the gravitational vector occasionally changes. But isn't this simply the kernel of a "just so" story? Haven't we simply postulated the existence of the phenomenon we wish in the context of a small amount of scientific verbiage? Is this really any better than simply saying that elves can walk up walls? My answer to these questions is that any attempt at scientific explanation of the anomalous is better than nothing. Furthermore, the more detail we can provide, the more convincing is the scientific explanation. At the same time an element of humility is important. After all, physics lacks any truly final answers. Although it may be psychologically unsatisfying to say gravitational vectors can change in an arbitrary fashion, we might just as equally ask, why does the gravitational vector always point to the center of the earth (actually it doesn't—a plumb bob in the Black Hills of South Dakota points somewhat off true, due to the nearby immense mass concentration)? What is gravitational force? Or, in Einsteinian terms, why does mass deform space? The conclusion is, we shall always come to a point where we can only say "that's the way it is."

In any event, however, we may still ask whether the concept of parallel universes is "doable." That is, is the scientific rationale for this concept sufficient to buttress the believability of the story?

Perhaps the most common entry to parallel universes in speculative fiction involves the traversal of a black hole. A black hole is a region of space-time whose density is so great that light cannot escape. Thus, the region is a perfect absorber of photons and, consequently, a true black body. Such objects should be detectable on the basis of their ability to "bend" light in the vicinity or to deform the orbits of companion objects. Indeed, strong candidate black holes have already been advanced, such as Cygnus X–1.

At the center of a black hole resides the singularity. In Einstein's equations this is essentially the result of division by zero, resulting in infinite density in zero volume. About the singularity or other interior regions of the black hole, we can say nothing, since all electromagnetic radiation, our information channel, is trapped within. Actually, there is an exception to this principle. Micro-black holes of sufficiently small radius can decay by quantum processes. In this case photons can escape and information concerning the interior could theoretically be obtained. However, the only time in the history of the universe when sufficient temperature and pressure conditions necessary for the origin of atomic-nucleus-sized, or smaller, black holes could have occurred was the Big Bang itself. The half life of the smallest of such micro-black holes is sufficiently brief that within a few million years after the Big Bang most such objects should have decayed. Actually, proton sized black holes may still be evaporating today. However, experimental observations indicate a constraint on the frequency of such "evaporations" of about one per year in a volume of space equal to 3×10^6 cubic light years.[1] In effect, information concerning the interior of any black holes extant today is effectively denied us.

Now this is a particularly attractive situation for the science fiction author. Since we can know nothing of the interior, we cannot even assume that the ordinary physical laws of our universe apply there. It is a short step to assume that they do not; that is, black holes represent portals to alternative universes with perhaps very different physical laws and histories.

But is it at all reasonable to think that traversal of a black hole is physically feasible? Two phenomena suggest the unlikelihood of survival of such a venture. First, for ordinary size black holes, tidal forces would make plasma of any object approaching very closely to the hole. That is, the differences in gravitational potential along the linear dimensions of an approaching object would literally rip it to shreds. The effective dimension along which such potentials are exerted in the earth-moon system is the diameter of the earth. That is, the difference in gravitational potential produced by the moon's mass, between diametrically opposite points on the earth's surface, is sufficient to generate the oceans' tides. The corresponding dimension for the application of significant tidal forces in the vicinity of a black hole may be a matter of millimeters or less. Now some authors have suggested means of circumventing such tidal forces. One might, for instance, interpose sufficiently massive objects between your ship and the hole, a strategy suggested by Robert Forward.[2] Of course, this still does not obviate the problem of traversing the hole, merely of approaching it. Alternatively, it has been suggested that the only black holes that are traversable are ones of truly stupendous size, such as, perhaps, the probable one at the center of our galaxy, since tidal forces vary as the inverse square of the affecting mass.

But even so there is yet another lethal problem associated with close approach to a black hole. Candidate black holes are intense sources of X-rays, and, apparently, synchrotron radiation. This radiation is apparently produced as matter is sucked into the black hole. Thus, black holes are extremely energetic regions and any ship approaching one would require shielding of heroic if not impossible proportions.

So the black hole approach to alternate universes appears fraught with peril. Are there any other potential routes? It appears that one route might be through time travel. This may sound like achieving the improbable through the intervention of the impossible, but what we should ask is why time travel should be considered impossible. The typical answer is the paradox generated by traveling backwards in time to kill your own grandfather. The abolition of your grandfather should result in the abolition of your act of abolishing your grandfather. Therefore, alterations of the past, in so far as they affect the present, would be expected to be phenomenally difficult if not impossible. Some authors have suggested that this in turn means that the past is inviolable, although observable. This implies you can visit it, but not affect it. Indeed, the visit itself may be incorporated into history, as in Moorcock's *Behold The Man*[3] An alternative, however, perhaps most elegantly described by Gregory Benford in *Timescape*[4] [It should be noted, however, that the basic theme can be traced at least as far back as Asimov's *End of Eternity*[5]] is simply that paradoxes generated by time travel engender new alternative universes. Each moment, then, is a branch point for a potentially infinite series of parallel universes. So with time travel we can generate any number of alternative universes.

But how do we obtain time travel? Once again, the most common scenario in science fiction is to exceed the speed of light. By Einstein's equations this would indeed be equatable with reversing time's arrow. Now, indeed, one of the will o' the wisps pursued by some physicists in recent years has been the tachyon, a hypothetical particle traveling at immense trans-light velocities, which has as much difficulty slowing down to the speed of light as ordinary matter has in obtaining the speed of light. However, after throwing quite a bit of money at the problem through searching for potential interactions of tachyons with other particles, the search was abandoned. One of the most telling arguments against the tachyon was a communication paradox. Observer A sends a transmission to observer B at ordinary light velocity. Observer B receives the message and decides it is irrelevant. Subsequently, he sends a message via tachyon mail to observer A instructing him not to bother to send the original message. The tachyon message is delivered before the original message is sent, resulting in nontransmission of the original message, which was the precipitating event in the entire sequence. So paradox is unavoidable. But, in a Benford-like scenario, we simply say that receipt of the tachyon message buds off, at that point, a new universe in which the original message is not sent, with corresponding alterations in the experiences and memories of all parties concerned. Thus, the paradox, but not the magic, goes away. Still such scenarios as the above require the intervention of hypothetical particles like tachyons or the attainment of translight velocity. The energy costs of even approaching the speed of light in a material vehicle are extreme to say the least. So this particular scenario appears quite difficult to achieve.

However, there is yet another possible way to achieve time travel. Some years ago a physicist by the name of Frank Tipler examined the theoretical structure of space-time in the vicinity of a very massive, rapidly rotating cylinder.[6] Essentially, if one were to rotate a cylinder of pure neutronium at one half the speed of light, space-time in the adjoining vicinity would be sufficiently disrupted so as to allow the execution, if you will, of the grandfather paradox (*vide supra*). It should be noted that only an approach to the vicinity of the cylinder is necessary, penetration or actual contact with it is not necessary. Sending a reasonable amount of matter back in time would require an immense expenditure of energy. However, sending information back, in the form of electromagnetic radiation, would be quite feasible. Thus, assuming the avoidance of tidal effects, time travel in the physical universe is theoretically possible, with no violation of relevant physical laws.

So we can safely conclude that there is actually a fairly strong *a priori* rationale for the "doability" of the parallel universe scenario.

Still, we must ask whether the differences between our universe and others, as they are painted in works utilizing the parallel universe mechanism, are sufficiently sketched out and densely detailed so as to qualify as science fiction as opposed to fantasy. One subgenre in the parallel universes class is that in which one historical detail undergoes alteration. The classical example here is Dick's *Man in the High Castle*.[7] Other examples include Benford's *Timescape*, Harrison's recent *West of Eden*[8] and, of course, *A Connecticut Yankee in King Arthur's Court*.[9] By the pragmatic criterion detailed above most works of this kind easily qualify as science fiction since the alleged historical event is typically a quite possible variant on what actually did happen in our particular version of the scheme of things.

A second subgenre is that in which there is explicit traversal of multiple universes. The classic example is Laumer's *Worlds of the Imperium*.[10] Others include Pratt and deCamp's Harold O'Shea Stories,[11] Farmer's pocket universe stories,[12] Heinlein's *Glory Road*[13] and *The Number of the Beast*[14] and, of course, Zelazny's Amber series.[15] Certain of these novels may be classified as science fiction since there is some attempt to rationalize anomalies (*Worlds of the Imperium, Nine Princes in Amber*). Others (*Glory Road, The Incomplete Enchanter, The Number of the Beast*) are thinly disguised fantasies, with no real attempt at explanation of the counterrational events that transpire therein. Even the Amber series can be criticized on this ground. In the second volume much is made of the fact that gunpowder does not ignite in Amber. Corwin laboriously hunts through Shadow until he finds a variant universe that can provide a substitute for gunpowder usable in Amber. But we are never given any rationale for why ordinary gunpowder does not function in Amber. Is there some basic difficulty with the oxidative process? If so, what implications does that have for the atmosphere of Amber? Or, for that matter, what are the implications for respiration and metabolism in the Amberites? Another example is the mythical, symbolic use of the unicorn, surely one of the most traditional fantasy elements. In light of the difficulty in classifying this work as science fiction or fantasy, it is true in more than one sense that cannons (canons) do not function very well in Amber.

All in all, it appears that there *is* a difference between fantasy and science fiction. That difference is perhaps most evident in the parallel universe genre, a genre which, although appearing to have solid roots in the science fiction camp, nonetheless demarcates the border between fantasy and science fiction. When the anomalies of a parallel universe are explained and rationalized in some detail, we have science fiction. Otherwise, we have fantasy. A corollary here is that it cannot suffice to treat fantasy as science fiction transpiring in a parallel universe. Rather, fantasy is distinguished from science fiction on the basis of the author's willingness or unwillingness to ground plot elements in some simulacrum of physical law.

Still there is a kind of logic and a sense of lawfulness that is evident in much fantasy. Admittedly, a spider the size of Shelob in *The Lord of the Rings*[16] would be disallowed on the basis of scaling considerations, since structural strength increases as a function of the square of linear dimensions (cross-sectional area) whereas mass increases as the cube (volume). Therefore, increasing the radius of a spider by a factor of ten increases surface area and support strength by a factor of one hundred, while mass is increased by a factor of one thousand. On the other hand, there is a peculiar satisfaction in the destruction of Sauron through the immolation of the One Ring in the fires of Mt. Doom. What is the nature of this satisfying lawfulness? Certainly, it is a form of lawfulness, since fantasies typically exhibit a high degree of internal consistency (magical objects tend to work in the same way no matter who utilizes them, villains are consistently evil, and the pure in heart ultimately win out). But I would contend that it is not a lawfulness likely to be explicated in Newton's *Principia*,[17] but rather in Frazer's *Golden Bough*.[18] For the lawfulness is typically the lawfulness of sympathetic magic. Thus, the destruction of Sauron's emblem of power is synonymous with the destruction of Sauron. But these laws of fantasy are not physical laws; more likely they represent an elemental lawfulness in the human psyche. And for the explanation and understanding of this lawfulness I suspect we must turn to the social sciences, particularly psychology and anthropology for an explanation. What is phobic reaction except an expression of sympathetic magic? Why is the ghost a universal element of every human culture ever studied? Perhaps when we achieve a deeper understanding of psychosocial law, we will find that it is as fully reflected in fantasy as physical law is reflected in science fiction.

High Tech and High Sorcery: Some Discriminations Between Science Fiction and Fantasy

Michael W. McClintock

Which shall it be, Passworthy? Which shall it be?

—H. G. Wells

At first it seems easy to decide, for usually, now, the specimens come labeled, by conventional icons, at least, if not by the literal terms. Sometimes titles alone are adequate indicators: *Timescape* or *Starship Troopers* will not name works of fantasy, nor will *The Wood Beyond the World* or *A Wizard of Earthsea* name works of science fiction. The covers of mass-market paperbacks mostly function within a consumer guiding iconography: spaceships, robots, or rivets mean science fiction; a quaint village, an old man with a very long white beard, or a sword held by a mostly naked person mean fantasy. Although memorable first sentences are rare—perhaps they are being eschewed—throughout contemporary and post-modern literature, some do reliably announce the sort of text that follows them: "In the nighttime heart of Munich, in one of a row of general-address transfer booths, Louis Wu flicked into reality," Larry Niven, *Ringworld*. "The unicorn lived in a lilac wood, and she lived all alone," Peter Beagle, *The Last Unicorn*. These works I have mentioned or cited seem generically consistent by the most elementary standard of consistency: they give the reader what the reader has come to expect of the type of thing they seem to be. To the extent that such typology is reliable, we may as well take it to be licit.

But what sort of thing will come after this opening? "Like a glowing jewel, the city lay upon the breast of the desert. Once it had known change and alteration, but now Time passed it by" (Arthur C. Clarke, *The City and the Stars*). A reader with one sort of literary experience will hear, not unreasonably, echoes of Orientalism, perhaps of *Vathek* or of Dunsany. Even a reader with more conventional tastes probably would not expect those sentences to lead him into a novel featuring a high-speed subway, a Central Computer, a flight to the center of the galaxy, artificial intelligence, and moving walkways that are stationary at each end. But as Arthur C. Clarke said, some fifteen years after writing *The City and the Stars*, "Any sufficiently advanced technology is indistinguishable from magic."[1] The wonderful walkways of Diaspar bemuse the reader who gives them much attention in the same way that a garage door opener would bemuse a Victorian stablehand. The spaceship that carries Alvin and Hilvar to the central suns is no more explicable by our knowledge or rigorous speculation than would be the flight of a winged horse. Why should we call *The City and the Stars* science fiction if we call *A Voyage to Arcturus* fantasy? What sort of thing shall we say *Star Maker* is?

Seventy or eighty years ago—ten or fifteen years ago—the question had no urgency. Even the distinction of fantasy from other sorts of narrative is not ancient. Although "fantasy" was used to mean some sort of fiction as early as the fourteenth century, the word more often denominated a mental activity of faculty. The appearance of "fantasist" and, with it, the clear sense of fantasies as intentional products of craft or art is recent; the earliest citation of "fantasist" in the *Oxford English Dictionary* supplement—it does not appear in the dictionary proper—is from 1923, when it was used of Oscar Wilde. The term "science fiction," of course, appeared six years later and became widely current during the 1930s. Some scholars, especially several who labored as apologists for science fiction in the years when it was necessary to make a case for paying attention to these works, took pains to distinguish science fiction from fantasy.[2] But those who took scorn for science fiction to be simply intellectual self-condemnation apparently felt no need to assert this division. Both Sam Moskowitz and Donald A. Wollheim have called science fiction a "branch of fantasy."[3] James Gunn has referred to it as "a mutated form of fantasy."[4] In his preface to the 1933 collection of his scientific romances, H. G. Wells suggested that the only difference in kind between his work and predecessor fantasies was a single substitution: "Hitherto . . . the fantastic element was brought in by magic . . . . But by the end of the last century it had become difficult to squeeze even a momentary belief out of magic any longer. It occurred to me that instead of the usual interview with the devil or a magician, an ingenious use of scientific patter might with advantage by substituted."[5]

Once the scientific romance—or science fiction or science fantasy or speculative fiction or speculative fabulation—became available as a possible thing to write and read, the substitution could be made either way: magic for science as well as science for magic. There might also occur mixes in various proportions, and either science or magic might go disguised as the other. For instance, in James Blish's *Black Easter* the magician Theon Ware discusses his practice with a client as an accountant might discuss mathematics; indeed, he uses just that comparison: "With books and the gift, you could become a magician—either you are or you aren't, there are no bad magicians any more than there is such a thing as a bad mathematician." (Blish, p. 26). Ware goes on to explain that all magic is done by controlling demons, "specifically fallen angels." (p. 28). The work is difficult, exhausting, and dangerous, but the instructions in how to do it are available to anyone who will do the research. The structure, although not the particulars and consequences, of the disaster that proceeds from Ware's final conjuration is the same as that of, say, the atomic disaster narrowly averted in Robert A. Heinlein's "Blowups Happen" or the ecological disaster that is not averted in John Brunner's *Sheep Look Up*.

Tricking out magic in the lab coat of science or the control panels of technology may be easier than what Blish did; it seems, at any rate, to be more common. Varley's *Titan/Wizard/Demon* trilogy, Malzberg's *Men Inside*, and almost anything by Alan Dean Foster or Jack L. Chalker will serve as recent examples. *Titan*, for instance, seems at first to be the same sort of technological wonder story as *Ringworld* or *Tau Zero* or *Rendezvous with Rama*. An exploratory mission to Saturn discovers what at first they take to be that planet's twelfth moon. It turns out to be a huge torus, or wheel, thirteen hundred kilometers in diameter, spoked, hubbed, hollow, artificial. Most of the novel is taken up with adventures among its marvels. But the expedition commander and her sidekick discover that this structure is the body of an intelligent being who tells them that her name is Gaea and that she is a Titan. In effect, she is a goddess. Although Varley, in the subsequent volumes of the trilogy, reveals Gaea to be more caliph than supreme being, the powers and facilities to which she—

and, eventually, her supplanters—have access are all but explicitly magical—among others, shape changing, superlatively long life, creation of living beings. Varley associates many of his wonders with known physical principles; Gaea's physical structure is held together by cables, for instance, and her inner parts that are not touched by sunlight (reflected through windows by mirrors) are frozen. But for the grounds of Gaea's existence, Varley relies upon mysticism: "Her thoughts whirled faster than light through a crystaline matrix of space the very existence of which defied the edicts of human physics" (*Wizard*, p. 337). "Crystaline matrix of space" has about the same referentiality as "mithral," the elvish metal in *The Lord of the Rings*, or "ulfire" and "jale," the colors from beyond the spectrum in *A Voyage to Arcturus*.

If there is, for the construction of fictions, no more elemental difference between technology and magic than Clarke's and Wells's remarks suggest, it is idle to pursue the question of distinguishing between science fiction and fantasy. The two sorts of thing are as interchangeable as the example of *Titan* suggests high tech and high sorcery to be. But the practice of readers and of publishers (who must sooner or later be responsive to readers) suggests that they perceive, despite contiguities and overlaps, some difference here between two sorts of fiction. That practice, of course, is the labelling I mentioned at the beginning of this discussion. The differentiated labels have been available at least since Wells began referring to some of his works as "scientific romances," but until the late 1940s there were, indeed, too many labels, reflected in the titles of the pulp magazines where most of the material was published: *Astounding Stories of Super-Science, Air Wonder Stories, Marvel Science Stories, Bizarre Mystery Magazine, Fantastic Adventures, Futuristic Stories, Science Fantasy, Space Stories, Strange Adventures, Strange Stories, Uncanny Stories, Unusual Stories, Weird Tales*, and at least, over the years, a hundred and fifty others. Codification developed, as it will, gradually; by 1938 *Astounding* was committed on its cover to science fiction, but its companion, *Unknown*, never incorporated fantasy in its title. After World War II, however, Donald A. Wollheim started the *Avon Fantasy Reader* (chiefly reprinting material from the prewar *Weird Tales*), and in 1949 Anthony Boucher and J. Francis McComas founded *The Magazine of Fantasy*, which, after its first issue, became *The Magazine of Fantasy and Science Fiction*. In the last title the linking of fantasy and science fiction announces that two different sorts of thing are being labeled.

Since the time when Boucher and McComas refined the title of their magazine, distinction between science fiction and fantasy has, for three reasons, become a significant topic. First, most works of science fiction or fantasy appear, either originally or as reprints, in mass-market paperback form, and that publishing field is dominated by categorization. Marketing procedures that rely in large measure upon habitual or impulse buying will also tend to rely upon standard-ization of the consumer goods. Those procedures, too, will tend to reward products that easily fit into established locations on the racks and to penalize items that don't. The market will first recognize, then require distinction between related products. If science fiction and fantasy are somehow different from each other, and if readers, in some way noticing the difference, tend to prefer one or the other, thus gradually developing two readerships, then eventually B. Dal-ton and Waldenbooks will make the difference definitive. Barry N. Malzberg and Samuel R. Delany, among others, have discussed the consequences of this mechanism for the production of science fiction—and, easily mutatis mutandis, fantasy.[6]

Closely associated with the effect of the marketplace is the influence of films, although the influence is in some ways opposite to the effect. Because of the expense of their production, films will necessarily be fewer than books and must be sold—rather, the view-ing of them must be sold—to larger numbers of people (almost the identical principle that underlay the Victorian rental library and that now underlies the video rental business). Thus, films exhibiting high box office grosses wil be imitated. But, to the extent people tend to be contemptuous of later work they perceive as mere repetition of a particular popular success, this imitation must be of structure, form, style, technique rather than of specific content. Special effects, cine-matography, relationship to current popular interests, and the per-sonal qualities of the performers are apparently independent com-plications. These factors, in combination with subsequent producers' unavoidable uncertainty about precisely which elements of the ear-lier hit were most responsible for attracting viewers, encourage amal-gamation of elements, broadening a genre and reducing the number of differentiable genres. A concomitant phenomenon is that a no-table and expensive disappointment may discourage future producers from attempting the same sort of thing, even if the causes of the failure were actually particular rather than generic.

Although relations between film and literature are often indirect and haphazard, the contemporary film seems especially potent in the evolution of taste and the development of audience expectations, to which publishers and professional writers will respond. The most abject hack is still unlikely to describe the roar of a starship in the depths of space, but in—for instance—*The Tar-Aiym Krang*, Alan Dean Foster is willing to describe a kind of space fighter as "weaving" and "peeling off" (p. 93, p. 94) as if it were a Spad or a Spitfire.

Because the effect of the marketplace and the influence of film continue to exert themselves upon science fiction and fantasy, prediction of their final consequences—even prediction that any consequences will be final—would be rash if not vain. But I shall, however rashly, suggest two possible sorts by way of introducing the third reason for discriminating between science fiction and fantasy. If the influence of film predominates, science fiction and fantasy may be forcibly merged, costing us at least one genre—two, if the synthesis turns out to be neither fish nor fowl. But if the effect of the marketplace is determinative, commerce between the categories will become difficult or impossible, perhaps costing us—we would never know—some rich individual works. Either expense would be injurious, especially if it were paid by science fiction.

We may be unable to avoid payment; as Alastair Fowler insists, genres are mutable, and among the several ways in which a recognized (or suspected) genre may vanish from our ken are subsumption or displacement by another.[7] Such change, as observed, may almost appear organic, like cross-pollination or interbreeding—or mongrelization. But in literary as well as in human genealogy the tree is only a visual, not a structural metaphor. We fecundate by coming together, not by branching. The metaphor Fowler employs, following, as others have, Ludwig Wittgenstein, is the family: "Representatives of a genre may . . . be regarded as making up a family whose septs and individual members are related in various ways, without necessarily having any single feature shared in common by all" (p. 41). The genetics of genre, Fowler argues, is literary tradition, the transmission of structural codes by influence and imitation and reaction and, simply, reading. A genre, like a family, exists only in terms of its members and matters only to the extent that it is recognized, a process that requires acquaintance with several members and is only imperfectly reliable. Here we approach, though not from his direction, Damon Knight's impatient scanting of definition: "it means what we point to when we say it."[8]

An Aristotelian enhancement of Knight's dictum would provide a better operating principle for study: we can say at the outset that science fiction (or fantasy) is the genre composed of those texts that have been called science fiction (or fantasy). Readers, then, and writers and publishers and, eventually, scholars convoke a genre by their association of some works with others. To distinguish between two genres is to note absences as much as presences. To associate the members of a genre we see something of some works in other works, as we see something of parents and grandparents in a child, but to see that one genre is not the same as another genre is in part not to see such resemblances and, of course, to be aware of not seeing them. This is a process of approximation, even, occasionally, of squeezing to fit, and it is unhappily susceptible to blurring, but definition of class and category has served us no better. At least the blurry approximation has the virture of allowing us more easily to fit theory to experience.

One of the common experiences of science fiction is what the title of James Gunn's history suggests: *Alternate Worlds*. Near the end of that book Gunn refers to "the exclusive preserve of the science fiction writer—the future and other lands unknown" (p. 239). Sometimes the future is coming very soon, and the lands are not very distant, as in Michael Crichton's *Andromeda Strain*, say, or Gregory Benford's *Timescape* or Gunn's own novel, *The Listeners*. Similarly, the world of a fantasy may sometimes almost be mapped onto our own, as in Fritz Leiber's *Our Lady of Darkness*. In both sorts of case, however, the distance is never quite zero; the time is usually a few seconds off (not, I concede, in the case of Leiber's book). The response to the objection that as much may be said of any fiction is fairly straightforward with respect to fantasy. The part of a fantasy's fictive world that cannot be mapped onto our own is excluded from our world by exactly the principle, whatever it may be, that includes it in the fictive world. In *Our Lady of Darkness* curses work literally, if they are done properly, as do magical spells in *The Last Unicorn*, *Black Easter*, and Ursula LeGuin's *Wizard of Earthsea*. Here may lie the seed of one distinction between fantasy and science fiction, since the fictive worlds of science fiction seem less distinctly removed in principle from our own. Benford's *Timescape*, generally regarded as science fiction, presents a fictive world which depends upon no principle that we could confidently exclude as part of the underpinning of our own. Although the novel appears to rewrite history, it also demonstrates that in principle, according to our own—not a fictive world's—physics, we cannot know certainly that our own history is not in fact being rewritten, our own reality being revised, at any moment.

Insofar as a genre depends upon reader recognition, however, the contrast between *Our Lady of Darkness* and *Timescape* jumbles rather than differentiates, because to most readers working curses are likely to be more sensible than the tachyons of Benford's novel. Curses are familiar; tachyons are fantastic. Yet just here is the germ of the distinction: a world that tachyons may alter will be immune to curses. The fictive worlds of each of our kinds have a presence absent in the fictive worlds of the other kind. The worlds of science fiction admit technology but usually not magic; the worlds of fantasy admit magic but usually not advanced technology. If Clarke's Third Law in fact ruled in this matter, the mutual exclusion should make no difference, for sorcery and technology would interchange indistinguishably with each other. Perhaps in the films of George Lucas and Steven Spielberg they do. But parlance and practice, the labels and the signals of generic code, argue that this is not the case for literate science fiction and fantasy. Something there is in technology that does not love magic, and magic is at least as hostile to technology. Here, then, appears to be the distinction between the fictive worlds of science fiction and those of fantasy: the principles of control are different. In fantasies, magic works; in science fiction, technology does. (And in both sorts of world, what matters most is control.) In magical worlds the usual forms of transportation are horses and sailing ships or some kind of magical locomotion; in technological worlds we find spaceships or moving walkways that are stationary at each end. The quintessential magical weapon is the sword; the off-the-shelf technological weapon will be some sort of gun. The age of magic is almost always past; technological time is almost always future. The root distinction is the relationship, mediated by magic or by technology, of the characters to the worlds they inhabit. By magic or by technology, the characters will try to control their worlds. But technology is always independent of the person of the operator; magic never is—except in *Black Easter*, where magic is a technology. Even when an author does not (usually because he cannot) explain the workings of a technological device—hyperdrive, say—those workings are assumed, by author, readers and characters, to be generally explicable and replicable. But working magic is customarily assumed to require some special personal capacity. Anyone who does technology becomes thereby a technologist. But you must in some way be a magician before you can do magic. Technology gives personal power; magic requires it.

Thus a fantasy world is just the sort that can be controlled by personal force and familiar natural powers—fire, wind, earthquake, rain. The sword is the exemplary tool (not just weapon) of such worlds because it has no working parts and because it extends a man's hand only a few feet. The iconic spaceship, nearly all moving parts, extends a man's reach across light-years but also contains him. What must be controlled in fantasy is simply evil, homely however black, but in science fiction the antagonist may be blind and recondite forces, the cold equations of Tom Godwin's paradigmatic story.

The conclusions of two exemplary works, often taken to represent both high ambition and high achievement in the two genres, will illustrate a consequence of this distinction. In each case, a hero comes home.

"At last they rode over the downs and took the East Road, and then Merry and Pippin rode on to Buckland; and already they were singing again as they went. But Sam turned to Bywater, and so came back up the hill, as day was ending once more. And he went on, and there was yellow light, and fire within; and the evening meal was ready, and he was expected. And Rose drew him in, and set him in his chair, and put little Elanor upon his lap.

"He drew a deep breath. 'Well, I'm back,' he said" (Tolkien, *The Return of the King*, p. 311).

"Alone, Shevek turned back to the observation port, and saw the blinding curve of sunrise over the Temae, just coming into sight. 'I will lie down to sleep on Anarres tonight,' he thought. 'I will lie down beside Takver. I wish I'd brought the picture, the baby sheep, to give Pilun.' But he had not brought anything. His hands were empty, as they had always been" (Le Guin, *The Dispossessed*, p. 338).

Both Sam and Shevek have been principal actors in events that profoundly alter their worlds; each returns quietly, simply, and alone to his wife and child. For Sam, homecoming is not only an end to adventure; it is virtually an end to events. Tolkien provides a chronological sketch of Sam's later years, the effect of which is to show that Sam need never again struggle, make hard choices, face evil (pp. 377–78). The harvest of his labor with Frodo, helping to bear the One Ring to its destruction, is a tranquility that marvelously neither stultifies nor corrupts. For Shevek, whose author provides no sheltering postbellum chronology, the adventure may be done, but he enjoys no promise that events have ceased. By his physical journey to Urras, his intellectual journey to instantaneous communication, and his ethical journey to revolution, he has gained just the right to go on doing. A reader following Sam to the end of his story finds hearth and home; a reader travelling with Shevek finds that "freedom is never very safe" (p. 336).

Magical worlds are basically safe; technological worlds are not. No fantasy concludes with the clear triumph of evil, but a science fiction may end in disaster or the continuing risk of it. The conclusion of no fantasy threatens its reader, and little or nothing of the reader's ontological or epistemological assumptions will be placed truly at hazard. But even the shabbiest science fiction at some point touches our world without insulation and thereby puts this world critically in doubt. Although fantasy is, in principle, the wider and more flexible—as it is the elder—genre, in contemporary practice science fiction is the more sophisticated, distinctly the more mature form.

Science Fiction and the Semiotics of Realism

J. Timothy Bagwell

Readers of Aristotle's *Poetics* will recall his assertion in Chapter XXIV that "the use of impossible probabilities is preferable to that on unpersuasive possibilities" (Golden and Hardison, p. 45). Aristotle is making a distinction between plot and subject matter, and his point seems to be that it is more important for the former to be convincing than for the latter to be believable. Aristotle is talking about epic (and secondarily about tragedy), and he imagines an extreme case in order to make his point. However, this extreme case is precisely that of science fiction. Even allowing for variations in definition or emphasis of the two poles, I think most readers of science fiction would agree that it must deal with what is currently impossible and that it must do so in a way that is plausible or "probable." Because the first criterion is one shared with other literary genres such as the fairy tale, our best bet, if we wish to understand the peculiarities of science fiction is to investigate the second, the probability of its plots. However, if we ignore the first criterion, the impossibility, we will misunderstand the kind of probability we are dealing with.

Any generic distinction that is purely canonical in nature, that is, it attempts to divide works into neat categories, is probably doomed from the start, doomed either to failure or to a useless reductivism. It is more useful to think of genres as in works than the other way around, that is, it is more useful to think of genres in terms of things like narrative functions, structures, and conventions that may or may not be operative in particular works and in various combinations. However, I would like to cite a particular story as an example of science fiction, not so much because the story has great literary merit as that it demonstrates thematically science fiction's uncomfortableness with the fantastic, and so draws its own generic boundaries.

I have in mind an episode of *Star Trek*. An enormous hand literally grabs the Enterprise as it makes its way across space. It is the hand of God, or as it turns out, of someone who claims to be a god, namely, Apollo. What he wants from the crewmembers of the Enterprise is worship; in return, he offers a pastoral paradise and immortality, more or less the same offer that Calypso makes to Odysseus. And Kirk, like Odysseus, rejects this offer in favor of struggle and mortality, and eventually succeeds in escaping.

The hidden agenda of this story is revealed in the succession of theories about Apollo. At first the crewmembers assume that, however powerful he might be, he is lying about his identity, because Apollo is a merely mythical figure. In the process, they tell us that, in the fictional world of this story, the gods don't exist. In contrast to numerous stories in which gods appear to disbelieving mortals, here the impossibility of the appearance is a part of the story. At the same time, the fictional world of the story is conveniently identified as a "realistic" one. (I'm not saying that the story is realistic, but that "realism" is one of the ground rules of its fictional world.)

However, Apollo's evidently unlimited power leads the crewmembers to consider the possibility that he is Apollo, the Apollo of legend. Now at this point, the story demands that we accept two mutually exclusive propositions: that Apollo is mere legend and that he really exists. If the story ended here, it would not be very different structurally from countless episodes of *The Twilight Zone* based upon the unignorable fact of the impossible.

But the *Star Trek* episode does not stop here; in fact, the central conflict of the plot is less the crewmembers' captivity than the mystery of Apollo himself. The solution to the conflict (and indirectly to the problem of captivity) is the discovery that Apollo's power is based on technology, on a machine that can be rendered inoperative by a well-placed shot from the Enterprise's phaser banks. The common motif of the defeat of the alien is coterminous in this story with the reduction of a god to a good but not perfect manipulator of the forces of nature, that is, of the creator of nature to someone subject to its laws. The story historicizes myth, only to detheologize it.

I think it is significant that the story not only demystifies its Apollo, but also the Apollo of classical mythology. What seems to be threatening is not so much the god as the human need to imagine a god, that is, the need to fantasize. In fact, as it turns out, the "gods" departed the earth in the first place because mankind stopped believing in them. Now a god who rules by virtue of an almost unlimited ability to transform matter and energy does not need belief, even if he were likely to be denied it. These, however, are gods who need belief. As Kirk says, after Apollo has been defeated, "We've outgrown you." In this story, then (and in many others), science fiction defines itself in opposition to fantasy precisely by means of a plot structure in which the fantastic is first introduced and then demystified.

The distinction will become clearer if we look at an example of fantasy, one whose structure is equally transparent. I am thinking of an episode of *The Twilight Zone*, "Nightmare at 20,000 Feet", in which a gremlin appears to a plane passenger. This story defines itself as fantasy also by rejecting another genre or, in this case, other genres: the fairy tale and psychological realism.

The story is roughly as follows. A man on a plane sees a creature, which he eventually identifies as a gremlin, tampering with one of the engines on the wing outside his window. The man has a history of mental illness and is unable to convince anyone else of what he sees, although it's not clear what action might be taken against a gremlin. Eventually, the plane lands safely, but the final shot is of a bent plate on the wing above one engine.

The story is not a fairy tale, because the nonexistence of gremlins is thematized in the story through the reaction of the man, who only with great difficulty overcomes his own disbelief. No one else can see the gremlin. But then why is this one poor soul tormented with a special ability to see what can't be seen? The only answer (barring psychosis) is that this character is structurally the scene of a brutal juxtaposition of realism and fantasy.

The psychological explanation of the gremlin as a hallucination, while it would explain the gratuity of this isolated manifestation, is also rejected by the story. That is the point of the final shot of the bent plate. The ground rule of the fictional world of the story seems to be the following: an event will be impossible, but it will occur anyway, and furthermore it will not be subject to any verification that would neutralize its impossibility.

Now impossibility, it should be remembered, intuitive assumptions notwithstanding, is a feature of a realistic world, not a fantastic world: gremlins are not impossible in a fairy tale, only in something that is a species of realism. Thus, if we take these two stories as typical of science fiction and fantasy, respectively, we see that it would be a mistake to say that one is realistic and the other fantastic. In fantasy, this juxtaposition is irreducible. In science fiction, however, it is *aufgehoben* by what we might call the "Explanation." Thus, I am in agreement with Samuel Delany when he writes of fantasy and science fiction in terms of "could not happen" versus "has not happened," respectively (*The Jewel-Hinged Jaw*, p. 44). I would simply want to define these concepts in terms of plot structures rather than content.

I therefore have to disagree with Scholes and Rabkin's assertion that science fiction is a matter of "what it has in it," of its "elements," whereas fantasy is a matter of "structure" (*Science Fiction*, p. 170). Science fiction is a species of realism, true, but its realism is a matter of structure, not merely of scientific content. In fact, science fiction can be understood in terms of the functioning of content as form.

This point can be illustrated with one of the best and most "scientific" works of science fiction around: Gregory Benford's *Timescape*. If we break down the plot of the story into its components, we can isolate three that exist in a structural relationship: the feat of communicating through time (and other speculative events); the subplots dealing with love, marriage, and academic politics; and the information mustered to explain the feat of communicating through time.

Component two we can dispense with immediately: love, marriage, and academic politics are the stuff of genres other than science fiction, though they help to identify the fictional world as realistic. Component one, communicating through time, might at first glance seem appropriate subject matter for (and hence constitutive of) science fiction. But each event might occur in fantasy. The bloom, considered apart from its biochemical explanation, is not too different from the plague that threatens Thebes in *Oedipus Rex* (or the blight on the world in Le Guin's Earthsea trilogy. As for communication through time, people have a tendency to wander in and out of the past without explanation in *The Twilight Zone*. And Stephen R. Donaldson presents us with a fantasy version of parallel universes in *The Chronicles of Thomas Covenant*. That leaves component three—

the explanation—as the only possible candidate for what makes Benford's novel science fiction.

Now if this information (the explanation) is the content that constitutes science fiction, several qualifications are in order. This content is not the content we might have expected to find doing the job; the major speculative or "scientific" events of the story could, as we saw, appear in fantasy. Second, this information must, according to the rules of science fiction themselves, be incomplete. Science fiction that does not go beyond what science currently can explain is not science fiction at all. That means that the explanation in science fiction, indispensable though it may be, is never—and could by definition never be—adequate. Benford's explanation, despite its brilliance, is no exception: if his novel explained how to communicate through time using tachyons (theoretically hypothesized particles that have the speed of light as their lower limit), he would have gone for a patent instead of a copyright.

If I am right, then we cannot distinguish fantasy from science fiction by saying that in the latter, unlike the former, the fantastic is explained. If we recognize the difference between what is possible (in terms of science) and what is probable (in terms of plot), then we can say that the explanation is an essential part of the plot of science fiction. But when we talk about explanation, we are talking about narrative codes, not hard science (though it is likely that hard science is itself a narrative code). It may be that the narrative code of realism is facilitated by the inclusion of what is recognizable as hard science, but that is because, in science fiction explanation, content functions as form.

According to Robert Scholes and Eric Rabkin, fantasy involves "the thrill of seeing the *believed* unreal become real." If I understand this point, they are not actually saying that the unreal becomes real, but that the unreal occurs or is made manifest without ceasing to be unreal: the unreality of the fantastic must be coded into the narrative, as it is, for example, in Alice's astonishment at finding talking flowers. Scholes and Rabkin claim that "this direct reversal of the ground rules of the narrative world is the structure that marks the fantastic," and this structure is so essential that, if need be, authors will claim that things that really exist don't, as Jules Verne does with the submarine in *Twenty Thousand Leagues Under the Sea*.

In SF, the impulse is to do just the opposite: the unreal is not emphasized, but rather explained; or to be more accurate, the fantastic in SF is coded as real rather than as unreal, without being any more or any less a code. Science fiction, then, involves the thrill of seeing the unreal become the believed real.

Science fiction is the imposition of the code or style of realism on the fantastic, but this notion needs emendation in light of the fact that fantasy is an imposition of the code of *unreality* on the fantastic. The fantastic is not properly the domain of fantasy or SF or both, but ought to be recognized as a neutral literary resource manifest also in mythology, allegory, metaphor, and even realism (insofar as the concepts of the fantastic and the fictional overlap). Fantasy is, no less than SF, a special case, a special use of the fantastic.

SF is an superimposition of the narrative codes of realism on the fantastic: that is to say that it is the form, not the content of SF, that is realistic. That this is so becomes clear if we contrast SF with another such juxtaposition of realism and the fantastic: what is called magical realism. In Gabriel García Márquez' *Innocent Erendira* there is a scene in which a character causes glass objects to glow by touching them. There is no explanation for this phenomenon, only a comment: "those things happen only because of love" (p. 32). If we contrast the use of the same fantastic content in magical realism with fantasy on the one hand and science fiction on the other, then we see that the difference is essentially a narrative one. Alice would notice and thematize the unreality of glowing glassware, which would identify the narrative mode as fantasy. In science fiction, the phenomenon might be explained in terms of quantum mechanics, which does not tell us any more, but evokes a different context. In García Márquez' story, the phenomenon is studiously ignored, which is not to say that in magical realism the fantastic is uncoded. Just as the unreality of the fantastic must be thematized in fantasy, so it must be invoked and then overlooked in magical realism: it is the narrator's very lack of surprise that surprises us. In reality, glowing glassware would not be so readily accepted.

If we say that the realism of science fiction is a matter of code rather than fact, of form rather than content (or of content as form), then we begin to see a way out of the paradox that arises from the double requirement that science fiction be at once probably and (currently) impossible. Just as fantasy, according to Scholes and Rabkin, must thematize unreality, "regardless of what, in the world outside of the fiction, might be unreal," so SF must explain reality, regardless of what, outside of the world of the fiction, might be real. In other words, SF is not obliged actually to explain unreality (that would be impossible), but rather merely to appear to explain it or at least to accept thematically the presence of or need for explanation. The more the explanation partakes of what we already know, the better it will appear, which is why it is still true that the better the science, the better the science fiction. This truth should not blind us however to the fact that the explanation, except in the most conservative, unimaginative speculative fiction, must be at some point blend into or cross the threshold of the unknown. This crossover must be handled very carefully, for if it is not disguised the narrative structure of science fiction will crumble.

A complete study of the techniques for coding fantastic events as explained realistically, despite its obvious merits, lies outside the scope of this essay. However, to support my assertion that such coding is an essential feature of the form of science fiction, I would like to sketch out a few of the more obvious techniques:

1. Characteristic of "realistic" storytelling is the inclusion of excessive or superfluous detail. In contrast to medieval allegory, say, in which every detail is significant, life presents us every day with countless experiences that are not integrated into our current teleologies. Ergo, such details in a literary work (as long as they do not become symbols) suggest the lifelikeness of the fictional world, and provide reassurance that the narrative is objective.

The same holds for science fiction, except that the inclusion of unnecessary details makes up for the exclusion of some necessary ones. Now if some of these superfluous details are themselves fantastic in nature (dilating doors, ion drives), not only is the science fiction world realized but the need for explanation is circumvented. Consider, for example, this passage from Isaac Asimov's *Robots of Dawn*:

> Baley did sleep—eventually, after Daneel demonstrated how to reduce the field intensity that served as a form of pseudo-gravity. This was not true antigravity and it consumed so much energy that the process could only be used at restricted times and under unusual conditions.
>
> Daneel was not programmed to be able to explain the manner in which this worked and, if he had, Baley was quite certain he would not

have understood it. Fortunately, the controls could be operated without any understanding of the scientific justification. (p. 41)

By positing the details of pseudogravity outside the symbolic framework of the story as superfluous, the narrative is excused from accounting for them; at the same time, their inclusion assures us that everything is accounted for.

2. A fantastic occurrence can be coded as explained even when it isn't. For example, once again, *Robots of Dawn*:

> It was the "Jump," the passage through hyperspace that, in a timeless, spaceless interval, sent the ship across the parsecs and defeated the speed-of-light limit of the Universe. (No mystery in words, since the ship merely left the Universe and traversed something which involved no speed limit. Total mystery in concept, however, for there was no way of describing what hyperspace was, unless one made use of mathematical symbols which could, in any case, not be translated into anything comprehensible.)
>
> If one accepted the fact that human beings had learned to manipulate hyperspace without understanding the thing they manipulated, then the effect was clear. At one moment, the ship had been within microparsecs of [earth], and at the next moment, it was within microparsecs of Aurora. (p. 45)

This is both not an explanation and a lot of explanation. This explanation amounts to a thematization of the reader's own ignorance; what matters is not so much the explanation itself as the fact (or gesture) of one (even though it is only a fact in the fictional world of the story).

A future setting of a science fiction story can itself function in this way: the future functions in the fictional world as a time when the unexplained will have been explained. The time of science fiction is almost always the future anterior. Here, there is a trade-off: the more distant the future, the more radical the unreal may be; however, the nearer the future to our own time, the greater the potential for shock effect (as in *Timescape*), which I will discuss in a moment.

3. A related technique is the thematization of the mystery of the fantastic itself. One of the best examples of this technique in recent literature is found in *The Roadside Picnic* by the brothers Strugatsky. In this novel, mysterious aliens have left mysterious things behind on

earth, things which courageous stalkers, at great personal risk, find
and sell. The realism of the story is largely a function of the stalkers'
frustration in their attempt to explain the things they find. Frustration, however, implies that an explanation exists (if only for the
aliens), and so the artifacts are coded as explained. The explanation
exists within the fictional world "somewhere."

4. Another way of avoiding explanation is the technique of
explaining one thing in such detail that the reader's attention is drawn
away from another thing that is unexplained. For example, if you
spend enough time describing the ecology or the alien populace of a
distant planet, you may neglect to explain how you got there, even
though getting there theoretically requires FTL. *The Left Hand of
Darkness* is primarily about interplanetary politics and sexuality, and
Le Guin explains in great detail what is relevant to these themes. The
question of space travel is not of primary relevance, but the detail of
her other explanations leads us to assume that a good explanation
exists (in the fictional world).

5. Probably the most common method of explaining a fantastic
occurrence in science fiction is to fictionalize the explanation itself.
There can be the explanation of fiction, but there can also be the
fiction of explanation: in this case, the explanation of the fantastic is
itself fantastic. Such would be the explanation of FTL as the result of
the development of interdimensional hyperdrive: interdimensional
hyperdrive is as much in need of explanation as FTL (I just made it
up), but it can occupy the structural position of an explanation
relative to FTL in the narration of a story. Thus, content functions as
form—and it does so, however invalid it might be as science.

6. All explanations in science fiction are fictional to some extent; otherwise, they would not be science fiction but science. This is
the case, I would argue, even when the explanation is based upon
rigorous science. To say that an explanation is fictional is not to put it
down—there are good fictions and bad fictions, and the more convincing the science, perhaps, the better the fiction. Still, it is perhaps
worth isolating a sixth technique for the coding of fantastic events as
realistically explained: that in which much or all of the explanation is
scientific. Gregory Benford's novel *Timescape* comes to mind again
as a sort of limiting example of this technique.

Science is prized highly by readers of science fiction, as is science
fiction that seems to offer the hope that it might someday become

science. I wonder, though, if that means that the element of fiction is relatively unimportant. One has only to imagine that Benford's novel was openly speculative, that it was written in the future tense, that it acknowledged the missing pieces of its scientific puzzle. I think it is clear that the story would no longer be science fiction. This suggests to me that the science in science fiction is like a real toad in an imaginary garden, an important element of a well-constructed fiction. It may make sense to insist that science fiction be constructed with the right ingredients; it doesn't make sense to insist that it not be fictional.

Science fiction will appear to have failed its task only if we make the unreasonable demand that it be science and not fiction. That was certainly not my purpose in arguing that realism in science fiction is a matter of narrative codes. On the contrary, only if we recognize science fiction as a literary genre can we hope to legitimize it as a genre that is "literary." The science in science fiction does not replace the usual concerns of literary art, but rather facilitates them according to the demands of a specific genre with a specific artistic function. It is probably pointless to argue the merits of fantasy and science fiction relative to one another; however, it does make sense to question the function of the imposition of the codes of realism on the fantastic. It is clear that science fiction must be speculative, but why must it be realistic?

It is not, as Le Guin argues (in *The Language of the Night*) because of a male American fear of dragons. What Le Guin understands by a fear of dragons is a distaste for pleasure for its own sake. Mere fantasy, so goes her argument, violates a masculine work ethic, and so men impose the rational explanation of technology.

But the best literature has always been that in which it is difficult to distinguish what pleases from what instructs, in which *dulce* and *utile* function in happy harmony. There is as much escapist science fiction as there is escapist fantasy: literature that only entertains is simply bad literature, whatever genre it belongs to.

Furthermore, Le Guin is wrong about fantasy. Fantasy in the broad sense, myth, allegory, and fairy tale, is almost never merely pleasurable, but rather highly instructive. Fantasy in the more narrow sense defined by Scholes and Rabkin—coded impossibility—is, like science fiction, an incursion of the fantastic into the realistic, coded in a certain way, with no less a hidden agenda.

The truth of fantasy, in the broad sense, is almost always a psychological or cultural one. This is probably no less the case for science fiction. The truth of science fiction is a human truth. But science fiction, in its experimental capacity, can be understood as attempting to go beyond the human (whether to comment upon the human from an external point of view or to project new fantasies that pave the way for psychological or cultural growth). But where in the real, that is, natural, world can we look beyond the human? Two obvious places are technology and space, that is, in nature made novel through alteration and nature made novel through discovery (especially through discovery of paradoxically intelligent but nonhuman life forms).

A good example of such speculative realism is Le Guin's own story *The Left Hand of Darkness*. Le Guin imagines a race of "humans" whose gender is not determined once and for all at conception, but rather a matter of current emotional situation. Imagining a society not divided up into men and women allows Le Guin to comment on ours, which is, and to make us aware of how much our way of thinking and our relationships with others are determined by that fact.

Thomas Berger has also written speculatively about human sexuality. In *The Regiment of Women*, women are the dominant sex. Reversing stereotyped sex roles allows Berger to illustrate both the absurdity of those stereotypes and the absurdity of reversing them as a solution. In fact, the motivation for much of what happens in the plot is formulaic rather than realistic: take your worst sexist nightmare and turn it around. As a result Berger's novel is "unscientific": he does not explain how this speculative situation came to be, and he exaggerates female chauvinism so much that we feel we are in the world of caricature, that is, of satire.

Despite the fact that Berger's novel is very realistic, as soon as we begin to see the formula, as soon as we begin to read the story as satire, we begin to read differently. Knowing how to read fantasy is precisely knowing how to look beyond implausibility to a truth that is allegorical: fantasy is not realistic, it is apt. The meaning of fantasy, then, is very much a part of the "real world"; in a sense, the fantastic is dispensable in fantasy.

In science fiction, on the other hand, the fantastic is carefully preserved; its status as "mere metaphor" is perpetually denied by the

Explanation. It is the very insistence that the fantastic is real that preserves its speculative impact upon us. The function of science fiction as a plot structure is not to reveal to us how things are but to change our way of thinking about how things are.

In this sense, science fiction is in the modernist tradition of Brecht's epic theater and metafiction. Modern writers have frequently been concerned that the world of the reader not be usurped by the fictional world of the text. This concern has led to various forms of antiart, aleatoric art, and self-referentiality. The solution for Brecht and for writers of metafiction such as Barth and Borges is to undermine the fictional world of the text, to have it self-deconstruct from within by thematizing the manner in which it is constructed from without by author and reader. One way of thinking about such literary techniques is as a rejection of fiction. Another way, more useful to my mind, is as a thematization of the reader and the reader's world within the fiction. This is the function, I would argue, of the Explanation in science fiction at its best. Far from being merely escapist, science fiction can engage the real world in a unique and powerful way. As in Brecht's epic theater, the ultimate goal of science fiction is to make the reader reflect upon gaining self-identity rather than losing it.

It is worth remembering, though, that the reader's world is itself to a large extent fictional, at least to the extent that it is a function of various unreflected codes that condition its interpretation. The message of science fiction is that these fictions can change. We read Berger, we laugh, we shake our heads, we recognize ourselves. Le Guin's novel asks a question. Her reader is encouraged to view finishing the novel not as a conclusion but as a beginning, as a demand for reflection. Her speculative world is not an "as if" but a "what if?"

Filling the Niche:
Fantasy and Science Fiction in
Contemporary Horror

Michael R. Collings

In a recent interview, Whitley Strieber justified his craft by arguing that the value of horror-fantasy lies in its ability to let the reader explore the boundaries between the known and the unknown, to investigate those niches between fantasy and reality that exist within our own world:

> There's this theme in my books that things are hidden in the cracks of life. When you get down into it, you find a whole other world, a complete reinterpretation of our reality.[1]

Strieber's attitude defines a major movement in contemporary fantasy—the increasing interaction between science fiction and fantasy. This interaction is not one-directional, of course. Novels may begin within a science-fictional world, then gradually transmute into something new, as in Stephen King's *The Stand* (Doubleday, 1978). The opening chapters are an exercise in science fiction: a superflu destroys 99.4 percent of the world's population, and humanity must confront the consequences of a technology turned destructive. The later chapters, however, emphasize the irrational, as characters dream and their dreams become the focus of a second crisis, one entailing fantasy rather than science fiction. The novel concludes with an almost theological apocalypse and incorporates characters largely incompatible with a science-fictional framework.[2]

Another possibility entails a movement from overt fantasy to something resembling science fiction. Piers Anthony's magical, fantastic Xanth, for example, lies physically embedded with the real world of Mundania; the interaction of the two realms underlies the

48

seven-volume series.³ In a sense, however, Xanth only suggests a conscious interaction, since Mundania has few uniquely science-fictional characteristics. In the Proton-Phase trilogy, on the other hand, Anthony fully investigates the relationship between the two genres.⁴ Proton is the science-fictional analogue to Phaze. Stile, able to cross between the two at will, is simultaneously a character of science fiction and of fantasy, of technology and of magic. And in the final volume, Stile must act in both frames in order to save each.

Anthony's series in progress, the Incarnations of Immortality novels, continues his experiments with generic interaction.⁵ Here science fiction and fantasy exist in the same physical and temporal universe. Magic has reasserted its right to stand beside science as a mode of knowing. In the second volume, *Bearing an Hourglass*, Norton (incarnated as Time) moves easily through the worlds of Bat Durston and the BEM, and of the Evil Sorceress and the Damsel in Distress—only to discover that both worlds are illusions generated by Satan, who depends upon science and magic for survival. The novels at times seem schizoid, as if Anthony has not yet fully mastered the difficult task of altering his reading protocols within a single text; the reader is occasionally unprepared for the shift from one set of generic expectations to another.⁶ Yet Anthony's ambitiousness in treating fantasy and science fiction simultaneously merits attention.

The most consistent generic blending, however, occurs in con-temporary horror fantasy, as authors consciously shift reading proto-cols. In *The Mind Parasites* (1967), Colin Wilson evokes a race of Lovecraftian "great old ones" and ancient buried cities of monolithic structures, only to subvert the Lovecraftian mythos by revealing that all of this merely distracts the hero from discovering the true alien invaders, the Mind Parasites. The novel becomes an "aliens from outer space" exercise, with overtones of Arthur C. Clarke's *Child-hood's End*. In Wilson's later novel, *The Space Vampires* (1976), aliens discovered in a derelict ship take on the emotional and psycho-logical colorings of the vampire tradition, only to be revealed at the end of the novel as fugitive entities from a distant galaxy.⁷

Similar techniques occur in a number of other recent novels, including F. Paul Wilson's *The Keep* (1981) and *The Tomb* (1984); Dean R. Koontz' *Phantoms* (1983); and Peter Straub's *If You Could See Me Now* (1977) and *Ghost Story* (1979). But the sense of a generic shift figures preeminently in the novels of Whitley Strieber: *The*

Wolfen (1978), *The Hunger* (1981), *Black Magic* (1982), and *The Night Church* (1983). Even *Warday* (1984), which seems strictly science fictional, incorporates a generic shift into pseudodocumentary. In each case, Strieber begins within traditions associated with one genre and demands that the reader apply certain assumptions or reading protocols. Then the novel shifts, undercutting what has been established, and moves into a new genre. What had seemed elements of horror fantasy—werewolves, vampires, demons—becomes an explainable part of the real universe. The horror-fantasist, Strieber argues, must rebuilt the traditions from the ground up, setting them into contemporary society where they *"really would genuinely fit."* The niches for them exist, he continues: "I *know* that there could be Wolfen if nature had chosen to take that course. They could exist and they could succeed."[8] In *Warday*, Strieber suggests that our conception of nuclear war may be as much fantasy as anything else; by writing his novel as documentary, he creates a deeper sense of verisimilitude. Anyone, he says, could describe the war. His concern lies with the consequences, and with making those consequences believable for this readers.[9]

The point here is that several contemporary horror-fantasists have begun to subvert the genre. Strieber's best work—*The Wolfen* and *The Hunger*, for instance—depends upon a shift from fantasy to near-SF. When the transition remains tangential, as in *Black Magic*, the novel risks failure. Perhaps the best imagistic illustration of this strategy occurs in Peter Straub's *Shadowland* (1980), in which the protagonist, Tom Flannagan, describes one of two key locales in the novel. Carson School, he says, was "an old Gothic mansion on the top of a hill, to which had been added a modern wing—steel beams and big plates of glass. The old section of the school somehow shrank the modern addition, subsuming it into itself, and all of it looked cold and haunting."[10] The second critical locale, Shadowland (the magician Coleman Collins' estate), is described similarly: "It looked like a Victorian summer house which had been added on to by generations of owners: a three-story frame building with gables and corbels and pointed windows, flanked by more modern wings."[11] Like Carson School and Shadowland, horror-fantasy has become a dual structure, dependent on the traditional appurtenances of horror and terror—on vampires, werewolves, demons, monsters of all sorts—*and* upon an infusion of the rational and the objective. By generating such a dual structure, the horror-fantasist recaptures terror for an audience at once distanced from it by increasing sophistication of world view and inured to it by constant exposure to everyday reality.[12]

Over sixty years ago, Dorothy Scarborough differentiated between what she called "old" ghosts and "modern" ones. She noted in particular that the old ghost, best represented in the fiction of Anne Radcliffe, became "a subterfuge to cheat the reader." In such fiction, Scarborough continues, ghosts with a "histrionic temperament" used "make-up of phosphorus, bones, and other contrivances to create the impression of unearthly visitation. Recent fiction is more cleverly managed than that."[13] The "modern" ghost (what Jack Sullivan calls the "new" ghost) is in fact entirely supernatural. Sullivan credits Joseph Sheridan Le Fanu with introducing this figure into English horror-fiction; Le Fanu's ghosts "stubbornly refused to confine themselves to the shabby psyches of aristocratic neurotics, yet somehow managed to emerge from within as well as invade from without; [they] could not be explained away, yet [they] would have nothing to do with what Oliver Onions once called 'the groans and clankings of the grosser spook'"[14] In other words, these critics differentiated between apparitions which could be (and were) explained away on some rational level, and apparitions which represented an authentic incursion of the fantastic into the real.

Yet almost paradoxically, the direction taken by Strieber, Straub, Koontz, both Wilsons, and others seems essentially reactionary. Refusing to allow their creatures to remain supernatural, they consistently explain their creatures. There is no true ghost in *Ghost Story*; instead, there are "nightwatchers," entities which have coexisted with humanity for millenia. There are no werewolves in *The Wolfen*; instead, we find an alternate canine evolution that has similarly parallelled human development, living off the detritus of humanity as we in turn live off cattle. There are no true vampires in *The Hunger* or *The Keep*; instead, we find Miriam Blalock, possibly the sole surviving specimen of an alien species, its blood incompatible with human blood, yet its life inextricably connected with humanity. In *The Keep*, this pattern develops even more completely. Wilson weaves into the texture of the narrative virtually every element of traditional vampire lore, culminating with the crisis of faith experienced by the Jewish Professor Cuza when the supposed vampire cringes at the sight of a crucifix; after all, if the crucifix is a figure of power, then the religion it symbolizes must be likewise. Wilson then reverses the narrative as he reverses the creature's name, revealing that Molasar/Rasalom is not a vampire. The creature has no fear of the cross, but has used the vampire tradition to manipulate Cuza. The crosses embedded in the walls of the keep are not even crosses: they represent the sword hilt, a remnant of power from a civilization predating humanity. The creature is an evil survivor of an alien race. When he is destroyed, the remaining alien, Glaeken, undergoes the transformation that makes him human, and there are no more creatures (except, of course, the Hitlers of humanity's own making).

In each instance, beginning with Colin Wilson's invaders from the moon, the Mind Parasites, we find a fully developed horror tradition suggesting that we are dealing with Lovecraft's eldritch "great old ones," or werewolves, or vampires, or whatever. Then the text shifts, explaining the apparition or creature, but simultaneously affirming its existence and linking it with an objective, technological, science oriented universe. The "ghosts" are rationalized, not by referring to phosphorus and old bones, but by identifying hitherto unknown species, coexistent with yet unrecognized by humanity. In Strieber's novels, in fact, the creatures' existence is verified by scientific means. In *The Hunger*, Miriam Blalock submits to a blood test that establishes her alien nature. In *The Wolfen*, the scientist, Ferguson, sees and describes the wolfen; even more critically, the novel concludes with a situation unique in the long history of the wolfen: a body has been left behind for humans to study. Unlike the corpses in many horror traditions, it does not disintegrate into ashes or disappear in a puff of smoke. In *The Night Church*, Jonathan's research into brain activity results in him giving himself and Patricia brain scans which reveal that they are the monsters they fear, the results of the Night Church's millennia-long attempts to breed a demonic analogue to humanity. In a term reflecting C. S. Lewis' "un-man" in *Perelandra*, Strieber refers to Jonathan as the *anti-man*. The existence of the creature has been verified, the creature defined, and he is the antithesis of humanity.

In essence, these novels build upon the horror traditions developed during the past century and a half, then appropriate more recent conventions of science fiction to defuse the horror and paradoxically make it more horrific. It is one thing to read about Dracula-type vampires or Chaney-type werewolves; but it is difficult not to laugh afterward, as much in humor as in relief.[15] But when Wilson reveals that the Lovecraftian paraphernalia of *The Mind Parasites* only disguises an alien force within us that prevents humanity from reaching its potential, we feel less relief. When he similarly reveals in *The Space Vampires* that the apparatus borrowed from Stoker's vampire tradition was a conscious disguise assumed by alien intelligence, we are free to add our contemporary fear of the unknowns of space to our inherited responses to the vampire legends. In Straub, hauntings occur, not because of ectoplasmic entities traditionally called ghosts, but because of the undying malevolence of the night-watchers, alien shape-shifters. And in *The Wolfen*, Strieber moves a step further and argues that we accept the traditional legends of the werewolf and the vampire precisely because of our imperfect perceptions of the wolfen and their occasional human allies.

In each instance, the fantastic is undercut, and a rational, orderly, scientific explanation substituted. Then the novels may freely exploit the fear and terror inherent in the conventions of horror fantasy—the reader's fear of unexplainable creatures which rise from nowhere and can (perhaps) never be entirely defeated—yet simultaneously develop an even greater sense of terror by revealing that there is a place for such a creature, even within a well-ordered, technological society.[16] And there is a paradoxical sense of relief in discovering that the creature is ultimately knowable, that we may to begin to understand its motivations and purposes and (again perhaps) either defeat it or coexist with it. Overlying these responses, however, is the threat that such creatures, explainable though they might be, represent to our society. In this sense, the final paragraphs in Strieber's *Wolfen* might be the most horrific of all. The wolfen sense their temporary defeat and respond by howling:

> High above them on the Third Avenue Bridge a repair crew was deploying its equipment. When they heard the sound the men stared wordlessly at one another. One of them went to the railing but could see nothing in the darkness below.
>
> Then the howl was answered, keening on the wind as pack after pack looked up from their haunts in the City's depths and responded to the powerful sense of destiny that the sound awakened in them all.[17]

There is no relief here; the creature has not been dispatched with a silver bullet. Instead, humanity faces a threat inherent in science-fictional narrative: a sentient species capable of meeting humans on their own terms.

An additional point that deserves mention is that films have been made from most of these novels. Generally, the authors had little control over the content of the films; both Straub and Strieber, in fact, have spoken out against alterations made in their narratives.[18] In most instances, the films were inferior to the novels, primarily because the single element that distinguished the narrative from traditional horror—the interaction of science fiction and fantasy in defining the creature—was deleted. The film version of *The Keep* is about an unexplainable thing with red laser eyes (one student referred to it as "Gumby on steroids"); the sense of "alien preexisting humanity" has disappeared and the movie suffers. The film version of *Ghost Story* is both strong and well-cast; but it fails to recreate horror. It startles, but only by cutting to disintegrating faces and slimy flesh. The deeper horror of some thing waiting fifty years to destroy the Chowder Society is largely lost; when the car is pulled from the lake bottom and the body allowed to topple out into the snow, the ghost disappears. A decaying, sentient mass of tissue at the bottom of a frozen lake may generate momentary fear in a darkened movie theater, but it cannot create the sense of a continuing, malevolent presence.

It seems, then, that the interaction of science fiction and fantasy is particularly fruitful in this one subgenre, at least. The inherent contradiction between the rational and the irrational, between inspiring horror and quelling uncertainty, defines the power of these novels. It does not seem coincidental that the authors who have chosen to incorporate this admixture of science fiction into their horror fantasies are among the most popular—and commercially most successful—in the field. Their novels provide readers with two essentially antithetical experiences simultaneously: they generate terror based on well-known horror conventions, and then connect those traditions directly to the scientific, rational world the reader knows and understands.

Fantasy and Science Fiction: A Writer's View

Roger Zelazny

I have often wondered whether I am a science fiction writer dreaming I am a fantasy writer, or the other way around. Most of my science fiction contains some elements of fantasy, and vice versa. I suppose that this could be annoying to purists of both persuasions, who may feel that I am spoiling an otherwise acceptable science fiction story with the inclusion on the unexplained, or that I am violating the purity of a fantasy by causing its wonders to conform to too rational a set of strictures.

There may be some truth in this, so the least I can do is try to tell you why I operate this way, what this seeming hybrid nature of much of my work means to me and how I see this meaning as applying to the area at large.

My first independent reading as a schoolboy involved mythology—in large quantities. It was not until later that I discovered folk tales, fairy tales, fantastic voyages. And it was not until considerably later—at age eleven—that I read my first science fiction story.

It actually did not occur to me until recently that this course of reading pretty much paralleled the development of the area. First came fantasy, with its roots in early religious systems—mythology—and epical literature. Watered-down versions of these materials survived the rise of Christianity in the form of legends, folklore, fairy tales, and some incorporated the Christian elements as well. Later came the fantastic voyages, the utopias. Then, finally, with the industrial revolution, scientific justifications were substituted for the supernatural by Mary Shelley, Jules Verne, H. G. Wells. I had actually read things in the proper chronological order.

I feel now that this colored my entire approach to the use of the fabulous in literature. The earliest writings of the fantasy sort involved considerable speculation from a small and shaky factual base. A lot of guesswork and supernatural justifications for events came into play. I accepted these things as a child would—uncritically—my only reading criterion being whether I enjoyed a story. About the time I discovered science fiction I was somewhere near the threshold of reflection. I began to appreciate the value of reason. I even began to enjoy reading about science. In a way, I guess, I was a case of ontogeny recapitulating phylogeny.

I have never gotten away from a fondness for all of these forms— I suppose because my thinking has been touched by all of them. Emotionally, I find it difficult to draw distinctions between science fiction and fantasy because I feel them to be different areas of a continuum—the same ingredients but different proportions. Intellectually, however, I understand that if the fabulous elements involve the supernatural, or are simply unexplained in terms of an intelligent person's understanding of how natural laws operate, then that particular story should be considered a fantasy.

If the fabulous should be explained, or indicated to be explainable in terms of the present state of human knowledge or theory—or some extension thereof—I can see how a story of this sort can be considered to be science fiction.

When I write, though, I generally do not think in terms of such facile compartmentalizations. I feel that fiction should mirror life and that its *modus* is that classical act of *mimesis,* the imitation of an action. I concede that it is a distorting mirror we use in science fiction and fantasy; nevertheless, it should represent in some fashion everything which is placed before it. The peculiar virture of a distorting mirror is its ability to lay special emphasis upon those features of concensus reality which the writer wishes to accent—a thing which in many ways places what we do close to satire, in the classical sense— making the science fiction and fantasy worlds special ways of talking about the present world. Another is the particularly wide range of characters this practice permits me to explore.

Not only do I not like to think of my stories in terms of separate science fiction and fantasy categories, but I feel that for me it would actually be harmful in terms of the creative act to drive such a wedge into my view of the continuum. According to John Pfeiffer, author of *The Human Brain,* "There is an entire universe packed inside your skull, a compact model of your surroundings based on all the experiences you have accumulated during the course of a lifetime." Of necessity such a model is limited by the range of one's perceptions and the nature of one's experiences.

Thus, the world about which I write, the world to which I hold up my distorting mirror, is not the real world in any ultimate sense. It is only my limited, personal image of the real world. Therefore, though I have tried hard to make my version of reality as complete a model as possible, there are gaps, dark areas which exist in testimony to my ignorance of various matters. We all possess these dark areas, somewhere, because we have not world enough nor time to take in everything. These are a part of the human condition—Jung's shadows, if you like; unfilled addresses in our personal databases, if you prefer.

What has this to do with the fabulous—with fantasy and science fiction? My feelings are that science fiction, with its rational, quasi-documentable approach to existence, springs from the well-lighted, well-regulated areas of our private universes, whereas fantasy, in the tradition of its historical origins, has its roots in the dark areas. Somewhere, I already hear voices raised in objection to my implication that fantasy springs from ignorance and science fiction from enlightenment. In a way it is true, and in a way it is not. To quote Edith Hamilton, "There has probably not been a better educated generation than the one that ushered in the end of Athens." Yet it was these same highly rational Greeks who passed classical mythology along to us, in its most powerful, sophisticated forms, while providing material for early chapters in world history books.

Fantasy may take its premises from the unknown, but what it does with them immediately thereafter is subject them to the same rational processes used by any story teller in the working out of a tale. The story itself then unfolds in a perfectly clear-cut fashion.

I am not saying that the dark areas represent things which are ultimately unknowable, but only that these are representations of the unknown within the minds of individual authors—from the nameless horrors of Lovecraft to the mental processes of Larry Niven's Puppeteers. I doubt that any two authors' world models coincide exactly. And I feel that the generalization and representation of these clouds of unknowing in literature is a basis for fantasy.

I wish to take things one step further, however. I can hardly deny the effectiveness of a good story which is purely fantasy nor of another which is purely science fiction, in terms of the distinctions as I see them. As I said earlier, I tend not to think of such distinctions at all while I am working. When I am writing a story of some length my personal sense of esthetics usually causes me to strive for closure, to go for the full picture, to give at least a nod to everything I regard in that version of reality. As a consequence, my stories reflect the dark areas as well as the light ones; they contain a few ambiguous or unexplained matters along with a majority of things which follow the rules. In other words, I tend to mix my fantasy and my science fiction. Looked at one way, what I write is, I suppose, science fantasy—a bastard genre, according to some thinking on the matter. I am not sure what that makes me.

I followed this pattern in my first book—*This Immortal*—by leaving certain things unexplained and open to multiple interpretations. I did it again in my second book—*The Dream Master*—only there the dark areas were in the human psyche itself rather than in events. It was present in the Peian religion and its effects on my narrator Francis Sandow in the otherwise science fiction novel *Isle of the Dead.* In *Lord of Light,* I wrote a book where events could be taken either as science fiction or as fantasy with but a slight shifting of accent. And so on, up through my recent novel *Eye of Cat,* where the final quarter of the book may be taken either as fantasy or hallucination, according to one's taste in such matters. I write that way because I must, because a small part of me that wishes to remain honest while telling the calculated lies of fiction feels obliged to indicate in this manner that I do not know everything, and that my ignorance, too, must somehow be manifested in the universes which I create.

I was wondering recently where this placed me within the general context of American incarnations of the fabulous. I began reviewing their history with this in mind, and I was struck by a serendipitous insight into our relationship to the grand scheme of things.

We did it backwards.

American fantastic literature began the pulp magazines of the late 1920s. From that time on through the 1930s it was heavily indebted to other sorts of adventure tales. We can regard this as a kind of *Ur*-science fiction, whence rose the impetus which has carried all of the rest.

What happened then in the 1940s? This was the time of the

"hard" science fiction story, the time of the sort of story referred to by Kingsley Amis as having the "idea as hero." Isaac Asimov and Robert Heinlein in particular exemplify this period when the idea, derived from science, dominated the narrative. At initial regard, it should not seem strange that our science fiction entered its first recognizable period with what was the latest phase in the historical development of fantastic literature—that technologically oriented form of the fabulous narrative which had to await the appropriate development of the sciences. But what happened next?

In the 1950s, with the collapse of many of the science fiction magazines and the migration of science fiction to the paperback and hardcover book markets, along with the freedom from magazine restrictions thus obtained, came a shifting of concerns to the sociological and political areas. The idea was still hero, but the ideas were no longer derived exclusively from the physical sciences. I think of Edward Bellamy and of Fred Pohl. I think of Thomas More and of Mack Reynolds. I think of Nietzsche and of some of Freud's character studies (which I can only classify as fantasies) and I think of Philip José Farmer. Looking back even further to the pastoral genre I also think of Ray Bradbury and of Clifford Simak.

Moving—ahead, I suppose—to the experimental work of the 1960s, I recall the *Carmina Burana,* the troubadours, the minnesingers, the lyrical literature of self of an even earlier period.

And the 1970s? We saw a resurgence of fantasy—fat-volumed trilogies detailing marvelous exploits of gods, warriors and wizards—a thing which is with us still, and which in recent years, as with Tolkien, has taken on the overtones of ersatz scripture.

American fabulous literature appears to have recapitalated phylogeny in reverse. We worked at it steadily and have finally made it back to the mythic beginning—which is where I came in. I have a strange sense of *déjà vu,* of my lost past recaptured, on reading much of the current material in the area.

Such are the joys, you might say, of being able to select my own examples. True. I can point to numerous exceptions of every generalization I've made. Yet I feel there is something to what I have said or I would not have sketched this tendency in even this wavery impressionistic outline.

So where do we go from here? I see three possibilities and a whimsical vision: We can drop back into the *Ur-* and write adventure stories with just the fabulous trappings—which is the direction Holly-wood seems to have taken. Or we can turn around now and work our way forward again, catching up with H. G. Wells sometime around the turn of the century. Or we can fall back upon our experience and strive for a synthesis—a form of science fiction which combines good storytelling with the technological sensitivity of the forties, the sociological concerns of the fifties, and the attention to better writing and improved characterization which came out of the sixties.

Those, I say, are three possibilities. A less likely avenue might be to do the latter and also to incoporate the experience of the ancient 1970s, when fantasy reached what may have been its greatest peak in this century. That is, to use all of the above with a dash of darkness here and there, to add to the flavor without overpowering the principal ingredients, to manipulate our fancies through a range of rationality and bafflement—in that our imagination needs both to fuel it, and a fullness of expression requires the acknowledgement of chaos and darkness opposed by the sum of our knowledge and the more successful traditions of thought to which we are heir.

I feel that it is this opposition which generates the tensions and conflicts of the human mind and heart implicit in all particularly good writing, secondary to the narrative line itself but essential if that nebulous quality known as tone is to sound with veracity in the search for mimetic verisimilitude. This quality, I feel, is present in the best writing in any genre—or in no genre at all, for labels are only a matter of convenience, and subject to revision by manufacturers or college catalog editors. One must, of course, feel strongly about such matters when attempting to recast the field in one's own image, for one would hate to dim the vision of those hard, gemlike authorial virtues of narcissism and arrogance.

Will science fiction and fantasy go this way? Partly, it depends on who is writing it—and to the extent that I see many talented newcom-ers in the area, I am heartened. The most gifted writers seem to be the ones who care the least what you call one of these things we are talking about, other than a story. Their main concern is how effec-tively a tale has been told. The area itself, like life, will go through the usual cycles of fads, periodic overemphasis of a certain sort of theme or character—as well as fat books, thin books and trilogies. The best stories will be remembered years later. What they may be like, I can't really say. I'm not in the prediction business.

Part 2
Gestations

The Gestation of Genres: Literature, Fiction, Romance, Science Fiction, Fantasy . . .

Samuel R. Delany

At the Strasbourg International Colloqium on Genre, in July 1979, French philosopher Jacques Derrida began his essay, *"La Loi du genre"* with *Ne pas meler les genres* (Genres are not to be mixed). The essay proceeds by a series of intellectual feints, turns, and interrogations of its own rhetoric, readings of Gérard Genette's *L'Absolue littéraire* and of Maurice Blanchot's limpid fable of vision and blindness, law and the failure of narrativity, crime and the impossibility of punishment, *"La Folie du jour,"* to suggest that such a law—"Genres are not to be mixed."—is, for genres, madness.

Derrida goes on to write: "What if there were, lodged within the heart of the law itself, a law of impurity or a principle of contamination? And suppose the condition for the possibility of the law were the *a priori* of a counter-law, an axiom of impossibility that would confound its sense, order and reason?"

Excerpting synoptic statements, definitive conclusions, or, indeed, any expressed notion that smacks too much of intellectual closure is notoriously difficult with Derrida's writing, which tends to proceed in a style that reminds me of nothing so much as a white moth in a white cloud, beating its wings against the mist, only to be repelled by it, again and again, as if its particular luminosity were a species of negative light. But in this essay Derrida comes as close to an unself-subverted statement as he does anywhere: "I submit for your consideration the following hypothesis: . . . Every text participates in one or several genres, there is no genreless text; there is always a genre and genres, yet such participation never amounts to belonging. And not

because of an abundant overflowing or a free, anarchic and unclassifiable productivity, but because of the *trait* of participation itself,
because of the effect of the code and of the generic mark." Just
before the final movement of his essay, Derrida concludes: "One
cannot conceive truth without the madness of the law"—just a paragraph before declaring, " . . . it would be folly to draw any sort of
general conclusion here."

What I take Derrida to be saying here and elsewhere in his paper
is more or less what Joanna Russ once wrote to me in a letter, after
she'd read one or another of my attempts to fix, from the vast gallery
of SF rhetorical figures, the specificity of various reading protocols
and the generality of their organization: "Worrying about the purity
of the genres," she wrote, "is like worrying about the purity of the
races." I suspect she is right. And I'm afraid I may just be the proof,
in both cases, that the horse is already well out of the barn.

But before we leave Derrida's at once dazzling and daunting
display of self-subversion and self-interrogation, on the occasion of a
consideration of literary genres that has occupied the central spot-
light of much recent thinking on genre theory—before we retire to
more marginal remarks on generic marks and their problematics
within the paraliterary precincts of SF, fantasy, and the like—there is
one other passage in this interrogation of *La Loi* that I would like to
recall for you:

> Outside of literature or art, if one is bent on classifying, one should
> consult a set of identifiable and codifiable traits to determine whether
> this or that, such a thing or such an event belongs to this set or that class.
> This may seem trivial. Such a distinctive trait *qua* mark is however
> always *a priori* re-markable. It is always possible that a set—I have
> compelling reasons for calling this a text, whether it be written or
> oral—re-marks on this distinctive trait within itself. This can occur in
> texts that do not, at a given moment, assert themselves to be literary or
> poetic. A defense speech or newspaper editorial can indicate by means
> of a mark, even if it is not explicitly designated as such: "Voila! I belong,
> as anyone may remark, to the type of text called a defense speech or an
> article of the genre newpaper editorial." The possibility is always there.
> This does not constitite a text *ipso facto* as 'literature,' even though such
> a possibility, always left open and therefore eternally re-markable,
> situates perhaps in every text the possibility of its becoming literature.
> But this does not interest me at the moment.

Here, in this moment, guided by a gaze cast from the brilliant center of literary and philosophical endeavor beyond the margin to what is "outside of literature and art," I glimpse precisely what interests *me*. Between what "may seem trivial" and what "does not interest" Derrida "at the moment" is what I want to look at with all the interest I am capable of mustering.

Let us re-mark it here:

The generic mark, for Derrida, is a mark that no text escapes, implicitly or explicitly, and is yet a mark always outside the text, not a part of it—such as the designations "science fiction" or "fantasy" on the book spine or cover—a mark that codifies the text on bookstore shelf or under hand, calling into play the codes and reading protocols by which the texts become readable. Readers of Derrida's other works will recognize that this "mark" plays a part similar to a whole host of Derridian terms, running from "supplement" in *De la Grammatologie* to "perergon" (or 'the framing') in some of his later essays on art.

Well, where do we go to examine these endlessly remarkable marks, outside of literature and art, that lie in that delicate state of in-betweenness, over every text but belonging to none, where, from the point of view of literature, the trivial careens into the uninteresting? I would ask you to consider that odd upper margin in my own text where the title of this paper sits: "Literature, fiction, science fiction, romance, fantasy . . ." Where do we go to find this inelegant and aneuphoneous set of overlapping marks, some of them clearly on the far side of the literary/paraliterary border? I have simply copied them—re-marked them—from the signs on the edges of the shelves of my local bookstore. And what they mark—what is remarkable about them—is a marginal situation that we who are interested in the workings of genre, especially the interpenetrations and speciation of the paraliterary genres of science fiction and fantasy might do well to fix, at least momentarily, at the center of our attentions.

These generic marks are the material trace of the inarguable fact that, in the last decade, we have seen the partial miosis, if not the complete metastasis, of at least three genres. Literature has recently spawned an odd and awkward offspring called "fiction" (how many bookstores have you been in of late that have the two sections clearly marked?) that already threatens to throw off—if it has not already done so—two further subcategories, "horror" and "romance." Certainly all these terms have venerable and staid meanings in the greater history of our language to which all of us, here, certainly have etymological and historical access. Yet, as they emigrate into the workings of our national book production that contours not only the reading habits of our nation but the millions of dollars and the millions of volumes that bear those marks, not to mention the many more millions of words that are organized by contemporary writers in expectation of the sort of reading those marks have come to call up, meanings change, shift, slip, slide in response to a series of social and economic forces that are, certainly, in their irreducible iterations little different from those that have codified the material reproduction and the critical reduction of all texts over the ages, and thus contoured the protocols by which those texts were read. And science fiction, which for many years bore a small, tumerous excrescence, sometimes called "fantasy" and sometimes "sword and sorcery," has nearly completed the division into two shelves, "SF" over here and "fantasy" over there, as distinct as peas and potatoes in adjoining green grocer stalls—at least in many bookstores around the country.

To examine these generic off springings even as they spring up around us is to see, as Derrida has told us, that none of these genres are pure, even at birth. ("Every text participates in one or several genres.") We say that "horror" springs from "fiction," but clearly the particular horror genre that Stephen King and Peter Straub have constituted between them, with its fallout among several dozen writers, from V. C. Andrews to Michael Macdowell, owes as much to science fiction as it does to Henry or M. R. James—as King himself is the first to acknowledge.

The contemporary "romance," which we cited, is really two modes: there is the Harlequin and Silhouette romance, whose origins can be traced back to a sub-genre that fibrulated through the 1960s without ever gaining a mention in *Publishers Weekly*, that is, the "nurse novel," which was published at the rate of two a month from one minor paperback house, three a month from another house, their production methods more or less identical to those that Harlequin and Silhouette have now parleyed into the largest single reading experience in the United States, dwarfing on the statistical level the privileged textual canon spot-lighted under that more and more beleaguered and ill-bounded category "literature." The second mode is the historical "romance," or "bodice buster," which has made Rosemary Rogers the most widely read writer in the American and English languages, her worldwide sales, a few years back, soaring beyond the all-time record of both Shakespeare and the Bible, a position she shares with (in close second place) Stephen King. But how much of interest can be said of either of these two forms of contemporary romance without citing their immediate predecesor, the contemporary "gothic,"—the single light in the window and the nightgowned heroine aflight on the rocks or shore or downs—a paperback mode that, a decade ago, seemed destined to reappropriate true generic proportions, but that, somehow, never got beyond a kind of cult memory of Anne Radcliffe with a nod to Georgette Heyer.

The current fantasy genre was spawned in the wake of the Tolkien craze of a few years ago, but it also has resonances with Lord Dunsany, James Branch Cabell, William Morris and George MacDonald—indeed, a whole marginal literature of the hundred years between the European revolutions of the mid-nineteenth century and World War II—again, an area of writing that has been kept alive by the enthusiasm of SF editors and readers since the 1920s against endlessly changing tides of tastes.

The historical relation between SF and fantasy, evinced by their current proximity on the shelves carrying both modes in many American bookstores today, is itself a manifestion of the historical coherence of the editorial complex that has overseen both. The relation goes back to the happy accident that *Amazing Stories*, a SF magazine, and *Weird Tales*, a fantasy outlet, were founded at approximately the same time in the 1920s. Add to this the accident of H. P. Lovecraft's interest in using both SF and fantasy forms to tell a horror story and his epistolary energy in conveying his interests and enthusiasms to other writers and, by the middle thirties, you have a whole range of pulp writers who are now seriously interested in both modes; and there grew up among them an editorial complex to support that interest, an editorial complex that has remained stable and coherent to this day.

This is the light which illuminates the fact that Stephen King assumed that his first published novel, *Carrie*, was an SF novel about a girl with telekinetic powers. It was only because the extra-SF

editorial organization at Doubleday, hungry to repeat the commercial success that had attended *Rosemary's Baby* and *The Exorcist*,
decided not to place the book in the standard SF line but to publish it
as a non-SF related horror novel that the artificial ceiling SF at one
point imposed on it sales was broken through to begin the Stephen
King phenomenon.

It should be clear in the light of these generic developments, that
sexual reproduction—syngamy—at least in its usual disexual model,
simply does not cover the confused insemination, gestation, and
never wholly complete parturition of contemporary genres and
subgenres. Indeed, the biological process of syzygy, which Theodore
Sturgeon brought to our attention during the "golden age" of SF, is a
better explanation of generic speciation. We get a new genre when
two old genres, joining, loose their membranous separation, mix and
interpenetrate on some intimate genetic level, which results in a spurt
of growth, multiplication, and the separation of modes, some of
which, against an economic and social environment supportive
enough, are able to flourish and become genres.

What are the forces that bring this flourishing about? Exposure,
advertising, and commercial success—the privileged processes of our
specular capitalism—seem to have been necessary to effect this most
recent split of the subgenres, "horror" and "romance," from capitalism's handmaid and gadfly, "literature," through the transitory
genre of "fiction." The services the texts themselves seem to supply
and stabilize is, in the case of "horror," a surreal showcase for an
endless string of brand names, by which readers recognize the world
around them and participate in the commercial success of the text in
question; at the same time they are reassured that there is something
in that world that is too horrible to deal with, too strange to understand, that will subvert all attempts to change, better, or improve; in
the case of "romance," what seems to have happened is that, in a
nation which has been in the midst of one sexual revolution or
another at least since the end of England's Edwardian Era, the
absolutely safe package for heterosexual carryings-on has once again
been found, placing them at just the right historical distance, in just
the proper linguistic cloud of aspecific rhetoric and with just the right
underlining of emotional and physical violence (read: punishment)
to make them palatable to its largely troubled, dissatisfied, and
generally underpaid female readership—a job the most literary of

genres, the novel, has had to do in one form or another at least since *Pamela*.

Science fiction, as usual, works differently. First, the coherence of the SF editorial complex created a stabilizing factor absent from these other neogenres. Ten years ago, the major publishing houses did not have "horror" editors or "romance" editors. Today they do—indeed, a rule of thumb to help us understand what we are reading, what we are buying in the bookstores around us, might be this: when generic changes become apparent in bookstores, there have always already been business changes to contour them at the editorial and distribution levels. Sometimes these changes are causative. Sometimes they are responsive. But they are there, and the gestation and speciation of contemporary genres are opaque without some understanding of them.

Many publishing houses have had science fiction editors for twenty to thirty-five years, and that editorial complex, now in the dying SF magazines, now moving its members from publisher to publisher, represents a comparatively stable group, bringing in new-comers slowly, providing a certain training, and even a certain weeding out.

Many people assume today that the Tolkien craze of a few years ago operated according to the same model that more recently brought King and Rogers to popularity. They imagine a book discovered by a "literary" editor with a particularly commercial bent: the text is selected, reproduced, advertised, published, and becomes exorbitantly popular—and imitated, finally, in a successful enough manner to establish a genre.

While this was indeed Roger's situation (and thus gives that phenomenon a vitality very few in academia are prepared to wrestle with), it is already an oversimplification of the King phenomenon, and covers the Tolkien phenomenon not at all.

The Tolkien craze could never have occurred without the stability of the SF editorial complex. Tolkien begins, after an initial appearance as a medieval scholar turned children's writer, with a set of eccentric volumes, written at the center of academic Britain, which had a limited but enthusiastic popularity with—in the 1960s—SF's small, marginal fantasy audience, in the United States and England, a popularity that endured for nearly seven years, during which it was observed and remarked by the whole SF community. Only at this

point did an established SF editor decide to make them available in
paperback—a move no commercial general paperback editor would
have been likely to make.

The resultant eruption of general popularity, spilling far beyond
the usual SF audience, not to mention far beyond what, in those
years, were its fantasy margins, makes a situation that is easy to
confuse, in its general social and economic outlines, with the later
situation of horror and romance. The difference, however, is that
here, what we have was a highly stable, specialized editorial tradition
(in the person of Donald A. Wollheim) that was able to stabilize and
organize the general reproduction, so to speak, of a highly specialized and, finally, intellectual text that would otherwise have been lost
to the general readership—rather than a general fiction editor pro-
moting a commercial find to an explosive and overwhelming popularity.

I think this stable editorial complex—which still oversees jointly
fantasy and SF—is the reason that the fantasy field today is growing
slowly and steadily, by the production of works of comparatively high
quality, for example Wangerin's *Book of the Dun Cow* and Ford's
Dragon Waiting. But I think the same social forces that have created
"horror" and "romance" as modern genres are at work in the proliferation of contemporary fantasy in the economic wake of Tolkien,
bolstered by the success of Donaldson and Anthony, all of which
finally pay for the spread of less commercially successful works that
nevertheless serve to educate and stabilize the audience over a given
period. We must also note that this editorial stability feeds into an
initial reading audience that has its own historically mediated stability of a much greater density and responsiveness than the "horror"
audience (with which it largely overlaps) or the "romance" audience
(from which it is largely distinct, save for a few intriguingly anomalous cases). A genre that explodes onto the social scene with the help
of films and television as horror has exploded can only be stabilized
by the audience's lowest common denominator.

The general model that controls the current speciation of "fantasy" and "science fiction" into separate genres is, for better or for
worse, the following: the readership of "science fiction" is editorially
perceived to be about 70 percent male and 30 percent female. The
readership of fantasy is perceived to be about 30 percent male and 70
percent female. In response to this over the past decade, the SF

editorial complex has allowed some editors to specialize in fantasy—though that same complex, almost without exception, has tended to move such editors slowly but inexorably to a secondary position.

Del Rey Fantasy is the first and certainly strongest attempt to establish a separate fantasy imprint. The economic reason for this is simply that instead of one lead title every month, Del Rey books can now present two: one fantasy and one science fiction. There is, of course, great pressure from distributors to prevent this: in the larger scheme of things, there are only a limited number of lead slots. And if fantasy takes one of these over, that it is one less slot for some other publisher, some other genre. Del Rey has only been partially success-ful. And that, in a word, is why only some bookstores today have separate bookstore shelves devoted to fantasy. But it is also why the SF editorial complex is still on the lookout for texts that will support the notion of a separate and discrete fantasy genre. And that is doubtless why writers will write them.

It would be silly to predict the outcome of these various generic speciations (and business conflicts); all of them are only more or less complete in their gestations. Ten years hence or twenty years, any one might have vanished, including science fiction; and any one might stabilize at a slow and developmental growth, contouring a whole interpretive space around the text toward a range of values we can not possibly predict today. But there is another possibility: all of them might move toward some homogenized set of unified and codified readings that could easily turn Derrida's assertion, "all texts belong to a genre or to several genres," into a nostalgic memory of a closed historical moment in which there reigned an idealized plural-ity—though I suspect that the general size of the reading classes sets a lower limit to the homogeneity of generic reading protocols. At least I would hope so. But whatever their futures, I feel safe in predicting that they all will be different; that continuing and developing differ-ence is vouchsafed by the difference of their seeding processes, differences in the varied field through which they have been dissimi-nated, and the innate differences of the dissemination processes themselves.

For many years I have been arguing that science fiction is differ-ent from literature. And, like Derrida, I am not all that interested in such marginal texts, such as SF, becoming literature too quickly—at least before their fascinating and luminous impurities have been studied and stabilized for future readers. And for all its seedings in a marginal practice of imaginative writing, the fantasy that has been growing under the mark of SF until, recently, it has taken on an organizational mark of its own is, I suspect, worthy of the same respect. For, finally, I *am* speaking of respect. I feel that both SF and fantasy must be studied in a full awareness of their historical differences as well as their material conflicts and filiations, an awareness of the difference of their discursive organisations, stabilities, opacities, and responsivenesses, as they are contoured by everything from their individual interpretive tradition and specific semantic conventions to their hard-edged differences in text production and reproduction.

"Truth is inconceivable without the madness of law." Well, it has been remarked. However great a madness the law of genres ("Genres are not to be mixed.") happens to be, it is strategically indispensable for generic study, even as we admit the staggering impurities, overlaps, and miscegenations that make an appropriate mockery out of any attempt to pin down one text or another in a dead moment of rigorous taxonomy—where, one suspects, death is only inflicted so that the inexorable genre mark may, itself, now safely be removed.

For those critics who would make SF or fantasy "literature"—who would deny them their history and nurturence outside the subject-dominated precincts of literature as specific practices of writing with their specific and complex codic responses to the complex object of modern culture—seduced by the nonbelonging of the text to its generic mark, seem to me to be trying to snatch SF and fantasy out from under their mark to drag them through some genreless, unmarked space in which they will, it is hoped, become "just a text," before relocating them under another mark, which, in its illusory separability from the text, proclaims an innocence, transparancy, and purity, free of all history, that no such marking can have.

Within literature, I think the institution of literature itself makes this an impossible crime: here, in the marginal precinct of paraliterature, where we do not have the protection of a long-established scholarly tradition and a sophisticated critical elaboration, such violence is all too possible, especially when committed in the name of literary authority, even though it entail the greatest and most reprehensible of tortuosities, supressions, and evasions—for the impurities of any text are tenacious. The only thing that will kill them once and for all is concerted historical insensivitiy and ignorance.

Genres are not pure. They come to us, always already mixed. But that does not mean they cannot be studied in the specificity of their differences.

To say that science fiction (or modern fantasy) is not the same as literature (or the fantastic) does not mean that what is appropriate to literature is necessarily inappropriate to science fiction. ("There is no genreless text, every text belongs one or several genres.") A sophisticated awareness of that difference, of that multiplicity, of those impurities vouchsafe, however, a margin for criticism: it allows us to note when what applies to literature or the fantastic is misapplied to science fiction or fantasy. It preserves a field where critical distinctions can develop—in a larger field where too many of the greater social forces militate for an instant and insistent homogenization at the lowest possible denominator.

Konstantin Tsiolkovsky: Science Fiction and Philosophy in the History of Soviet Space Exploration

Michael Holquist

Science fiction has a special standing in Russian and Soviet history because both science and fiction have played a unique role in shaping that history. Literature in Russia has traditionally been accorded a status far beyond that enjoyed in other countries. Figures as diverse as Chernyshevsky in the nineteenth century and Solzhenitsyn in our own time have always been there to remind us that literature is constantly taking on tasks that in other cultures are performed by philosophy, social thought, and even theology: Russian literature, in short, has been pursued for purposes far exceeding the merely aesthetic pleasure it might provide. So much is generally recognized in the West. Much less attention has been paid to the extra-scientific motivation that is at the heart of much Russian science: much as literature has been required to do more in Russia than elsewhere, so science has been expected to provide more than merely scientific results. Indeed, the filiation of science and fiction is even more tightly woven: there is a very real sense in which some of the most important Russian science has been prosecuted for ends that must strike any outsider as precisely fictive. We may be more precise. Russian science, or at least an important strand of it, does its work (which may, of course, have the most actual scientific consequence) in a literary context that can be further specified as a branch of utopianism. The purpose of this paper is to provide a specific instance of this thesis.

On October 4, 1957, headlines of a size usually reserved to announce declarations of war gave us the news that the Russians had succeeded in placing a man-made satellite into orbit around the earth. The most immediate effect, internationally, was one of stunned surprise. Instantly a new word—a new Russian word—entered many other languages, including English: *sputnik*. It was to spawn a host of other words when, on December 6, 1957, Vanguard I, the rocket that was supposed to put the first American satellite into orbit, wobbled a few inches off the launching pad and blew up; the English language was instantly enriched with such other new terms as *flopnik*, *kaputnik*, and—my favorite—*stayputnik*.

The rest of the world was amazed by the success of Soviet scientists; and they were only slightly less appalled than the Americans themselves by America's initial blunders in what was immediately perceived to be a "space race."[1] The reasons why everyone was stunned by the Soviet triumph were essentially the same set of reasons that had caused everyone to be caught by surprise eight years earlier when, on September 22, 1949, the Soviets exploded their first nuclear device several years in advance of the most radical Western predictions of when they might do so. We were not prepared for what occurred in both cases because it was a widely held article of faith (and not only in the United States) that Americans had good science and the Russians bad science. This illusion was momentarily dispelled in the fifties, but it has come back to haunt us in current debates about our ability to implement a star wars defense policy as opposed to the presumed lack of technological sophistication that will keep the Soviets from ever being able to mount extraterrestrial weapons of such complexity ("They don't have the miniaturization!") In what follows I will be discussing some ideas that may strike the American reader as hopelessly utopian and far removed from today's problems. But I would remind such a reader that the scientific (which today also means political) effects of those ideas continue to be anything but imaginary.

Let us begin by remembering that like most other things, science came late to Russia. The seventeenth century is everywhere recognized as the watershed of modern scientific development, but it was over a hundred years later that anything resembling European science really got going in Russia as Peter the Great established his Petersburg Academy on the model of such already existing institutions in Paris and Berlin. When the Academy began in 1724 it consisted exclusively of imported foreigners, most of whom did not even speak Russian. Very soon, however, native scholars began to make their mark, especially in those areas that have continued to be particularly strong in Russia, such as mathematics.

But even the most brilliant and patriotic Russian scientists had to confront from the start the hostility of the Orthodox church. Clerical opposition is, of course, a notable factor in the history of science in most Western nations as well. But there are certain features in Russian intellectual and political history that give the Orthodox church's hostility to science a special edge. There are obvious peculiarities, such as the absence of any class within the church analogous to the Jesuits and the nonoccurence of a Counter Reformation in Russia. But more importantly, the czarist form of government was essentially a theocracy; thus the opposition between religion and science was characterized by the extra degree of urgency in Russia, for science was perceived as threat not only to the church but to the government.

This is not the place to rehearse the long, sometimes hilarious but more often tragic tale of relations between science and politics in prerevolutionary Russia. Suffice it that by the 1850s science had achieved the same ideological status for those opposed to the government as orthodox Christianity had for those who supported the government. Science had shaded into scientism, less an intellectual discipline than an ideology, a belief system, even a kind of religion.

A striking example of this tendency which bears directly on the history of Russian rocketry is provided by Ivan Kibalchich, the man who created the explosive device that killed Czar Alexander II in 1881. We can see in the assassination itself a realized metaphor for the government's fear that science, in this case in the form of a particularly ingenious bomb, was its deadly enemy. In the subsequent fate of Kibalchich, who was the explosives expert for assassins in the revolutionary People's Will group, we can see the degree to which science had for the radicals come to occupy the structural slot occupied by Christianity for Russian conservatives of the time. As Kibalchich awaited execution for his crime, he drew up his last testament, a document that took the curious form of a rough blueprint with a number of mathematical formulae attached to it. The design was for a "reactive motor," or what we would now call a jet propulsion engine—the first model of such an engine, in fact, that has been documented. Appended to the design was a note containing Kibalchich's profession of faith: "I believe in my idea, and that faith supports me in my fearful situation. If my idea (works), I will be happy to have performed a great deed for my motherland and for all mankind; I will meet my death calmly, knowing my idea did not perish with me, but will live on among humanity, for whom I was prepared to lay down my life . . ."[2]

I will pass over the obvious features Kibalchich shares (along with many other revolutionaries of the period) with Christian martyrs of the first century. But it should be noted in passing that just as there was an influence going in both directions between the way saints conducted themselves in actual experience and their portrayal in the highly formulaic literary genre of the saint's life, so was there a very intimate connection between the lived lives of Russian radicals and their portrayal in such nineteenth-century novels as those by Turgenev, Chernyshevsky, and other "civic-minded" authors. Among the first texts that would have to be considered in any history of Russian science fiction would have to be these Nihilist fictions about science. For the young Nihilists in such novels as *Fathers and Sons* or *What Is to Be Done?* live their lives in the service of an exalted dream of the future that will be brought about when science, unhindered by religion and the governmental and economic systems dependent for their authority on religion, will reign supreme. Hagiography as a genre helped to produce the kind of life saints actually lived: but as a genre it was, of course, influenced in its formal properties by practices obtaining in the lives of real saints. The same kind of biographical and literary reciprocity can be seen in the relation between revolutionaries and accounts of their lives. For all their opposition to orthodoxy and autocracy, the Nihilists shared with the government one fundamental assumption: that science could be used as a weapon against religion—or for it.

But the Nihilists were not alone in nineteenth-century Russia in putting science in the place formerly occupied by religion. They simply represent the easiest to perceive paradigm assumed by this transformation of values in the 1860s and 1870s. There were others outside both the radical and the conservative camps who sought to harness the power of the natural sciences—in support of religion. And it is these figures, far more peripheral in their own time than either the Nihilists or their opponents, who were to play a much larger role in the development of Russian space science (what the Soviets now call "cosmonautics"). If Kibalchich represents what might be called the Nihilist contribution to cosmonautics, the philosopher Nikolai Fyodorov (1828–1903) and his disciple, the physicist, engineer, and science fiction author Konstantine Tsiolkovsky (1857–1935) may be said to represent a utopian contribution to the philosophy, and more importantly to the practice, of Soviet space science.

This strand in Russian intellectual history is typified by its frequent appeals to categories traditionally associated with religion, and more particularly with Russian Orthodoxy. But these categories are then pressed into the service of a militantly antitranscendental and militantly materialist ideology that can most economically be described as a heresy springing from the emphasis Orthodoxy always placed on the human, physical status of Christ as a man. This ancient doctrine, in the context of the powerful new natural sciences of the nineteenth century, produced a radical humanism that sees in men the capacity to become god ("god-manhood").

It is really Fyodorov's story that needs telling, because Tsiolkovsky is a well-known figure in his own right, regarded by scholars everywhere as the greatest pioneering genius of modern space research.[3] Tsiolkovsky was the first to do most of the things necessary to make, launch, and sustain life inside rockets as we now know them. The list of his original contributions is overwhelming: he developed aerodynamic test methods for rigid air frames; he solved the problem of rocket flight in a uniform field of gravitation; he calculated the amount of fuel needed to overcome the earth's gravitational pull; he invented gyroscopic stabilization of rocket ships in space; and he discovered a method for cooling the combustion chamber with ingredients of the fuel itself (a method still widely used in most jet engines). As early as the 1870s he designed and built a centrifuge-like contraption to test the effects of rapidly increased gravitational acceleration on living organisms, demonstrating principles that would enable the Soviets to launch the dog Laika in their second sputnik and, in 1961, to send the first man into space. Tsiolkovsky also did original work on solid fuels, multiple-stage rockets, and space stations (a particular interest of his that has shaped much subsequent Soviet space policy).

A man with such a list of firsts to his credit has not gone unacclaimed even in the West. Less known is the fact that for all his contributions to science, Tsiolkovsky was not in the narrowly professional sense a scientist at all. On the contrary, he lacked formal degrees of any kind: he was a poor boy who succeeded in living his own Russian version of the Horatio Alger myth: without going to the university, he managed to pass the state examinations necessary to be certified a high school teacher. And he spent most of his life teaching school in obscure provincial towns, such as Borovsk and Kaluga, far from laboratories, libraries, and academic centers.[4]

There is, however, one important difference between Tsiolkovsky and the typical Horatio Alger figure. A detail left out of most accounts of his life is that for all his overcoming of adversity, he was not, in fact, a self-made man. Tsiolkovsky was educated by Nikolai Fyodorov, one of the greatest geniuses—if also one of the greatest eccentrics—that Russia, a country not short of geniuses or eccentrics, ever produced.

Tsiolkovsky's mother died when he was young and his father, who was an itinerant forester, was seldom home. Because Tsiolkovsky was deaf, he was in danger of receiving no formal education of any kind in a time and place where schools for the handicapped were unknown. But he managed to give himself something like a high school education at home. The university education for which he thirsted was quite out of the question. Nevertheless, in 1873, at the age of sixteen, he left Vyatka, where he had been living, and set out for Moscow, determined at least to study in a great library. As it happened, the chief cataloger at the Chertkov library was none other than the philosopher Fyodorov, who immediately recognized something special in the ragged young provincial.

Fyodorov himself was one of history's great autodidacts. Although he was the illegitimate son of Prince Pyotr Gagarin (and thus related to one of his father's collateral descendants, Yuri Alexeevich Gagarin, the first man to be rocketed into orbital space flight), he early chose to educate himself, a habit that stayed with him all his life. Never satisfied with the conventionalities of formal education, he left the lycée without a diploma, but managed nevertheless to pass with distinction the tests necessary to qualify as a high school teacher. After a brief period of itinerant teaching, he ended up in Moscow, where he worked as a librarian for the rest of his life.

During the day, Fyodorov, who lived with the utter simplicity of an anchorite, modestly cataloged books, along the way inventing a much more efficient way to do so. After the library closed, he

devoted himself to prodigious reading and presided over a discussion
club that included through the years many of the most distinguished
names in Russian culture. Dostoyevsky in his later years was an
admirer of Fyodorov, as were Tolstoy, Leonid Pasternak (artist-
father of the man who wrote *Dr. Zhivago*), and many others who
considered Fyodorov to be not only the most erudite man in Russia
(in addition to cataloging the books, he actually read them all) but
the wisest sage of his era. Even philosophy professors such as the
great Vladimir Solovyov listened to him as to a guru; he was not only
a teacher, wrote Solovyov, but a comforter as well.

Fyodorov took the teen-aged Tsiolkovsky under his wing, providing him not only with food and clothing but, what is more important, with an education: he set up a plan of study that roughly
paralleled courses in math and physics departments at the University
of Moscow, but which far exceeded those courses in their breadth
and depth. The philosopher and the boy were in daily contact for the
next three years; Fyodorov encouraged the budding scientist's
dreams, while not neglecting practical assistance, such as helping
Tsiolkovsky pass the qualifying exams and find teaching jobs, first in
one of Fyodorov's former posts at Borovsk, and then in Kaluga,
where Tsiolkovsky taught until he died.

Tsiolkovsky was thus influenced at an early age by the ideas of
Fyodorov, and Tsiolkovsky's great achievements were in fact exercises in applied philosophy. But what kind of philosophy is it that
would inspire a young man stuck in the provinces to begin drawing as
early as July 1878 (in one of the eighteen page exercise books still
used by students in Russia) sketches of the whole known solar
system, of asteroids with men floating in the weightless world inside
them? What philosophy might impel such a young man to think of
himself as a "gravity hater," who would take gravity itself as a bitter
personal enemy and who would conceive "free space" (the name
Russians use for what we call "outer space") less in its normal sense
as free of gravitational pull than as an environment in which freedom
could be realized as a political metaphor and in which the poor would
be equal to the rich?

A philosophy that would have such effects is the body of ideas
Fyodorov called "the philosophy of the common task." The root
idea, the one that attracted so many people to Fyodorov in his
lifetime, is that human beings do not have their natural home on

earth. Rather, they are organisms whose ecosystem is more properly the whole cosmos. In Fyodorov's view, everything is alive, from the gigantic suns of distant galaxies to the smallest pebble under our feet here on earth. Everything is organic: the biggest difference between the life of rocks and the life of human beings is that stones and people live at different velocities in time and at different degrees of consciousness in space. Because people have consciousness in the highest degree, it is their task to "regulate nature," not just here on earth but throughout the universe.

Humanity conceived as the center of everything that exists gains both in dignity and in responsibility. Human beings not only attain the prerogatives formerly attributed to God but shoulder His cares as well. All that is living is connected, as members of a family are related. Therefore the task of "regulating nature" must be undertaken only with compassion and love, for inasmuch as everything has life, we are related both to all other human beings and to matter as well. As human beings we have a moral as well as a scientific imperative to introduce order into the workings of the natural world. In Fyodorov's thought, ethical categories are inseparable from logical or mathematical categories; there is no split between the so-called human sciences and the natural sciences.

The "common task," then, is for people first of all to stop wasting time, effort, and lives in wars; we must stop killing each other, for the great common enemy in the cosmos is chaos, the rampant contingency that finds its most powerful expression in death, where death is conceived as entropy in the universe and as death of the person in individual human beings. Death is the enemy; it is what we should bend ourselves to overcoming, both for ourselves and all other people now living, and for our dead ancestors as well. This is perhaps the most radical aspect of Fyodorov's thought: the search for ways to bring back—physically to resurrect—all the people who have throughout time have passed into the grave. It was precisely this call to the common task of bringing back all our ancestors that attracted Dostoevsky to Fyodorov, and this idea pervades *The Brothers Karamazov*.

Fyodorov was so interested in all aspects of science, and science plays so central a role in his thought because he felt that only through science would the means ultimately be found to raise the dead. The regulation of nature, the point at which the human mind would introduce design and purpose into the workings of a formerly blind and chaotic nature, represents a new epoch in the evolutionary process: the conscious stage of evolutionary development.

Fyodorov's thought is in some sense a combination of Orthodox teaching about the holiness of matter and a Frankenstein-like conviction that, through science, men may become what Mary Shelley called in the subtitle of her novel, *The New Prometheus*. This strange mix is reflected in Fyodorov's style, which brings together elements of the archaic language of Old Church Slavonic and the latest professional jargon in the newest sciences. It is as if one were to describe the subatomic physics in the style of the King James Bible. Cosmonautics in particular interested Fyodorov, because he foresaw the need to find on other planets *Lebensraum*, as well as new sources of food and other necessities, for the immense population that would result from mass resurrection.

Such ideas lie behind not only the science but the fiction of Konstantin Tsiolkovsky. In fact, in Tsiolkovsky it is often hard to separate the two. Tsiolkovsky himself recognized this peculiarity of his work, but always argued the relation between fiction and science was best conceived as sequential. First he maintained came the fairy tale, the fantasy, and only then scientific calculation. A good example of what he meant is provided by the relation between his novel *Beyond the Earth* and the mathematical treatises in which Tsiolkovsky worked out the calculations for how much lift a rocket would have to have in order to escape Earth's gravitation.

Let us begin with the novel, which opens in a setting reminiscent of one of De Sade's hideaways: the year is 2017, but the setting is a castle hidden away in the Himalayan mountains, where a band of wealthy men have gathered in sort of monastery, their wants supplied by a large force of willing servants. But the *raison d'être* of this remote hideaway is not sex, but science (although Tsiolkovsky's brotherhood of seekers is no less obsessive in its pursuit of intellectual exploits than were De Sade's in pursuit of physical sensation. The roster of the company sonds at first like one of those jokes that play on differences between national stereotypes ("There once was an Irishman, a Frenchman, and a Jew . . . "). Not only is the company composed of an Italian, an Englishman, a German, an American, and so forth (and of course a Russian), but they bear such imposing names as Galileo, Newton, Helmholtz, and Franklin—all except the

Russian who is named simply Ivanov, but who plays the most important role.

The essential structure of *Beyond the Earth* consists in little islands of action (such as the launching or landing of a rocket) surrounded by oceans of talk, most of which is scientific or metaphysical. The science is rather formidable in places: Tsiolkovsky uses several of his actual mathematical formulas, using Ivanov as his spokesman. Events are kept to a minimum, and the story *qua* story is quickly told: Ivanov discovers the principle of jet propulsion, applies it to getting beyond earth's gravitational field, lectures his friends on how it can be applied in a large space vehicle. The others enthusiastically join his project, collectively design and, with the help of their many servants, actually build such a ship. They take off and explore the moon (which turns out to have diamonds and kangaroo-like fauna) before penetrating farther towards the sun. In the meantime they communicate their research back to earth and soon other rockets set out as colonists leave to populate new worlds in deep space. At the novel's conclusion, the original group of scientists return to the earth and celebrate in their Himalayan castle with a series of lectures and discussions.

The easy triumph of Tsiolkovsky's fictional scientists is in stark contrast to the setbacks experienced by Tsiolkovsky himself. *Beyond the Earth* was begun in 1896, but the ideas about the necessity of space travel and the actual mathematical formulas it contained go back to a work Tsiolkovsky had done thirteen years earlier in a monograph called simply *Free Space* (1883). Tsiolkovsky received no recognition at the time, and in fact was frequently dismissed as a crank. In 1883 there was a majority of scientists who doubted men would ever fly in conventional aircraft, so it is not surprising that Tsiolkovsky who dreamt of going to the sun in rockets at a time when the airplane had yet to be invented—was treated as a hopeless dreamer. It was only very slowly, and then through nonestablishment, amateur scientific circles that Tsiolkovsky gained any recognition at all. In 1891 he was asked to contribute two papers to a collection published by the physics section of the Natural Sciences Society of Amateurs, the first on the relation of wing length to lift in experimental aerodynamics, and the second on protecting delicate objects from jolts and shocks. This second paper grew out of Tsiolkovsky's attempts to design a rocket that could carry humans into outer space, as Fyodorov had argued was necessary if nature was to be regulated and the dead brought back to life.

Once again frustrated by lack of response from professional scientists, Tsiolkovsky tried another tack in 1895: thinking perhaps he could create more enthusiasm for space travel by describing in fiction some of the possibilities such travel would open, he published a collection of stories called *Fantasies of Earth and Sky*. The relation between his own pragmatic experimentation with centrifuges and mathematical formulae and his experiments in fiction that we see in this move typifies Tsiolkovsky's *modus operandi*: the inventor-scientist uses fiction as propaganda for the real, at the same time permitting its author to imaginatively fill in the gaps of his experimental program as it was progressing in his makeshift laboratory. Thus science fiction served real science as kind of thought experiment, an epistemological wind tunnel, if you will. For in these stories we find not only the first mention of artificial earth satellites but already the necessary math for predicting their orbit (incongruously using the traditional Russian measurements of *poods* for calculating engine thrust and *versts* to discuss distance between planets). Eight years later Tsiolkovsky published the paper that more than any other single contribution is responsible for realizing space travel, "The Probing of Space by Means of Jet Engines," which appeared in *Science Survey* of 1903. In this paper Tsiolkovsky presented a complete theory for a jet engine powered by liquid fuel which would give maximum combustion temperatures; he explained the necessity for streamlined design to insure maximum thrust, described his specific design for such a rocket, and provided the formula (still known as the "Tsiolkovsky formula") that established that a vehicle must reach at least 17,000 m.p.h. if it were to escape earth's gravity, plus other math related to motion of the rocket in space. But when Tsiolkovsky finally received his copy of that now classic issue, he was horrified to discover that through atrocious proofreading the math of his formulas was completely distorted.

He need not have worried, for no one read the article anyway, not only because of its technical sophistication, but because a typically Russian factor now intervened in the history of scientific research: censors had found something subversive—it is still not clear what—in the May issue of *Science Survey* and the government had forced the journal to cease publication. The whole May 1903 issue was confiscated by the police and it was only eight years later in 1911 that Tsiolkovsky was able to publish a second version of his paper, including long additions and painstaking corrections, in the new journal *Flight News*. Nevertheless, even his second paper predated the pioneering work on rocketry done in France by d'Essault-Pelterie (1913), in the United States by Robert Goddard (1919), or by Hermann Oberth in Germany (1923). In the years before the Revolution Tsiolkovsky had further problems in publishing both his fiction and his science: it is no wonder the last thing he did get out before the Revolution was a small booklet whose title sums up the whole lugubrious story of his career to that point, *Sorrow and Genius*.

A new and happier chapter opened for him after the Revolution. The excesses of Stalinism were so horrendous we have forgotten that in the years between the accession of the Bolsheviks to power and the introduction of the first Five-Year Plan in 1928 the Bolshevik Revolution released an enormous charge of creative energy in a number of disparate fields, most powerfully perhaps in the area of the natural sciences. Tsiolkovsky was one of the beneficiaries of this renaissance: in September of 1918, he was named a Fellow of the institution soon to be known as the Communist Academy (the party's answer to the Academy of Sciences). In 1920, a complete version of *Beyond the Earth* was finally published, and in the following years his work on solid-fuel propellants, "rocket trains" (multiple-stage rockets), and space stations appeared in a flood. In 1923 he was awarded the Order of the Red Banner of Labor. In July 1935 a film based on *Outside the Earth* was released, further popularizing rocketry in the Soviet Union. On September 13 of the same year Tsiolkovsky publicly announced that the Soviet government was to be the sole heir to his scientific papers. A few days later (September 19, 1935) he died heaped with honors.

Tsiolkovsky, the student of Fyodorov, is then the father of the Soviet space program. That program is full of triumphs, but has, like our own space program, its darker side. It is a tragic irony that Tsiolkovsky is precisely the man who would regard the current state of poised Soviet and American rockets with the greatest sorrow. Inspired by the utopian visions of Fyodorov, his was a great dream of progress that grew out of the deepest revulsion for war or any other kind of violence.

In the current climate of suspicion vis-à-vis the Russians, it is important to remember the life-affirming vision that played so crucial a role in the early development of the Soviet space program. For we once again face a common task, if not as in Fyodorov's vision of it to bring back our dead parents, then surely in the service of providing a future for our children.

Victorian Urban Gothic: The First Modern Fantastic Literature

Kathleen Spencer

> The record of what actually is, and has happened in the series of human events, is perhaps the smallest part of human history. If we would know man in all his subtleties, we must deviate into the world of miracles and sorcery. To know the things that are not, and cannot be, but have been imagined and believed, is the most curious chapter in the annals of man.
> —William Godwin, *Lives of the Necromancers*

In classifying literary genres, as other entities, the natural human response is to construct a bipolar system: mimetic literature as opposed to nonmimetic, science fiction as opposed to fantasy.[1] Yet neither of these systems is as neatly dyadic as we might think. Not only do both systems allow for an intermediate—a mediating—term, but the same genre can mediate in both systems: the fantastic, in which the ordinary everyday world of mimetic fiction is invaded by events or creatures out of the world of fantasy, creatures which violate our sense of the possible, of the real. The greatest difficulty in discussing the genre of the fantastic is, unfortunately, the term itself, which has become increasingly problematic with every new critical study of the genre. Some critics use *fantasy* and *the fantastic* interchangeably, while others consider one of the terms a subcategory of the other. *Gothic*, another term subject to this critical indeterminacy, is likewise often intermingled in the discussion of the fantastic. However, of the numerous competing models, the better-known theories of such critics as Todorov and Rabkin prove to be less helpful than that of Polish critic Andrzej Zgorzelski.[2]

The fantastic, Zgorzelski states, "consists in the breaching of the internal laws which are initially assumed in the text to govern the fictional world" (p. 298). All texts begin with metatextual information about the genre to which they belong: though not always in a single phrase, like the "Once upon a time" of the fairy tale, but nonetheless unmistakably, they signal their nature in the opening pages. In the case of the fantastic, the initial signals indicate a fictive world based on objective reality, what Zgorzelski calls "a mimetic world model." The subsequent entrance of the fantastic element breaches this model and changes it into a different world, one following different laws. The genre of the fantastic, then, consists of those texts which "build their fictional world as *a textual confrontation of two models of reality*" (p. 298; emphasis in original).

The most important marker of the fantastic—what separates it immediately both from mimetic fiction and from the major non-mimetic genres, science fiction and fantasy—concerns the tone or focus of the narrative itself: in the fantastic, the emphasis is on provoking the reader's sense of wonder or terror at encountering what is not only unexpected, but impossible according to the natural laws of the world they are reading about. When, for instance, Dracula appears in Picadilly Circus at high noon, the characters react initially with disbelief, and the kind of horrified vertigo which results from discovering that a legendary monster is real. At the same time, the author must find a way of justifying or making credible the improbable events of the story, to convince not only the characters but, within the confines of the text, the audience as well of the actuality of their experience. The proper response from characters and readers alike faced with such occurrences is: "This cannot be happening—but it is!"

By contrast, science fiction writers, who construct a text on a nonmimetic world model, direct their efforts "not towards making this world probable, but towards making it *ordinary*; not towards justifying the appearance of improbable events, characters or elements of the setting but rather towards making it appear *normal, everyday-like* within the suggested laws of the given reality" (p. 299). Though the setting and the characters are impossible by mimetic standards—moon colonies, alien creatures, intergalactic space ships, faster-than-light drive, even the future setting—the narrator and the characters accept the existence of such things as in accordance with the laws of possibility in the textual world they inhabit. Thus, readers of science fiction, faced with what appears to be a breach in the laws of the textual world, assume merely that they have not fully understood those laws and that the event, when explained, will turn out to be entirely natural.[3] The same thing holds true for readers of fantasy. However impossible a dragon or a flying horse or a wizard would seem in our ordinary world, in the world of the fantasy text they are taken for granted. They do not violate the laws of the fictional world in which they occur. Unpleasant or threatening a given magical manifestation may be, but it is not a violation of natural law.

The readers of the fantastic, on the other hand, while they must accept that the remarkable occurrences are actually happening, should never come to regard those events as normal or ordinary. The terror of seeing the laws of reality violated is the keynote of the genre. But it is not just the readers who respond with terror to the events of the text; they are instructed in their response by the reactions of the characters and the narrator. Both are naturally aware of the laws of their own world, the initially established mimetic world model, so that when those laws are breached by the fantastic, they respond with astonishment, disbelief, awe, terror—just as readers do in sharing their experience. The fantastic text itself, therefore, testifies repeatedly and in multiple ways that a breach has indeed occurred.

Given this general description of the fantastic, we can be more specific about the textual elements we can expect from a fantastic tale. In the beginning of the text, the ordinary conventions of realism apply. The world of the text refers to a recognizable world, full of realistic objects, customs, and institutions. The characters are, for the most part, not real historical personages but are realistic—a set of generalized characteristics appropriate to their period, class, occupation, and age, combined with individualizing traits. The events described must fall within certain parameters of probability, given the personalities of the characters and their situations; above all, events must obey the natural laws of our own physical world. The subsequent intrusion of the fantastic modifies some of these conventions and adds others. In the first place, the fantastic element must represent a genuine violation of the natural laws of the mimetic world model; that is, it must actually be what it appears to be—not a hallucination, not a dream, not the result of a tricked or overstimulated imagination. Furthermore, the characters or narrator or both must recognize the occurrence as violating the laws of their world.

Paradoxically, in order to make the fantastic event convincing, the author must apply the same techniques of verisimilitude that create the mimetic elements of the text. Surely one of the simplest and most effective of such techniques is the detailed, particularized description of objects and events, fantastic ones and mimetic ones alike. This technique is a variation of what Jonathan Culler, following Roland Barthas, calls a "descriptive residue," items in a story which tell us nothing about plot or character, whose only function in the text is to be there in order to denote concrete reality—"trivial gestures, insignificant objects, superfluous dialogue"—to represent the simple *thereness* of the world.[4] If such descriptions of ordinary objects can convince us of the reality of the text's world, they can also help us accept the reality of the fantastic elements which intrude into that world. The more specific and intimate details of appearance and behavior we are given, the more persuasive the fantastic occurrence will seem.

One of the aspects of the fantastic which contributes most crucially to the verisimilitude of the genre may well be the initial mimetic setting itself: if we recognize and accept the world and its characters as realistic, and enter into their perceptions and experiences, we thereby make an emotional commitment to the text as verisimilar, we commit energy to believing in it. Even when the fantastic challenges the initial mimetic world's credibility, the characters are experiencing the same doubts and dislocations that we are. Consequently, though our identification with the world of the text has been disrupted, our identification with the characters is not diminished but, on the contrary, reinforced. Rather than rejecting the text altogether, we instead experience that typical and paradoxical reaction to the fantastic: this, we think, cannot be happening, yet it is.

If the fantastic can be considered to mediate between the mimetic and the nonmimetic, it can also, from another point of view, be seen as mediating between science fiction and fantasy. Partly this is a simple matter of plot: in some fantastic fictions, the intruding element comes from the science fiction realm—all alien invasion stories, for example, or nuclear war stories like Ted Sturgeon's "Thunder and Roses" or Nevil Shute's *On the Beach*. In other sorts of fantastic fiction, the invasion derives from the realm of fantasy—*Dracula*, or Somerset Maugham's *Magician*, or *Rosemary's Baby*, or almost any Stephen King novel you choose to name.

But there is another level too at which the fantastic mediates between science fiction and fantasy. In researching British fantastic fiction of the late nineteenth and early twentieth centuries, I discovered a new and distinctively modern form of the fantastic that developed in the 1880s: the urban gothic. This is a form whose popularity has grown steadily into contemporary times, represented not only by writers like King but by movies like *Wolfen, An American Werewolf in London*, and *The Hunger*.[5] These first urban gothic tales are set in the modern city, and derive a substantial part of their emotional power from the contrast between the materialist beliefs of most of the characters and the supernatural marvels or horrors happening before their eyes—a vampire prowling the streets of London, a three-thousand-year-old mummy reanimated and killing at the command of its master, or a magician using his powers to kill an enemy without detection or to conquer death.

The world in which these texts begin is the ordinary materialist world we know; and the characters, like us, believe in the power of induction, of rational thought operating on facts, to solve all problems and answer all questions. This is also the basic assumption underlying science fiction as a genre, that the universe is governed by rules 'which can be learned and used to achieve predictable repeatable results. But the characters in urban gothic tales find themselves confronting beings or events which cannot be explained by the natural laws they know, beings and events which are more like the ones to be found in the worlds of fantasy than those of science fiction. In order to deal with the fantastic situation, the characters must abandon the familiar laws as inapplicable, and must either learn an alternate set of laws (those of ritual magic, for instance) which will allow them to control the situation, or they must experiment to discover what kinds of actions will produce the desired results. But in searching for these laws, the characters rely on empirical techniques. In *Dracula*, for instance, the key action turns out to be Mina's chronological arrangement of the documents in the case—Jonathan's journal, her journal, Dr. Seward's log, and various letters—an action which turns a pile of miscellaneous facts into a coherent body of data from which the two scientists, Van Helsing and Seward, can draw accurate conclusions. Thus, the texts of the Victorian urban gothic insist that, even in the realm of magic and unholy spirits, the scientific temper is still of use (though some of the more recent examples of the genre seem less sure of that). It is this characteristic combination of the rational and the irrational, of science and the occult, which leads me to argue that the urban gothic functions as a mediating form between science fiction and fantasy.

It is no accident that this form of the fantastic is an invention of the late nineteenth century.[6] In the first place, it is only then that the awareness of science and the power of the scientific method become relatively widespread in the culture; and in the second place, it is then that the experience of urban life begins to dominate public awareness in Britain. By 1850, as Raymond Williams points out, the urban population of England outnumbered the rural population—for the first time ever, anywhere in the world; and by the end of the century, the urban population was three-quarters of the whole. "As a mark of the change to a new kind of civilization the date has unforgettable significance."[7]

Living in such an unimaginably large city as London had become means that by definition one lives surrounded by strangers, by people who do not know or care about you and whose private lives are mysteries. Everyone knew there were dangerous parts of the city, inhabited by the poor and the criminal; but even the respectable middle-class parts of the city had their terrible secrets. Behind the distinguished mien of Henry Jekyll lurked the monster Hyde; other ordinary visages concealed black magicians, unscrupulous mesmerists, perhaps a werewolf—or a woman who looked twenty might turn out to be actually four thousand years old, a priestess of Isis whose youth has been preserved by human sacrifice. Over and over the tales of the urban gothic repeat this message: surface appearances cannot be trusted. The natural, reasonable, mundane world is only a thin film covering a realm of horrors which at any moment might break through to attack the unsuspecting, and it is the city, that indiscriminate, crowded, roiling mass of humanity, which creates a hospitable space in the modern world for such monsters, a place where they can hide unsuspected.

The modernity of the urban gothic is further marked by its other identifying characteristics besides the urban setting. Most important is the effectual thematization of the mystery plot and the omnipresent figure of the detective, that characteristically Victorian discoverer of secrets. The "detective" in an urban gothic tale may be a police officer or a private consulting detective like Sherlock Holmes, but more often he is a lawyer, a scientist, or a doctor—someone accustomed to gathering data, weighing evidence, and drawing conclusions. It is not uncommon, as in *Dracula*, for there to be several figures in the tale sharing the detective function. There are even several collections of tales about "occult detectives," that is, people with occult knowledge or abilities who specialize in solving problems in the spiritual realm. Most of these are doctors or psychiatrists, like Algernon Blackwood's John Silence, or Dion Fortune's Dr. Taverner; but some of them are psychical researchers, and a few, like Sax Rohmer's Moris Klaw, specialize in uncovering psychic frauds. There is even one woman among these occult detectives, a professional psychic—a White Witch, as she is described by her clients, though she prefers the title "supersensitive."[8] But, whatever their profession, all these characters function like detectives, finding answers to puzzles and proposing action to solve crimes.

The second identifiably modern characteristic of the urban gothic is its concern with contemporary science, both with an underlying "empiricist epistemology"—that faith in the power of inductive reasoning discussed earlier—and with the potential of scientific advances to revolutionize human life. One subset of the urban gothic, those stories whose plots center upon such scientific advances, provides a helpful contrast with science fiction. The typical "occult science" story concerns a scientist who makes a remarkable discovery or invents some device which promises to make dramatic advances in some aspect of life, but he dies and the discovery or invention is lost: either the crucial details have never been written down, or the notes get lost or destroyed or fall into the possession of someone incapable of understanding them (as at the end of Wells' *Invisible Man*). However, these occult science stories are very different from the usual science fiction or contemporary horror-fiction treatment of this plot in which such a character would be treated as the Mad Scientist, trying to discover something "man was not meant to know."The death of the Mad Scientist and the loss of his invention is thus a highly moral ending to these stories, meant to warn readers of the dangers of science run amok. In the Victorian tales of occult science, the scientist's invention is a potential good if not an actual one, and his death functions not to point the moral, but rather to explain why this wonderful invention or discovery is not broadly available. In other words, the scientist's death is generally a pragmatic device—a way to preserve verisimilitude. The major exceptions to this pattern are Stevenson's *Dr. Jekyll and Mr. Hyde* and Wells' *Invisible Man*, in both of which the scientist's death does make an explicit moral statement.

Significantly, the scientists in these occult science stories either are medical doctors specializing in the brain, nervous system, or nervous disorders; or they are physicists, chemists, engineers, or mathematicians investigating problems of perception, or nonmaterial aspects of communication, or altered states of consciousness—dream, trance, sleep. All of these people tend to be investigating, one way or another, the problem of individual identity and the unexplored territory of death: in other words, they all concern themselves with the mysterious connections between mind and body, spirit and matter—that ambiguous boundary where the occult and the scientific join. Thus, these stories manifest the characteristic blend which marks them as part of the Victorian urban gothic.

Another significant marker of the modernity of the Victorian urban gothic is the nature of the fantastic intrusions in these stories, which derive from such explicitly late-Victorian cultural phenomena as spiritualism and Theosophy, psychical research, and the contemporary occult revival (most notably the Hermetic Order of the Golden Dawn, which at the turn of the century claimed both W. B. Yeats and Aleister Crowley as members). These movements not only achieved widespread adherence throughout the culture, but also, through extensive public discussion of such experiences as seances and table rapping, had made their philosophical assumptions and their procedures common knowledge even among those who did not believe in them. The urban gothic stories about such issues include frank apologetics written by members of the various groups, *romans à clef* about contemporary occult circles, stories which make use of certain basic ideas about the existence of human spirits separate from the body without subscribing to the entire spiritualist or Theosophical doctrine, and simple potboilers (whose very existence in such numbers proves there was a significant audience for such stories).

Although I have made no study of the contemporary urban gothic, it seems likely to me that it is in such matters as subject that we will find the greatest differences between the original Victorian versions and the more recent ones Seymour Rudin examines. This is only logical. One of popular literature's most important functions is to express the anxieties of its culture; and while many of our own cultural anxieties have their roots in the late Victorian period—the common experience of alienation, the need to humanize large cities, fear of devolution or loss of humanity, the irresolvable debate between spiritualist and materialist models of the world—there are also significant differences between us and our ancestors. The world has changed in a hundred years, and the problems they grappled with have reached different stages in our time and manifest themselves under different guises. The Victorians' anxieties about the giant city concerned its appallingly rapid growth; ours deal with the problem of decay, and the horrible things that can grow out of decay. For them, science was still essentially a positive power, knowledge which would ultimately give humanity much greater control over the natural world than it currently had; but we have learned to our sorrow that in human hands science has as much power to work evil as good, and that our ability to control or make wise use of our own inventions is highly questionable. Thus, in Victorian urban gothic, the lonely genius struggling to wrest one of Nature's secrets into the light was a positive, if ultimately tragic, figure; for us, he is most often the Mad Scientist, an example of hubris and a warning to us all. Finally, the Victorian urban gothic does not demonstrate the contemporary fascination with material horror, with blood and violence; that motif becomes central only in the aftermath of World War I, and has since grown steadily as our vision of the world and our place in it gets progressively bleaker and more terrifying.

Burke observed in his essay on the sublime that terror is delightful only at a certain distance. But the urban gothic takes precisely the opposite tack: the supernatural terrors, the fantastic occurrences, derive much of their emotional power from the fact that they are happening here, now, next door, in the ordinary daily world—or a world that has always appeared to be ordinary—to people very like the readers themselves. As the distance disappears, the sense of the fantastic increases. These tales must give readers pleasure, or we wouldn't read them; but they are doing more than that. Stories about vampires in London, about sinister mediums, about ancient mummies being revivified, should be read as revealing—in the indirect, symbolic ways appropriate to art—the secret nightmares of comfortable bourgeois Victorians. Identifying those nightmares helps to explain both the increased popularity of all kinds of nonmimetic fiction in the nineteenth century and in particular the invention of a new kind of "contemporary" fantastic like the urban gothic. In turn, understanding the origins of the urban gothic as a genre distinct from, yet related to, both science fiction and fantasy will help us to understand the more recent versions of the urban gothic which express our own up-to-date nightmares.

Jewels of Wonder, Instruments of Delight: Science Fiction, Fantasy, and Science Fantasy as Vision-Inducing Works

Michael Clifton

When I was a boy, reading my way through the few juvenile science fiction books in the local library, I discovered Clifford Simak's *City* quite by accident in the separate, adult section all the librarians thought was too old for me. In a sense, they were right: the concepts and vocabulary were over my head, and I only half-followed the story. On the other hand, I had a good, intuitive sense of English syntax and knew what the individual words in the sentences were doing; I simply supplied most of the conceptual material out of my own abundant imagination. Because of this, I remember the book from that first reading as really marvelous, filled with strange and colorful scenes I could never quite remember clearly afterward. Yet on a subsequent reading—at the advanced age of thirteen or so, driven back at last by that remembered sense of magic—the book was not nearly as good. Oh, it was still first-rate, of course, but the half-glimpsed marvels were missing and, consequently, a great deal of what brought me back, book after book, to science fiction and, later, to fantasy.

This reaction of mine leads me toward a definition of a major function of both genres, which is, quite simply, to provide contact with the unconscious, the creative imagination from which all marvels spring, not simply for myself but for all of us. In order to defend this definition—and having done so, to argue that the two genres are collapsing into one in order to continue providing such contact for both authors and audience—it is necessary to be able to tell when, in fact, such contact occurs in literature: what forms it will take, what emotions will surround its occurrence, and so on. Fortunately, the means of determining just these things lies at hand, the offshoot of an earlier study to discover what was behind the shift toward and popularity of deep image poetry in this country in the early 1960s. From that effort emerged a pattern of contact with the unconscious that applies equally well to many of my favorite science fiction and fantasy writers. Based partly on my own meditative efforts, partly on Aldous Huxley's similar efforts with psychedelics and hypnosis, and partly on experimental efforts to discover the overlap of mystical states and drug experiences, the pattern—a visionary schema, in effect—forms the backbone of this paper.

Extrapolating from his experiences with both mescaline and deep hypnosis in his book *Heaven and Hell*, Huxley characterizes the two common features of all visionary experiences as light and bright colors, writing that everything "seen by those who visit the mind's antipodes is brilliantly illuminated and seems to shine from within. All colors are intensified to a pitch far beyond anything seen in the normal state"[1] Both these appear most often, according to Huxley, in the form of brilliant, intricately structured entities resembling flowers or gems (pp. 103–04). This leads him to generalize that the chief virtue of earthly jewels and blossoms—the secret of the huge attraction both have always had for mankind—is that they remind us, however dimly, of their visionary counterparts, whether they occur naturally or in a recreation, that is, "whatever, in nature or in a work of art, resembles one of those intensely significant, inwardly glowing objects encountered at the mind's antipodes is capable of inducing, if only in a partial and attenuated form, the visionary experience" (p. 105). For Huxley, in fact, the chief intent of certain forms of art is to provide just those hints and flashes of the unconscious: "in the realm of art," he writes, "we find certain works, even certain classes of works, in which the same transporting power [that is, the same as that of literal gems and flowers] is manifest" (p. 106).

With Huxley's schema in hand—a light, generally white or golden, together with the imagery of brightly colored gems or flowers—it is quite possible to label fantasy as one of the classes of works that is vision-inducing simply by listing some examples of such visionary imagery, which occur throughout the genre. Gems, for example, occur in everything from Fletcher Pratt's *Blue Jewel* to *The Lord of the Rings*, chiefly in the form of Tolkein's famous *silmaril* and *palantir*—the latter of which explicitly provides visions of distant landscapes. The hobbit Pippin, entering into what appears to be an involuntary trance-state upon gazing into such a gem—"it held his eyes, so that now he could not look away . . . closer and closer he bent, and then became rigid"—and Saruman the wizard's gradual corruption from constant gazing into one testify to the enormous appeal of its vision-inducing power.[2]

Tolkien's seminal work, in fact, provides a kind of focus for the other imagery in the schema typical of the genre. Bright light appears, together with a variant of the gem imagery, in the vial Galdriel presents Frodo. The entire realm of Lothlorien itself is not only golden but home to flowers of unearthly beauty, the *elanor* and *niphredil* (see the floating mats of flowers on the oceans of Venus in C. S. Lewis' *Perelandra*). Walking among these leaves the hobbit Frodo with heightened sensory perceptions and a sense of the interior life of things: he had never before "been so suddenly and so keenly aware of the feel and texture of a tree's skin and of the life within it. He felt a delight in wood and the touch of it, neither as forester nor as carpenter; it was the delight of the living tree itself" (I, p. 366). His emotions and perceptions, in other words, are those of a person transported; to use a more modern phrase, he is experiencing an altered state, a heightened, waking awareness of the unconscious.

It happens to him more than once during his long quest because Frodo is actually a bit of a visionary, experiencing both pleasant and unpleasant altered states of consciousness (ASC's) on a number of occasions, one of them, for example, in Elrond's house at Rivendell when listening to the voices and instruments of the elves:

> At first the beauty of the melodies and the interwoven words in the Elven-tongue, even though he understood them little, held him in a spell, as soon as he began to attend to them. Almost it seemed that the words took shape, and visions of far lands and bright things that he had never yet imagined opened out before him; and the firelit hall became like a golden mist above seas of foam that sighed upon the margins of the world. Then the enchantment became more and more dreamlike, until he felt that an endless river of swelling gold and silver was flowing over him, too multitudinous for its pattern to be comprehended; it became part of the throbbing air about him, and it drenched and drowned him. (I, pp. 245–46)

To read—or to write about—such an episode is to experience it vicariously, and it is just this, the vision-inducing quality Huxley defines, that is typical not only of *The Lord of the Rings* but of the genre Tolkien's work helped create.

Making the case for science fiction as another vision-inducing genre is not quite as simple as for fantasy since there is no single, seminal work one can approach as representative; there are, however, popular authors—writers who are evidently doing, and doing well, what their audience feels the genre should do—and examples from two such authors, Roger Zelazny and Brian Aldiss, should make the point.

Zelazny's novel *Doorways in the Sand*, written in 1976, is nearly as perfect an example of hard science fiction as one could desire: not only was it originally published in *Analog* and dedicated to Isaac Asimov, but each element of the story is either solidly scientific or a plausible extrapolation from current theory. It has a galactic federation, aliens both evil and friendly, glimpses of a technology far beyond us, a likable, intelligent hero named Fred Cassidy—and it has the "star-stone," a sentient, viruslike gem described as a "pseudo-stone, semiopaque or semitransparent, depending on one's philosophy and vision, very smooth, shot with milky streaks and red ones. It somewhat resemble[s] a fossil sponge or a seven-limbed branch of coral, polished smooth as glass and tending to glitter about its tips and junctures. Tiny black and yellow flecks were randomly distributed throughout."[3] The gem is a gift to the Earth from another race in the galaxy as part of what Zelazny calls "an interstellar *kula* chain," that is, an exchange of ceremonial artifacts analogous to that of certain Pacific islanders (pp. 29–30). It is therefore a means of "affirming the differences and at the same time emphasizing the similarities of all the intelligent races in the galaxy—tying them all together" (p. 30). It is, in short, an instrument of unity and functionally identical to the flowers of Lothlorien, by means of which Frodo also savors the existence of a life form different from himself.

By various haps and mishaps, this living jewel literally becomes a part of Cassidy, and the book is, in large part, the record of its repeated attempts to communicate with him, to rouse itself to full awareness, and the consequences thereof. The problem is that the star-stone can only communicate with him during marginal states of awareness, when he is either highly relaxed, asleep, or just waking. One of these dimly recollected attempts at communication, the "kinesthetic/synesthetic DO YOU FEEL ME LED?" remembered as "a penny's worth of spin and color" over his morning coffee (p. 32), for example, is typical of the sort of ASC achieved by means of psychedelic drugs or meditation.[4]

Zelazny is so nearly forthright about what he is doing, however, that one need not go to secondary sources for support. The first time the star-stone manages to communicate with Fred success- fully—during a moment in orbit when he is caught up in a "glorious sensation," a highly pleasurable sense of the "beauty of basic things, things as they are and things as they might be" (p. 45)—he is able to understand the conversation of two aliens speaking a language he realizes is nonterrestrial. Speculating about both this and other strange turns to his thought-processes, Fred asks himself, "Had some valve given way in my unconscious, releasing a river of libido that cut big chunks of miscellanea from the banks it rushed between, to deposit them in shiny layers of silt up front here where I normally take my ease?" (p. 47).

Once Fred manages to rouse the star-stone to awareness, follow- ing its instructions, his reward is to become its partner in a gal- axy-wide hunt for information: he becomes a professional traveler and seeker of marvels. And when he visits the first of these extrater- restrial, visionary landscapes, both the bright colors and the golden light Huxley's schema predicts appear together. Describing what he calls an "Epiphany in Black & Light, Scenario in Green, Gold, Purple & Gray" (p. 175), Zelazny paints a race Fred has with himself on another planet:

> Climbing from hold to green stone on the seaward side of the structure, he has contrived to race with the last of the day as it flees upward, tilts, prepares to jump. In the antic light of evening the top of the Tower of Cheslerei is the last spot touched by the daygold before its departure from the capitol . . .
> He draws himself up and stands, turning his head toward the sea, toward the light. Yes . . .
> He catches the final fleck of gold that it tosses. For a moment only he stares after it. (pp. 175–76)

Fred's reward for rousing to full awareness this interior jewel, in other words, is a momentary glimpse of the gold light visionaries of every time and place have described as a key element of their expe- rience; it is the same light Tolkien's hobbit sees.

Brian Aldiss' more recent *Helliconia Spring* also contains this light, as well as the other elements of Huxley's visionary schema, but in order to understand Aldiss' treatment of such imagery, it is first necessary to introduce the element of experimental psychology. During efforts to discover the overlap between classic mystic states and altered states induced by psychedelic drugs, researchers discovered that the common experience of those resisting the sudden flow of unconscious material was that of feeling one's self to be trapped behind a glass barrier.[5] Arguably, then, the presence of the usual light or bright colors under a sense of something glass may be equivalent to an ambivalent, rather than a wholeheartedly positive, sense of the unconscious; a vision is induced, to be sure, but the subjective sense of that heightened contact with the unconscious is dicey.

When one of Aldiss' characters descends into the underworld of a "brassimip," then, a huge tree consisting almost solely of passable, oversize roots, she is assailed by a "perfumed rotting smell that both repelled and attracted her."[6] Her reaction, in other words, is ambivalent, and the brassimip itself, actually an image of the unconscious, one which, in Aldiss' case, is at once pleasant and dangerous, a "refuge for several sorts of animal, some decidedly nasty" (p. 185).

But not all of them. In addition to the light and colors typical of such a place—she sees "spots of light, star-like—galaxies of red stars imprisoned in the tree" (p. 186)—the woman Vry brings back to the surface with her another inhabitant of the brassimip. Emerging in a state of heightened awareness similar to but less pleasant than the hobbit Frodo's—the "world seemed blindingly bright, the ring of axes intolerably loud, the scent of jassiklas unduly strong" (p. 186)—Vry gazes down at the animal she has brought with her, a *glossy*: "It was in a state like the phagor's tether [that is, the deep trance-state of an alien race], curled into a ball with its nose tucked into its tail, its four legs folded neatly into its stomach. It was immobile, and felt as if made of glass . . . through its dusty coat, striations of faded colour showed" (p. 186). The visionary colors Huxley predicts appear here under that sense of something glassy caused by resistance to the flood of unconscious material. Essentially, the little animal is a vision-in-embryo, an ASC held at bay by some underlying ambivalence.

Aldiss supports this interpretation of the *glossy* and its glassy feel by establishing it as, in fact, the embryonic form of the hoxney, the animal that captures the essence of Helliconia's long spring: "Of all the life that invaded the western plains, it was the hoxney that, in its sportiveness, most embodied the new spirit" (p. 219). It is in the insouciant hoxney, then, that the visionary colors appear forthrightly: "Every hoxney bore stripes of two colours, running horizontally from nose to tail. The stripes might be vermilion and black, or vermilion and yellow, or black and yellow, or green and yellow, or green and sky blue, or sky blue and white, or white and cerise, or cerise and vermilion" (p. 219).

The imagery of the most positive vision possible, however, appears in a hunter's chance encounter with the woman he desires in a place described as a "hollow, in the centre of which lay a deep pool surrounded by verdure." This secret place-with-a-pool is another image of the unconscious, and the sight of his beloved in it triggers an episode for the hunter in which all the elements of Huxley's schema appear, together with a hint of that sense of unity to which both Tolkein and Zelazny allude: "Batalix had broken free from one of the giant purple castles of cloud, to flood the land below with gold. The sentinel's rays scattered obliquely over Oyre's cinnamon skin, which was pearled about her shoulders and breasts with water drops. Runnels of water chased themselves down the mazes of her flesh, finally spreading to the stone on which she stood, as if to unite her, naiadlike, to the nearby element they shared" (p. 228). The hunter's reaction to the sight of her—"'Oyre, golden Oyre!' he called in ecstasy" (p. 229)—supports the notion advanced here of the passage as an analog of a visionary experience, as does Aldiss' description of their subsequent lovemaking: "There they lay in the secret place, serene, ecstatic, making love. The mud beneath them, plastering their sides, emitted comfortable noises, as if full of microbes all copulating to express their joy in life" (p. 230). In this image of the most positive sense of the unconscious, the very mud—the fertile chaos out of which all life (and creativity) springs—is caught up in a great sexual dance, a joy literally approaching orgasm.

The blurb on the cover of *Helliconia Spring* that declares it to be the work of a "professional visionary," then, is precisely right, not only for Aldiss but for Zelazny, Tolkien, and a great many other writers in both genres, and the schema that establishes both science fiction and fantasy as vision-inducing art forms can further be used to help explain the collapse of the old genres into the hybrid science fantasy.

The first reason for such a collapse is the general rule that, as Huxley puts it: "Familiarity breeds indifference" (p. 115). We all recognize this phenomenon in one form or another: that new album, the one we could not hear often enough, finally begins to pall; favorite passages from a novel or poem no longer much move us, and we wonder what caused our initial excitement. After so many years of wizards, so many marvelous gems or instruments, so many quests into the unknown—whether to another galaxy, the future, or to an alternate reality, no matter how wonderful—the old patterns or genres in their strict forms no longer give us quite the same lift. They are, in short, no longer vision-inducing, even in the attenuated form Huxley describes as initially possible for them. And when the original theme tires, both writers and audience look to variations for that fading exhilaration.

As a kind of corollary to this rule, the technology that is crucial to science fiction has had a key role in the loss of power to induce visions. "Modern technology," according to Huxley, "has tended to devaluate the traditional vision-inducing materials" (p. 115). Had he been writing during the Electronic Revolution today, however, with its LED displays, its moving lights and computer graphics, Huxley would more likely have written not that technology is devaluating the traditional vision-inducing materials (and forms), but that it is replacing them. The essential elements of vision—bright light and color in intricate patterns—are more readily and vividly available in any video game, or in the special effects of any science fiction or fantasy movie released these days, than they are in the pages of a book. One can always read of such things couched in technological terms—by visiting the Weapon Shops of Isher, say—but why bother when a quarter will buy you the literal lights (and with auditory stimulation to boot)? Such amusements are far more directly vision-inducing than any literary representation, and the accounts of unconscious marvels-as-technology have dwindled in proportion to the actual technology's ability to replace them. Consequently, a new genre has risen in which the role of technology per se is restricted: not science fiction but science fantasy is the current popular vision-inducing literary form for those of us who are both old-fashioned enough to demand our visions in print and sufficiently hardheaded to demand some initial, quasi-rational explanation for their occurrence.

But there is another reason for technology's dwindling role in science fantasy, which is that the visionary experience is not always pleasurable, whether it is attenuated or not. As Huxley explains, the presence of "negative emotions"—resistance based on fear, anger, or whatever—will cause the nightmarish inverse of the positive vision (pp. 137–38). Using the example of a French schizophrenic as representative, Huxley writes that, in the negative vision, "Everything that, for healthy visionaries, is a source of bliss brings to Renee only fear and a nightmarish sense of unreality. The summer sunshine is malignant; the gleam of polished surfaces is suggestive not of gems, but of machinery and enameled tin" (p. 134). The same elements of vision, light and bright colors, then, are indicative of an appalling rather than a pleasurable sense of the unconscious when they are seen in connection with machinery.

The epitome of this negative visionary experience is the sense of being dismembered in a machine; Poe's classic "The Pit and the Pendulum" captures the essence of it, but killing machines are present in modern science fiction as well, in that Demon Prince of Vance's who specializes in them, for example, or in Saberhagen's Berserker series. (One should note that Saberhagen's title contains an implicit recognition that what he is imaging with his deadly mechanism is an altogether unpleasant altered state, a "dangerous" form of trance similar to that of the traditional berserker.)

Given this odd connection between vision and machinery, that is, technology, it is possible to restrict the earlier definition of science fiction and fantasy as vision-inducing genres even further: a major purpose of both genres is not simply to provide a sense of contact with the unconscious but to provide a pleasurable sense of such contact. In order to do so, the role of the machine is necessarily diminished, and what emerges is a new genre in which technology is background: marvelous machines are no longer the focus but the bolster, providing an element of belief, a quasirational mechanism necessary for the suspension of disbelief, that relaxing of rational safeguards necessary to the enjoyment of any visionary experience, whether literal or literary.

In our highly technological society, there are essentially three reasons, following this visionary schema, why the old genres of science fiction and fantasy are collapsing into the hybrid science fantasy, the first of which is that the vision-inducing quality of overly familiar patterns diminishes; neither the old-fashioned space opera nor one more wondrous quest can any longer provide that necessary sense of the marvelous for those of us who have read too many. The second reason for this collapse of the traditional forms is that real, electronic technology is simply too vivid for any vision-in-print to compete, and the third, closely related to the second, is that a sense of machinery is associated with an awareness of the unconscious that ranges from the unpleasant to the appalling. While the presence in current science fiction of the killing machines that embody this vision argues that a negative sense of the unconscious is better than none at all for some readers, the simultaneous emergence of a new genre— one in which the visionary elements of bright light and colors appears at a safer distance from the machine—argues that most of us prefer our visions to be pleasant, attenuated or not.

The Tooth That Gnaws: Reflections on Time Travel

David A. Leiby

> The uncertainty of life and one's final lot has always been associated with mutability, while unforseen and uncontrollable change has been linked with time. Time is the tooth that gnaws . . .
> —John Dewey, "Time and Individuality"

Since H. G. Wells' *Time Machine* appeared in the last decade of the nineteenth century, writers of science fiction and fantasy, writers ranging from Asimov to Zelazny, have used the idea of man being able to travel into the future or into the past bodily as well as mentally to create time travel stories which fall into a variety of categories: stories that use time as an analogue for space; stories that speculate on the nature of time; stories that speculate on the end of man; stories that engage the reader in a mire of paradoxes; stories that speculate on causality by introducing time loops and alternate worlds; and stories that appear to be concerned with providing historical tours. Using the concept of a world in which the characters can travel in time enables writers such as Gerrold and Heinlein to experiment with point of view shifts that do not require any textual signal to the reader, scenes that characterize the protagonist by showing him interacting with one or more manifestations of himself, plots whose circular nature allows for the development of character as the old scientific romances rarely did, and themes that traditional stories can only treat in a metaphysical manner. Moreover, time travel is largely a point of intersection for fantasy and science fiction, because writers of both forms share the same metaphysics and hence the same literary techniques. To demonstrate the similarity of literary techniques in fantasy and science fiction and the dissimilarity of these techniques with those occurring in traditional literature, I shall ana-

lyze works by Faulkner, Wells, and Heinlein using two major philosophical conceptions of time.

The two concepts of time that form the basis of all stories in this
discussion were named the A-series and the B-series by J. M. E.
McTaggart in his famous argument to demonstrate the unreality of
time, an argument first published in 1908. Briefly, McTaggart says:

> Positions in time, as time appears to be *prima facie*, are distinguished in
> two ways. Each position is Earlier than some and Later than some of the
> other positions. To constitute such a series there is required a transitive
> asymmetrical relation, and a collection of terms such that, of any two of
> them, either the first is in this relation to the second, or the second is in
> this relation to the first. We may take here either the relation of "earlier
> than" or the relation of "later than," both of which, of course, are
> transitive and asymmetrical. If we take the first, then the terms have to
> be such that, of any two of them, either the first is earlier than the
> second, or the second is earlier than the first.
>
> In the second place, each position is either Past, Present, or
> Future. The distinctions of the former class are permanent, while those
> of the latter are not. If M is ever earlier than N, it is always earlier. But
> an event, which is now present, was future, and will be past.[1]

The first series McTaggart describes in the above passage he calls the
B-series, and the second series (with Past, Present, and Future), he
calls the A-series.

McTaggart has named two fundamentally different ways in
which we conceive of and talk about time. When human beings think
in the mode of the A-series, they conceive of time in a "dynamic and
tensed way, as being the very quintessence of flux and transiency."[2]
Thus, events that are future become present and then past. The
results of this process of temporal becoming appear in metaphors
that use the image of time as a river. However, when we think in the
mode of the B-series, we think of a static structure or order. The
same events "which are continually changing in respect to their
pastness, presentness, or futurity are laid out in a permanent order
whose generating relation is that of 'earlier than' or 'later than' (or
simultaneous with)."[3] This is the static or tenseless way of conceiving
time, in which the history of the world is viewed in a God-like
manner, all events being conceived as coexisting. Events can never
change their position in the B-series. If an event M is ever earlier than
an event N, then M is always earlier than N. The only change an event

can undergo is a change in its A-determination. Hence, M was present but is now past, and N was future but is now present. Such change has been described as temporal becoming.

In order to clarify these two conceptions of time and their significance in narrative, I offer the following analysis of the use of the A-series and the B-series in H. G. Wells' *Time Machine*. Although Wells provided only a sparse account of the structure of time in the Heinemann edition (the final version) of *The Time Machine*, he presented a more detailed (and more useful) description of time in an earlier version of the novel, a version which appeared in five installments in William Henley's *New Review* between January and June 1895. In the first installment, the Time Traveller describes the fourth dimension:

> To an omniscient observor there would be no forgotten past—no piece of time as it were that had dropped out of existence—and no blank future of things yet to be revealed. Perceiving all the present, an omniscient observor would likewise perceive all the past and all the inevitable future at the same time. Indeed, present and past and future would be without meaning to such an observor; he would always perceive exactly the same thing. He would see, as it were, a Rigid Universe filling space and time—a Universe in which things were always the same. He would see one sole unchanging series of cause and effect to-day and to-morrow and always. If "past" meant anything, it would mean looking in a certain direction; while "future" meant looking the opposite way.[4]

On the following page, Wells clarifies the significance of this concept of time for the inhabitants of the world he has created: "From my point of view the human consciousness is an immaterial something falling through this Rigid Universe of four dimensions, from the direction we call 'past' to the direction we call 'future.'" Note that events cannot change in relation to one another. Furthermore, in the *New Review* version of *The Time Machine*, the writer explicitly superimposes the A-series on the B-series; that is, the consciousness (a dynamic concept) "falls through" the Rigid Universe (a static structure). Wells posits an entity that moves and a continuum that does not move; consequently, he is just one step away from positing not only velocity ("falls through") but also acceleration, which is defined as a change in velocity with respect to time. But adopting a spatial analogy for time in the form of a Rigid Universe allows Wells to speculate on the possibility of acceleration without resorting to supertime to explain the second derivative.[5] Hypothesizing the existence of a supertime only leads to an infinite regression, since, for example, another term, perhaps super-supertime, would be required to explain supertime. The importance of this version of *The Time Machine* to the argument is that Wells provides a means of movement in time not previously available to man, albeit a fictional means of movement; man can simply accelerate (or decelerate) through the Rigid Universe if he wishes to be a time traveler. Thus, Wells offers the reader a world in which the inhabitants are not restricted to traveling along the B-series in only one direction and at only one velocity, that is, "the normal velocity of the consciousness as it moves steadily along the Time-Dimension with a uniform velocity from the cradle to the grave."[6]

In contrast to Wells, writers of traditional stories do not utilize these two philosophical concepts in the same way. Consider, for example, the thoughts of Quentin Compson, the narrator of the second section of William Faulkner's *Sound and the Fury*, as he speculates on the nature of time. At the opening of the second section, the reader finds Quentin thinking:

> When the shadow of the sash appeared on the curtains it was between seven and eight o'clock and then I was in time again, hearing the watch. It was Grandfather's and when Father gave it to me he said, Quentin, I give you the mausoleum of all hope and desire; it's rather excruciatingly apt that you will use it to gain the reducto absurdum of all human experience which can fit your individual needs no better than it fitted his or his father's. I give it to you not that you may remember time, but that you might forget it now and then for a moment and not spend all your breath trying to conquer it. Because no battle is ever won he said. They are not even fought. The field reveals to man his own folly and despair, and victory is an illusion of philosophers and fools.
>
> It was propped against the collar box and I lay listening to it. Hearing it, that is. I don't suppose anybody ever deliberately listens to a watch or a clock. You don't have to. You can be oblivious to the sound for a long while, then in a second of ticking it can create in the mind unbroken the long diminishing parade of time you didn't hear.[7]

Note the presence of both the A-series and the B-series conceptions in Quentin's musings. He points to the moving present in the first sentence when he reminds the reader that he is "in time again."

Furthermore, evidence of the moving Now (a component of the A-series) is as close as the ticking of the nearest watch. In addition, hearing his grandfather's watch prompts Quentin to visualize the B-series concept, "the long diminishing parade of time you didn't hear." Here events are arranged in order, either earlier than or later than other events in the parade. Because the event taking place in the privileged moment (the present is a privileged moment because all the utterances made then, as well as "all other events occurring then, are in the predominant position of having the capacity of being directly offered to that part of one's awareness that is being lived") prompts Quentin to visualize the past (a part of the parade of events), Quentin reacts by trying to discard the present.[8] He does this by first turning the watch upside down and then by smashing the crystal and tearing off the hands. However, his attempt to escape time is futile even on this metaphoric level because the watch continues to tick and to remind him of the past.

Quentin has two problems with the past: first, he cannot redeem the past; and second, he cannot stop trying to redeem it. Jean-Paul Sartre's description of Faulkner's use of the past and the present reveals some of Quentin's problem: "Faulkner's vision of the world can be compared to that of a man sitting in an open car and looking backward. At every moment, formless shadows, flickerings, faint tremblings and patches of light rise up on either side of him, and only afterward, when he has a little perspective, do they become trees and men and cars."[9] Given the world that Faulkner has posited for his creatures in *The Sound and the Fury*, Quentin can either continue "looking backward" or he can try to stop time altogether. Having failed to escape time, his "misfortune," by tearing the hands off the watch, Quentin at last escapes time by destroying his immersion in and awareness of the present; that is, he commits suicide.

In contrast to writers of traditional fiction, writers of science fiction time travel stories can create characters able to exploit time. Unlike Quentin Compson, these characters are not appalled by the "long diminishing parade of time"; rather, they hope to travel into the past or the future and improve their fortunes, as it were. And they do—accelerate or decelerate in time, all of which creates an unexpected type of experimental fiction. In fact, the science fiction writers' use of "an imaginative framework alternative to the author's empirical environment" largely determines the nature of their characterization, the kinds of plots they employ, the point of view they select in order to tell the story, and the themes they pursue.[10] In order to demonstrate one of these effects, I shall analyze the extraordinary effect of a character's ability to accelerate or decelerate in time on point of view in Robert Heinlein's novella "By His Bootstraps." The story begins:

> Bob Wilson did not see the circle grow. Nor, for that matter, did he see the stranger who stepped out of the circle and stood staring at the back of Wilson's neck—stared, and breathed heavily, as if laboring under strong and unusual emotion.
>
> Wilson had no reason to suspect that anyone else was in his room; he had every reason to expect the contrary. He had locked himself in his room for the purpose of completing his thesis in one sustained drive. He had to—tomorrow was the last day for submission, yesterday the thesis had been no more than a title: "An Investigation into Certain Mathematical Aspects of a Rigor of Metaphysics."
>
> Fifty-two cigarettes, four pots of coffee, and thirteen hours of continuous work had added seven thousand words to the title.[11]

Heinlein opens the story using a third-person, limited point of view; that is, the reader is privy to Bob Wilson's thoughts, but the reader does not know the thoughts of the fellow who has just stepped through the time gate behind Bob Wilson and who is watching Bob work. During the following discussion, the reader learns that Joe (the intruder) has come from a time some thousands of years in the future. Shortly, a second man (unnamed at this point in the story but later referred to as "Number Three") steps through the time gate into Bob's room. After a brief argument between Joe and Number Three, the bewildered Bob Wilson is accidentally knocked through the time gate and lands in the High Palace of Norkaal (some thirty thousand years in the future). Now Bob Wilson is prevented from at once stepping back through the time gate at once by Diktor, an inhabitant of the Hall of the Gate. When Bob is finally able to step back through the gate into his room, he does so with instructions from Diktor to send back to the Hall of the Gate the person Bob finds on the other side. Consequently, we readers learn, at the same instant the protagonist learns, that the protagonist is no longer Bob Wilson; the protagonist is now (some eleven pages later for the reader and one day for the protagonist) Joe, a double of Bob Wilson. Thus, the reader observes the initial scene of the story again, but this occurrence is presented by a narrator who relates Joe's thoughts—but not Bob's thoughts. Hence, the use of a world in which time travel is possible (in this case, the time gate enables the protagonist to move almost instantaneously some thirty thousand years into the future; Joe tells us in the opening scene that "time flows along side by side on each side of the Gate, but some thousands of years apart") allows Heinlein to shift point of view while maintaining the unity of the reader's time and the protagonist's time. This unannounced shift of perspective provides some rather startling effects in the story.

To begin with, this shifting point of view confronts the reader with an intellectual challenge of sorts. On the one hand, the reader wonders how this shift has been accomplished in such a subtle and intriguing fashion. As a contrast, consider the reader of *The Sound and the Fury* who may be momentarily disturbed upon beginning the "June Second 1910" section and finding the narrative voice considerably changed—Quentin speaking instead of Benjy. However, the visible shift in the text (the bottom third of p. 92 is blank; at the top of the facing page "JUNE SECOND 1910" appears—a title of any sort, let alone one printed in a larger font has not appeared since p. 1 of the novel; and finally, the diction level has changed from Benjy's musings that "the dark began to go in smooth, bright shapes, like it always does when Caddy says I have been asleep" to Quentin's reflections that include words like *mausoleum* and *reducto absurdum*) eases the transition for the reader. In "By His Bootstraps," this is not the case. The switch to Joe's point of view occurs quite subtly in the course of the text—that is without any superficial or artificial indicators. This phenomenon may cause the reader of Heinlein's novella to pause and ponder what has just occurred; even without having had any formal background in critical theory, the curious reader may speculate on the legitimacy of such a shift. However, if the reader means to continue reading, he does have to make an adjustment at this juncture. He must accept the idea that in the world of this text, a world that features the ability to accelerate or decelerate in time, and especially to travel into the past (as Joe does when he steps into Bob's room), shifts in point of view can occur in a different manner than they do in traditional fiction. Because the writer of this time travel story posited a world in which characters can travel into the future and the past, paradoxes of this sort—two temporal manifestations of the same character appearing in the same scene—can and do occur; consequently, one of the reading protocols of this type of science fiction requires that readers be able to cope with a shift of point of view that is caused by the protagonist's travel into the past to perceive his old self (from an earlier portion of the story) as an object.

Furthermore, this shift (from third-person, limited to Bob Wilson's thoughts to third-person, limited to Joe's thoughts) is accomplished without any discontinuity in the text, without any textual cues. That is, a common reading protocol for readers of traditional fiction is the understanding that a break in the text or a shift to another font or a shift to another announced date (at the top of a letter in an epistolary novel) may constitute a shift in point of view as well. However, the reader of "By His Bootstraps" has the quite different experience of shifting point of view without experiencing any discontinuity. The overriding benefit of this technique is that it forces the reader to accept the logic of the world which the writer has created. Because the kind of story most readers are familiar with features a single character's perceptions of the world, a single point of view, that is, readers are accustomed to a unified effect in the narrative. Because there are no artificial shifts via typographical breaks in "By His Bootstraps," the reader is predisposed by what he brings to the story before he begins reading and is conditioned by what has happened thus far in the story to feel the effect of unified time. The reader thus experiences a narrative which appears always to be generated by the consciousness of the protagonist; moreover, this effect aids the reader in his struggle to maintain close contact (identification) with the protagonist in a world populated with a paradoxical cast of temporal manifestations of the protagonist. Perhaps the most significant benefit of this technique is that shifting perspective without discontinuity as Heinlein does in this story, provides apparently natural grounds for the reader, grounds from which he can understand all that transpires in the narrative. As Heinlein dramatizes the same scene three times, the reader does not entertain concern because the same scene plays thrice, and the reader observes the protagonist from three different points of view without any discontinuity.

This repetition of a scene in a time travel story creates an effect quite unlike the repetition of a scene in a traditional story because in the case of the time travel story the reader is not required to shift to a new consciousness. For example, the reader of *The Sound and the Fury* eventually perceives that the scene at the branch (where Caddy has muddy drawers) occurs both in Benjy's section and in Quentin's section; however, the reader already knows that Quentin's account of the scene differs from Benjy's because Faulkner has indicated, via a change of style, that on the one hand, Benjy's consciousness is that of an idiot, and on the other hand, Quentin's consciousness is that of a freshman at Harvard. In Heinlein's story, however, the narrating consciousness has not changed; because the shift in point of view occurred without any sort of discontinuity in this story, the consciousness narrating the scene from Joe's point of view already has as part of its memory the scene narrated from Bob Wilson's point of view. Now the replaying of the scene in Bob's room constitutes a direct analogy to the experience of reading a text for the second time. In *The Implied Reader*, Wolfgang Iser has described the reading process which occurs when we read a text for the second time (in this case, we observe the same scene again):

> However, when we have finished the text, and read it again, clearly our extra knowledge will result in a different time sequence; we shall tend to establish connections by referring to our awareness of what is to come, and so certain aspects of the text will assume a significance we did not attach to them on a first reading, while others will recede into the background. It is a common enough experience for a person to say that on a second reading he noticed things he had missed when he read the book for the first time, but this is scarcely surprising in view of the fact that the second time he is looking at the text from a different perspective. The time sequence that he realized on his first reading cannot possibly be repeated on a second reading, and this unrepeatability is bound to result in modifications of his reading experience. This is not to say that the second reading is 'truer' than the first—they are, quite simply, different: the reader establishes the virtual dimension of the text by realizing a new time sequence. Thus even on repeated viewings a text allows and, indeed, induces innovative reading.[12]

Having read a text once, a reader has certain expectations and very little uncertainty regarding the outcome. In the same manner, Joe has read the text once and indeed has little uncertainty about the outcome. That is, the conception a reader has after finishing a text is roughly analogous to the B-series conception of time. Joe's conception of the first playing of the scene in Bob Wilson's room is also roughly analogous to a B-series. The relationships between events never change, and the reader perceives all events as coexisting—the scene is conceived as just that, a scene. Hence, these two conceptions of time aid the critic in understanding the particular significance of the repeated scene in a time loop story. This technique enables science fiction writers to present a character with the literal opportunity of reliving an event from the character's past and, perhaps, speculating on the possibility of altering the past.

Writers of traditional stories are at a decided disadvantage when they encounter the problem of speculating on causes and effects. They can, of course, set up thought experiments of sorts in order to spin out answers to questions regarding changing the past. However, writers of science fiction time travel stories have the advantage of being able to dramatize the problem by having a character agonize over his ability to alter the past. Even a character who has not pondered at length the problem of paradox in altering what has already occurred may hesitate, may wonder about the implications of interfering with the chain of cause-and-effect relationships that constitute the past. In "By His Bootstraps," the reader is encouraged to speculate on the possibility of altering the past just after Joe steps through the time gate into Bob Wilson's room (the second dramatization of the scene): "The man at the desk took another cigarette, tamped it on one end, turned it and tamped it on the other, straightened and crimped the paper on one end carefully against his left thumbnail and placed that end in his mouth. Wilson felt the blood beating in his neck, *sitting there with his back to him was himself, Bob Wilson*! [Heinlein's italics]"[13] When the scene begins to play again, Joe, whose thoughts we now read, begins to realize that he has been through all this before—as Bob Wilson. Then, his thoughts shift to cause and effect: "Wait a minute now—he was under no compulsion. He was sure of that. Everything he did and said was the result of his own free will. Even if he couldn't remember the script, there were some things he knew "Joe" hadn't said. "Mary had a little lamb," for example. He would recite a nursery rhyme and get off this damned repetitious treadmill. He opened his mouth."[14] But in fact, Joe cannot escape this treadmill; he cannot restructure the sequence of events that occurred once before in Bob Wilson's room. Thus, the reader is presented with a world in which the past cannot be changed even though the protagonist can literally be present at certain events in the past, observe them, and even participate in them. Joe is not constrained to just speculate on whether or not the past can be altered; on the contrary, in this world, he can experiment with cause and effect. First, he develops an hypothesis about causality, and then he immediately turns around and tests that hypothesis. The protagonist in "By His Bootstraps" at first thinks he has more freedom than a character like Quentin Compson in *The Sound and the Fury* would think; but, in fact, this supposed advantage of being able to travel into the past bodily to attempt to redeem the past betrays Joe because he, unlike Quentin, learns that there is no longer any use in speculating on the past. In Quentin's case, the potential for hope still exists because Quentin has not actually journeyed into the past only to learn that the past is indeed fixed. Thus, Joe's field of vision may not be as constricted as that of Quentin—that is, riding in an open car and looking backward, as Sartre has suggested—but Joe's attitude toward his own future must change drastically when he realizes, when he proves, that his past cannot be changed.

Although writers of traditional literature may focus on time just as numerous science fiction and fantasy writers do, the selection of literary techniques these writers of traditional literature have is limited by the metaphysics these writers employ. Because Faulkner presents a world with no future, with only a present in which his characters are obsessed with the past, and because he does not literalize the metaphor (his characters cannot travel in time bodily), he cannot experiment with scenes in which his protagonist travels into his own past and attempts to change it. Recall the opening of the second section of *The Sound and the Fury*, where Quentin Compson is thinking, "When the shadow of the sash appeared on the curtains it was between seven and eight o-clock and then I was in time again, hearing the watch" (p.93). Shortly after this, Quentin continues musing, "You can be oblivious to the sound [of a clock or a watch] for a long while, then in a second of ticking it can create in the mind unbroken the long diminishing parade of time you didn't hear." Being in time again means Quentin's consciousness must resume its frenzied search over the long diminishing parade of events which constitute his tortured past. However, writers of science fiction and fantasy time travel stories, having adopted a metaphysics that allows their characters to travel in time, may use literary techniques made possible by this world view and thus provide characters who travel so far into the future that they observe the end of man (Wells' Time Traveller) or so far into the past that they can meet themselves (Heinlein's Joe). Science fiction and fantasy form a unified field here. Whether the character's ability to travel in time springs from some scientifically extrapolated device (science fiction—Wells' time machine) or from some unexplained effect (fantasy—Heinlein's time gate) is of much less interest than the effects these writers can obtain by using unusual literary techniques; Heinlein's shift in point of view and thus his use of the rereading analogy allows him to develop his protagonist's character fully more rapidly and more convincingly than any writer of traditional literature could. Unlike traditional literature, both science fiction and fantasy promise hope by enabling the inhabitants of their fictional worlds to travel back and forth on the B-series (to travel into the past and into the future), and like traditional literature, sometimes both forms deliver only perpetual motion—the tooth that gnaws endlessly.

Frames in Search of a Genre

Frank McConnell

A poll conducted in the 1960s found that the most popular daily comic strips in America were, in order, *Blondie*, *Dick Tracy*, *Little Orphan Annie*, *Peanuts*, and *Rex Morgan, M.D.* I offer this fact as proof that evolution, at least in the arts, is not always downward. *Dick Tracy* and *Little Orphan Annie* have long since gone to that great syndicate in the sky, though neither without a final, sadly optimistic spasm of hoped for contemporaneity: Tracy was even drawn, near the last, in three-quarter face instead of the classic and inevitable, full and hawk-face profile, and Annie, though she never got eyeballs, did get involved with drug dealers and social radicals in her penultimate, etiolated days. This is known as profanation. Peace to their ashes, or to their dried ink. As with all truly popular forms of popular art, they were there and they were great when we needed them to be. *Blondie*, boringly, continues. *Peanuts* continues boringly and pretentiously: how many times must we hear Linus quote the Gospel according to St. John before we admit that Mr. Schulz is a well-read man? And Rex Morgan, the Ronald Reagan of comics—you don't trust him, but you can't dislike him—still acts out the interminable soap opera of his life and nonloves to the affectionate yawn of the cosmos. Mary Worth, at least—because of a change in writers—has moved to Santa Barbara. All of which is beside my point. My point is that you don't read these strips. Or if you do, you do because, like me, you are hopelessly nostalgic or because you are so hopelessly old-fashioned that you don't want to hear the rest of what I have to say. I'd like us, after all, to part friends, even if only in the first paragraph.

But if you're still with me, let me suggest this as preface and premise. In a culture increasingly torn between the alternatives of

119

science fiction and fantasy; magic and technology; the possibility of
infinite possibility and the risk of unfathomable guilt; in a culture at
the break of noon between aspiration and despair; in a culture like
that, one of our best guides to who we think we are and where we
think we are is the comic strip, which is to say the purest contemporary form of the joke. The joke or the cartoon, where SF and fantasy
meet, kiss, and dance—my favorite form of modern fiction.

   L'histoire drôle, the French, with their seemingly endless gift for
tediously irrefutable analytic brilliance, call it. It is a *histoire*: every
joke, every cartoon worth the cost of publication, is in fact a short
story ("This guy walks into a bar, see? And he's got this duck on his
shoulder, right? And the bartender says to him . . ."). Bultmann
distinguished between *Geschichtliche* and *Historische* utterance because the latter not only tells you where you are, it tells you in a way
you can't, except if you are a Philistine, forget for the rest of the day.
The greatest of Galilean *zaddiks* was also—and I say this with the
deepest reverence—a kind of *Historische*, religious stand-up comic.
What is the Kingdom of heaven like? Well, maybe a mustard seed.
See, a mustard seed when it starts out is, like, real small, you dig?
You can almost hear Peter chortling and digging Matthew in the ribs.
Damn! There he goes again.

   But *l'histoire drôle* is not only a *histoire*, it is also *drôle*. Violette
Morin, in a brilliant essay on cartoon jokes, concludes by invoking
Todorov's studies on fantasy, and by observing that while "literary"
fantasy is naturally enlightening, cartoon fantasy is naturally shock-
ing—not *éclairante* but *foudroyante*. The joke, in other words, has
this difference from the true story: it doesn't teach us, it simply jumps
out from around the corner and says "booga-booga!" to the soul.
Violette Morin's essay is, as I have said, brilliant. It is also wrong. A
better theorist of fiction, Barbara Herrnstein Smith, tells us in *On the
Margins of Discourse* that fiction is indeed, as Aristotle said, a
mimesis or imitation—not an imitation of *the real*, but rather an
imitation of so-called natural forms of discourse. Thus, the epistolary
novel is an imitation of letter writing, the drama is an imitation of
conversation, the Valentine's Day card is an imitation of saying "I
love you," and so forth. So what is the cartoon joke, *l'histoire drôle*,
an imitation of? I think, of that most natural and unnatural of human
activities, the act of storytelling and mythmaking itself.

   Let me begin with an example from *Garfield*. In frame one,

Garfield the cat, about to grab a vine hanging from the ceiling, thinks "I'm going to swing down this vine and steal Jon's [his owner's] chicken." In frame two, Garfield swoops down on the vine, grabbing the roast chicken off Jon's plate. In frame three Jon, bemused, stares at the ceiling and asks, "Where did the vine come from?"

Kierkegaard is about as perceptive about the nature of narrative, but not many others. There is, of course, the magic sword Beowulf finds when he is fighting Grendel's mother, that enables him to kill her. Where did the sword come from? There is the white gold wedding ring in Stephen R. Donaldson's *Thomas Covenant* cycle that makes Covenant the most important character in the magic Land. Where did the ring come from? There is the shield of Achilles, the garter of Sir Gawain, Cinderella's glass slipper . . . . There is Mark Twain's immortal comment that a character in one of James Fenimore Cooper's Leatherstocking tales is slain by a random bullet fired by the author.

The joke tells us, in one way or the other, that the universe— that very large machine that we know is out to get us—can be, if not conquered, at least circumvented by our very admission of its alienness. The joke, in other words, is man's first inkling and first denial of the irreversibility of the entropy arrow. *Raffiniert ist der Herrgott, aber böshaft ist er nicht*, said Einstein in a famous utterance: the Lord God is subtle, but he is not a trickster. Niels Bohr was not as sweet a man as Einstein but he would not have committed such a *gaffe*. Every joke, every fantasy, and every science fiction story tells us that the Lord God is *böshaft*. And since it has become my personal ritual to tell you that there is no such distinct entity as science fiction or fantasy, I shall do so once again and insist that all storytelling fits the crucial matrix of the joke.

Where did the vine in the Garfield cartoon come from? From the same place the universe, the scene of all stories, came from: from nowhere. Ilya Prigogine, Hugh Everett, and John Gribbin all entertain the possibility that the universe, from big bang to contemporary whimper, is a vacuum fluctuation, a random permutation of sheer probability that will eventually permute back to absolute, Brahman-like nonbeing. There is a free lunch, in other words, but it turns out to be a wake. I am, to be sure, Huckleberry Finnishly innocent of the mathematics behind this hypothesis. But since Jerry Falwell has denounced it from the pulpit as a hellish, damnable doctrine, I am sufficiently persuaded of its righteousness. The world, like the tales we tell about the world, loves to jump from around the corner and shout "booga-booga!" at us. Why else would the *Herrgott* have given elementary particles a quality called "strangeness?" The only real question is whether or not the joke is on us. If the joke is on us, we are writing what can roughly be called science fiction. If we get to share in the joke, we are writing what can roughly be called fantasy. There is a third alternative, but I haven't yet the courage to address it; bear with me.

There are two elementary forms of the joke: the one-liner and the shaggy dog story. Of course, the one-liner doesn't have to be restrained to only one line any more than the shaggy dog story has to involve an overhirsute canine. The distinction is in the punch line: the one-liner has one and the shaggy dog story doesn't. Henny Youngman's famous gag will illustrate the first model. "Women are funny, you know? Take my wife. Please." That "Please," I submit, is brilliant. It turns what promises to be a rambling set of anecdotes about women into an ironic statement of domestic less than bliss, at the same time effecting an epistemological leap in the interpretation of the word *take*: not "take her as an example" but "take her off my hands." (Arthur Koestler discusses jokes as synaptic leaps of this sort in his splendid and underrated *The Act of Creation*). The punch-line—or, in this case, punch-word—gives meaning, finality, the sense of an ending and even of a kind of epiphany to the joke. In a night club, the drummer would do a roll and a rim-shot to punctuate it. It is the equivalent of the Grand Unified Theory that would explain, once and for all, the interrelationship of the four elemental forces and the reason for, as Douglas Adams puts it, *Life, the Universe, and Everything*.

Tiddley-bum (one's approximation of a rim-shot).

How different is the shaggy dog story.

A little old man—Murray, say, is his name—is walking through the garment district in New York late at night. A UFO lands and an alien steps out.

"Ach," says Murray, "are you ugly! Where you from?"

"I am from Mars," says the alien.

"Mars, schmars. *Nu?* But you got seven arms. Everybody on Mars got seven arms?"

"Everyone on Mars has seven arms."

"Yeah, but *feh*! On each arm you got six fingers, like tentacles or something. Everybody up there got that?"

"Everyone on Mars," with a patient sigh, "has six fingers on each of their seven arms."

"Yeah, yeah, *sei gesund*. But on each of your fingers you got all kinds rings. Topaz, emerald, diamond, ruby. Everybody on Mars got rings like that?"

"Well—not the *goyim*."

As Murray himself might say; this, already, is a *joke*? "Not the *goyim*" is, maybe a punch line? What, there's Jews on Mars? That is funny? That is to do a rim-shot? What's the point? The point is that there is no point: no answer, no epiphany, no Grand Unified Theory. No rim-shot. If you love shaggy dog stories, you love them because they are celebrations of the fundamental unknowability of the cosmos, and therefore of its infinite capacity to surprise, delight, or murder us. And by cosmos I mean not only the galaxy, but also the neighborhood—yours or mine.

Robert Scholes and Frank Kermode both suggest that the distinctive form of the classical novel may be the idea of absolutely transmissible information (the punch-line model, in my reductivist argot), and that the postmodern novel, from Joyce to Pynchon, can be best described as a version of the shaggy dog story. What does Molly Bloom's "Yes" mean? Who is V? Where does the meaning come from? In his recent, brilliant fantasy *Jitterbug Perfume*, Tom Robbins narrates a conversation between two women, "Do you pray to God?" asks woman A. "Yes," says woman B. "Does he answer you?" "Yes—always." "What does He say?" "He says the check is in the mail." This, I submit, is not only very good theology but also a very good four-frame cartoon: it has been said that if Thomas Pynchon were a muppet, he would write like Tom Robbins. The punchline writer believes that the world owes us an explanation—benevolent or malevolent—of its workings. The despair of infinitude, says Kierkegaard in *Fear and Trembling*, is the lack of finitude. Such people like to listen to Mozart or the Beatles, read *Doonesbury*, and play bridge. The shaggy-dog writer believes that the final explanation, if we ever got one, would be incomprehensible anyway. The despair of finitude is the lack of infinitude, says Kierkegaard. Such people like to listen to Stravinsky and Thelonious Monk, read *Garfield*, and play poker.

Job believes fervently in punch lines. He demands one of the Lord God. The Lord God, speaking out of the whirlwind, tells him instead the greatest of shaggy dog stories. Why did all this happen to you? *Why?* Because. As the shortest and best shaggy dog joke in the world puts it: "Are we lost, Daddy?" "Shut up," he explained.

Literature is littered with left-to-dies, founded upon foundlings. Oedipus is abandoned, Moses is abandoned, Arthur is abandoned. Donald Duck never knew his papa drake, Garfield as all the world knows was found in the kitchen of an Italian restaurant—hence his lasagne addiction—and Opus, the saintly penguin of Berke Breathed's *Bloom County*, was abandoned by his mother on an Antarctic ice floe. If the joke is the model for fiction, and if fiction is the model for human consciousness, then the sub-subtext of both articulations is the quest of the son/daughter for the parent who will justify, validate existence itself. Am I lost, Daddy? Odysseus tries to get home. But Telemachus journeys out to find the father he seeks and who is seeking him. Joyce did not misread the aboriginal tale as much as he retaught us to read it aright. We begin and end all quests with Telemachus, Stephen Dedalus, thee and me looking for the punch line—or the lack of same—that will finally tell us whether we are lost.

If most literature and most jokes—by now you know that to me they are the same—express the search of the son for the father, then *Lear* is the elemental joke turned inside out. For years I wondered why that play, of all plays, is the most truly terrifying. (Doctor Johnson said he could never read the last act again, and he was right.) Now I know. The play is about being a father. And that means it is about organizing, not being organized by, your universe. And *that* means it is about delivering, not waiting for, the punch line or non-punch line the universe ultimately has in store for you. It is a play about the difference between science fiction and fantasy.

The Duke of Gloucester has only sons—one good and one bad. Lear has only daughters—two bad and one good. Male chauvinism aside (Milton might have given Lear even more bad daughters), it is important that both old men choose the wrong moiety of offspring, and both pay for their wrong choice.

But how differently they pay. Gloucester lives through a tragedy. Having given his love to the wrong son and having been horribly blinded (this, apparently, is a professional hazard of tragic

heroes), he can deliver the best tragic punch line in English literature: "As flies to wanton boys are we to th' gods; / They kill us for
their sport." The universe is meaningful, even if inimical, and to
suffer because the Lord God is subtle, even if sadistic, is at least to
suffer for a reason.

That is what Gloucester knows. Lear knows worse. When Cordelia is strangled because of an absurd oversight ("great thing of us
forgot" is Shakespeare's immortally silly line), Lear, entering with
his dead daughter in his arms, can manage one imperishable line,
perhaps the most difficult of all lines to deliver: the single word,
"Howl," repeated three times.

It is an anti-punch line. It is the question, "Where did the vine
come from?" It is Lear's, once-uttered indelible affirmation that
there is no affirmation; that the world is a zero-sum game; that death
is death, and death and death indeed; and that all life from the birth
and perishing of star systems to the birth and perishing of those like
you and me is accidental, pointless, devoid of even the consolation of
a cosmic rim-shot.

This is the way the world ends: not with a tiddley-bum but with a
howl.

Or is it? Every morning I buy the San Francisco *Chronicle*. Each
day in the San Francisco *Chronicle*, on the comics page, at the top of
the page, I read what has become known in my household as "the big
three"—*Doonesbury*, by Garry Trudeau; *Garfield*, by Jim Davis;
and *Bloom County*, by Berke Breathed. Of course, I read everything
else on the comics page—Lynn Johnston's *For Better Or Worse*, Phil
Frank's *Travels with Farley*, and so on. And, in the Los Angeles
Times I read Tom K. Ryan's *Tumbleweeds*, William Overgard's very
strange and extraordinarily hip *Rudy*, and Gary Larson's *Far Side*. If
I were ordered to deliver a course on the theory of fiction and the
theory of narrative, I could not think of a better reading list.

Doonesbury, which thinks it is a fantasy, is actually a novel in
spite of itself: *un roman malgre soi*, if you think Gallicisms lend
authenticity to the obvious. The ongoing story of Mike Doonesbury—patron saint of the Yuppies—of Uncle Duke, patron saint of
the chemically addicted, and of everybody else in Trudeau's imaginative menagerie is, notwithstanding Trudeau's year-and-a-half retire-
ment, a chronicle of the late 1960s sensibility. Remember that back
then we all thought there were answers: the war in Vietnam was

wrong, civil rights was (were?) right, and we all read *Dune* and *The Autobiography of Malcolm X*. Those are two great books, and that was, even allowing for the fear and the pain and the ugliness, one great decade. It was a Gloucester decade, a punch line decade; a decade in which we believed that, however hostile the universe might be to our chances for survival, there was still a point to the hostility. When *2001* was released in 1968, only John Simon had the good sense, in his initial review, to describe it as a "shaggy God story." The rest of us tried to figure out what the monolith meant, and whether it was Louis Quatorze or Louis Quinze furniture in that galactic motel room at the end, and why HAL was so disturbed in the first place. The rest of us, in other words, not being gifted with John Simon's universal distaste—rather like the absolute solvent, which nothing can hold—believed that there was a reason for what was going on. *Why Are We in Vietnam?* Norman Mailer had asked only a few years before. Well, to ask why is to suggest that there ought to be a why?—is that not so?

Of course, there wasn't; any more than there was a why for the carnage Ezra Pound memorialized in *Mauberly*. But we thought there was, and those of us who went through the decade thought and think there was, and so does Garry Trudeau. One of his recent running gags in the reborn *Doonesbury* is the implantation of a liberal heart into the mind and body of a conservative. It makes, perhaps every other day, for great fun; but it is also rather grimly confessional. Trudeau's strip has not been nearly as funny since he has come back—and it hasn't been, I suggest, because the age of the punch line is, at least temporarily, over.

It is now the age of Reagan, and of *Garfield*: the vain, self-satisfied, eternally hungry fat cat. Garfield looks like a punch-line strip, and is actually a shaggy dog—or shaggy cat—one. Where did the vine come from? *Garfield*, actually, is ritualized; and ritual, as any liturgist will tell you, is inimical to punch lines.

Garfield is a three-frame strip, and *Doonesbury* is a four-frame strip. This makes a very large difference in the respective psychic realities of the two mythologies. In four frames you can set up a situation, a complication of the situation, a pause, and a summation. In what may be the best and most Swiftian cartoon ever, Mike Doonesbury and the eternal hippie, Zonker Harris, are staring across the field. Frame one: Zonker says, "It's a very nice day today." Frame two: Zonker says, "They say it was a very nice day one year ago today at Kent State." Frame three: silence. Frame four: Zonker says, "Have a nice day, John Mitchell." If this is not the moral use of language—which is to say, a holy thing—then I do not know what is. Frame one: Garfield strolls into the yard, saying, "Hello, flowers, hello trees, hello grass." Frame two: Garfield passing an extinct bird says, "Hello, daisies, hello, Apteryx." Frame three: Garfield does a double take. You see, I hope, the difference. I do not mean to privilege one or the other form of the joke. But Garry Trudeau, I think, could write great science fiction and Jim Davis could write great fantasy. Or put it this way: Zonker thinks there is a point to it all, while the Great Gar knows there isn't.

I suggest to you that all artists are disingenuous. Plato, braver than I, simply observed that all poets are liars. Samuel R. Delany wants us to believe that his novels, from *Nova* through *Dhalgren* to *Stars in My Pocket Like Grains of Sand*, are science fiction. And Roger Zelazny wants us to believe that the *Nine Princes in Amber* series is fantasy. Of course, we all know that there is no real distinction between the two forms. A story is a story, and a joke is a joke, and the *Iliad* and the *Odyssey*, the best punch line and the best shaggy dog stories, respectively, ever told, were created by the same committee. But, as good readers of the comics, we also know that the distinction, though false, is useful. Life is like that. Ask any lawyer.

You will recall that I gave you the option of exiting this discussion at the beginning. But I would be disappointed in you if, at this point, you were not mumbling to yourself, "Okay, fine, for sure—but what the heck is he trying to *say*?" Harold Bloom, in *Agon*, defines fantasy as that form of mythmaking in which the pleasure-pain principle predominates over the reality principle but, through overdetermination, collapses back into the very *thanatos*-drive it came into existence to overcome. That is a brilliant, since Bloomian, and baffling, since Bloomian, description of the mechanism of fantasy and the daily life of Garfield. What the heck I am trying to say, in other words, is that from the Homeric poems and the Torah to yesterday's comic page, all storytelling is storytelling, and that the differences matter less than the similarities. And if you tell me the jokes you laugh at, I will tell you how you stand with the universe. Or if you tell me what animals you laugh at, to paraphrase, by their brutes you shall know them.

Subtle is the Lord God, but a trickster he is not, said Einstein, that greatest of believers in the punch line theory of reality. But Pan was a trickster, and so was Anansi the Spider who, when he migrated from Africa to America, changed his name to Brer Rabbit. So were a number of deities, all of whom are, in their ways, the tutelary deities of fantasy, and of the comic strip. I am not fond of people who are fond of Snoopy, and I like almost everyone who likes Fred Bassett (Garfield, of course, is *hors de combat*). There: you have my personal metaphysics. I believe in the radical unknowability of the universe, in the Second Law of Thermodynamics, in the ineluctability of the darkness that is going to descend upon us all, and in Thelonious Monk and Garfield. And that is what fantasy believes in. I find it significant that there are no animals in *Doonesbury*: in a punch line universe, the trickster figure, the innocent who observes that the Emperor is naked, is not welcome, not any more welcome, indeed, than poets in Plato's *Republic*, the Mule in Asimov's *Foundation* trilogy, or Hobbits in *The Lord of the Rings* as it might have been written by Doc Smith or Jerry Pournelle. Tricksters, like charm particles, muons, and monopoles, upset as much as they clarify, and teach us that the pleasure-pain principle is really not different from the reality principle. Penguins, cats, and bassett hounds are not supposed to talk; neither, by the way, are subtle serpents in certain gardens. And if they do, what they have to tell us is our own alienness, our own strangeness in an otherwise ordered and healthy cosmos. The serpent, after all, did not lie to Eve. She did eat the fruit, and she discovered exactly what the serpent told her she would discover: that she was not the woods she wandered in. Then—and only then—did she receive her name, Havah, meaning "life" or, specifically, "human life."

The story of the Fall in Genesis is shot through with the gaping absence of a tiddley-bum. Because what Adam and Havah enter, thanks to the ministrations of the serpent, is nothing less than human history—where, one suspects, YHVH meant them to be all along, to where fantasy always returns us (Thomas Covenant will awaken from his dream of the Land, Garfield will rediscover and redemonstrate the law of gravity), and where we live our lives without more than the hope of punch lines, Grand Unified Theories, or reasonable answers out of the whirlwind.

But there is more. I told you that there are two kinds of jokes;

and then I told you that there is a third alternative. It is now time to discuss that third alternative. It is what that very bright man, Christian Metz, calls the "witticism." It is also the hope of imaginative salvation.

If we are torn between the alternatives of the punch line and the shaggy dog universe, then we are damned and doomed. "We live in an old chaos of the sun," writes Wallace Stevens. Indeed we do. But we need not accept it. The witticism is harder to illustrate than the two classic forms of the joke, just because it is the point at which consciousness intersects with reality, rather than judges reality. I will try to give you an example.

A few years ago, I found myself separated from a wife of twenty years and in the company of a lady of whom I am, to this day, very fond. It was a time for paranoia, guilt feelings of Olympic proportions, anxiety attacks, and whatever other bad things you can imagine. 'A friend, whose kindness I will never forget, left a note in my office simply telling me that he knew what I must be going through, and that he was there if I needed to talk to him. I had not spoken to anyone—anyone—since my private apocalypse. So, that afternoon, I called my friend. When I said "Hello," he laughed and said, "Frank! What's new?" That is a witticism. It is not a punch line, because it doesn't give any final answer to my plight. It is not a shaggy dog line, because it does not tell me that the point is that there is no point. It arises out of the absurd, unending possibility of friendship and is therefore like a manifestation of grace. A *mitzvah*. It is a moment when the joke—or the fiction, or the imposed structure, call it what you will—no longer impinges upon but guides and heals reality. Most of us who are still sane—and we are all last-ditch soldiers in the wars of consciousness—*are* still sane because we have been lucky enough to encounter our share of witticisms along the way

The shortest and the best witticism in the world you will only understand if you are Jewish (I consider myself very reform): it is the word, *Nu*? accompanied, of course, by a shrug of the shoulders. John Ashbery has a poem entitled I HAD THOUGHT THINGS WERE GOING ALONG WELL: the poem reads, "But I was mistaken." Another witticism; perhaps a shrug, like Kurt Vonnegut's "So it goes" in *Slaughterhouse-Five*, or like the Road Runner's invincible faith that, though coyotes do kill and eat road runners, he will not be killed and eaten by Wile E. Coyote. Where does faith like this come from? From the same place that the vine comes from. You will not mind if I discuss the Road Runner as a paradigm of religious belief, since I have already sufficiently indicated to you that I regard all human culture as having approximately the structure of a Caesar salad. I am merely offering you another anchovy.

Early in his book, *Religion*, Leszek Kolakowski observes that "a religious world perception is indeed able to teach us *how to be a failure.*" That strikes me as one of the smartest things I have ever read. The Fool in *King Lear*—wiser than Cordelia, holier than Lear, and bitterer than Gloucester—knows the same thing. He doesn't drop punch lines and he doesn't tell shaggy dog jokes, he utters witticisms. He tries to train his king in failure, how to shrug and say *Nu?* to the onmivorous universe, how to find what lies beyond the pleasure-pain principle and the reality principle.

And what might that be? The knowledge, I suppose, that though we are here by accident we also have a right to be here by accident, and that the nostalgia of infinity for finitude and the nostalgia of finitude for infinity are both, properly considered, the longing of being for meaning. And what the best fiction, and the best jokes, and the best science fiction, and the best fantasy tell us is that that is a longing whose very passion is its own fulfillment.

In the late eighteenth century, in London, someone was marauding the city and murdering cats in the most grisly ways. Dr. Samuel Johnson, when he heard of this, expressed disgust and anger at the sadism and then, stroking his own cat, said, "But they won't get Hodge. No, they won't get Hodge." It is a punch line at Johnson's expense: the great man was incapable of separating his own feelings from the feline carnage abroad. It is a shaggy dog story: what does it matter if one cat more or less is disemboweled? But it is also a witticism: a lesson in failure: an observation that the silliest or grossest of violent acts still can touch the heart and still can move the human spirit to pity. As such, I submit, it is a great joke and a very human story.

Do not mind that it is also, like *Garfield*, about a cat.

Part 3
Fields

The *And* in Fantasy and Science Fiction

George E. Slusser

A bureaucratic matter first brought to my attention the complex function of *and* in a phrase like "fantasy and science fiction." The case in point is this: I needed to find a term that would define (in the sense of *circumscribe*) the field of activity for a potential research center that would deal with "speculative" art in general. Without thinking, drawing perhaps on an instinctive sense of this field, I proposed "science fiction and fantasy." This drew immediate protest from colleagues who felt it should be "fantasy and science fiction." What they meant by this reversal of terms was, I realized, not only that fantasy was the broader category, but the primary one. Seeking an area of operation, I had instead a value judgment, where priority in order means primacy in the generic sense. Fantasy was there first, and the fact that it has been around longer gives it a measurable value. This may be common logic for genre theorists. What it did however is highlight the real question: What did I mean when I said "science fiction and fantasy"? Why did I, despite this logic of priority, so easily invert these terms?

To think about this is to focus not on the terms themselves, but on the *and* that connects them—on the function of conjunctions in the designation of groups of literary types. If such types do not stand alone, the question is: In what ways do they join? What sort of conjunction is possible? For those who defend the phrase "fantasy and science fiction," the conjunction is clearly one of comparison. Fantasy is "greater than" SF; SF is "lesser than" fantasy—the *and* allows us to measure the value of forms relative to each other. This *and* tends toward becoming an *or*. Indeed, in the taxonomic lists and diagrams that are the end result of much genre thinking, the *and* of classification, no longer stated but simply implied, has effectively

133

become an *or*—absence now marking the separation of forms into discrete categories or niches.

The *and* in such compounds as "fantasy and science fiction" however remains a coordinating conjunction. The insignificant *and*, in fact, is the key word; marking the intersection between terms, it establishes the system of coordinates that not only allows forms to become "vectors" but permits those vectors to position themselves in literary space. More than forms, compounds such as "fantasy and science fiction," or for that matter "realism and fantasy," become, by means of the coordinating *and*, sets of interactive curves. Classic discrete genres, such as Aristotle's tragedy, are defined essentially in terms of formal structure (complete actions) or modes of discourse (catharsis). What I suggest here however is that, when combined, generic types can only be defined, in the fullest sense, as themes. The original sense of this word, *tithenai*, is to place, locate. And this is exactly what the *and* does—it governs the shaping, in its binary structures, of specific configurations of what is possibly the fundamental human pattern. This pattern is not one of action or of speech, but of placement in space-time: the pattern of equilibrium. And I would further suggest that, once combined, it is not the types (that is, the terms—*fantasy* and *science fiction*) that have thematic primacy, but the *and*. For they are merely designations, called into being by the nature of the shapes the *and* governs: products in a sense of the field of conjunction.

My initial question, however, if qualified, is still there: does it make a difference (in the topographical sense this time) which term comes first in the set? For the *and*, as intersection, should be invariable, the equal sign in the equation, and as such a mark of equilibrium. But this holds only to the degree that the equation remains unlocated. If the terms are abstract or general ones, such as *openness* and *closure*, their coordination results in a system that is homeostatic, that is, where terms can be interchanged without effecting the balance. The minute we recast this system in human terms, however, we locate it. And by so locating it, we necessarily choose (if only implicitly) an order and direction for its terms. Pascal, for instance, does this by placing man, in the role of coordinating *and* sign, between his "two infinities." In this position man is now called upon to guarantee a relationship of proportionality, of median balance, between the infinitely large and infinitely small worlds. Yet as Pascal puts it, the silence of these infinite spaces terrifies. Because Pascal's man fears what he must connect, that fear relocates the system along a clear vector: that of open silent spaces and man the reluctant agent of closure. Today's terms—*entropy* and *organization*—are the legacy of Pascal's fears. And in this series the first term has become dominant, indicating the general "turning" of all things (including the human) toward a uniform state of disorganization. A further shift, locating the system now squarely in the human area of communication, gives us the terms *noise* and *information*. And the vector makes clear just how little balance remains in this coordination. For information, once the defining factor in the very concept of communication, now cast as a form of human closure, is relegated to the role of reaction, resistance, to the disorganizing openness of noise.

If such location is a historical act, it is so in terms of a history of shapes rather than measurements. And rather than shapes, perhaps we should speak of designations. For to designate terms—here literary forms or types—is to locate them, to vectorize them into a field, and in doing so create the shapes that trace their interactions. History here, if anything, is metahistory: the history of consciousness of our act of locating generic terms in relation to the coordinating *and*. No form is an island. And genre designations have always marked (if only by exclusion) the attitude of the designator toward a correlated set of forms. There has always been location; only awareness of this act is modern.

This analysis applies to any generic term—Aristotle's definition of tragedy, with its emphasis on closure in a field of possible coordinations such as "tragedy and epic," is an act of location. But I will apply it to *realism* and to *fantasy*. The two terms, implicitly, have always been coordinated. In their modern connection however, they have been relocated. That relocation may explain the baffling changes each term undergoes. In its medieval usage, *realism* designates a universal mode of perception—the creation of ideal forms. The "real" is the organized, in relation to the "nominal," which indicates a mode of dealing with phenomena which is relative, "fanciful." *Fantasy*, on the other hand, in its original Greek sense, designates a mode of perception that is essentially open—the mimetic capacity to represent simply what is visible to the eye. This binary set, in its modern context, has been relocated from a general space to a more particular one. The function of closure in realism, relocated in the individual point of view, inflects toward a fascination with the relative and contingent, is collapsing in essence toward an open structure. And fantasy, moved in proportion by the tensions of instability of the connecting *and*, inflects toward closure: here the creation of a private seeing space within the mind, one that now designates itself, in relation to so-called real space, an other, or alternate, world.

This relocation, I would argue, results in a vectorization of terms crucial to our understanding of literary types as sets—sets not of forms, but of locations, of designations of place within a basic field, in short, of themes. Many theorists see genres creating their own formal space. I argue that all genres occupy the same space, one not determined by a noun, seeking to bestow on a shape the singular existence of a form, but by the conjunction *and*, connecting shapes as coordinate entities. In light of this *and*, genre theory itself, in its search to fix by naming, has itself inflected toward a sort of nominalism. The *and*, on the other hand, has, beyond genre, come to mark the place, the necessary field of literary activity. As such it is the basic theme, that of typing and naming, that governs all other themes—all designations that are acts of placing, of relocation. Through the presence of the *and*, forms become aware they are binary. This means they cannot designate their space unless they realize they are connected to another form, that their location or relocation must change the placement of that form in relation to the basic binary set—that of openness and closure.

Realism's awareness of the *and* is implicit, something revealed in its shadowy fascination with those contingencies and singularities its traditional placement rejects. Fantasy's corresponding awareness is, however, more radically and overtly contradictory—an act of naming where the singular renames itself as ideality, totality. Because it is so paradoxical, fantasy's demand for closure makes us radically aware of the *and* that governs its existence. Yet that existence, paradoxically unstable and connected, makes us aware, as does no other type, of the problems of connection themselves, the instabilities of the literary field. Fantasy then is a catalyst. Urging us to rename its complement, it creates new bindings—I call them catastrophe and complementarity—and new namings—I call them horror and science fiction. In doing so, it generates new fields of literary activity: fantasy and horror, and fantasy and science fiction. These are the subject of this essay.

The Logic of Fantasy

Definitions of fantasy usually consider the term either as a particular, historically determined form or as a general faculty of the human mind. I want to investigate an area between these two. No one can deny that fantasy is a historical form, one born in history, and the product, in literature, of a new historical vision, emphasizing the effects of evolutionary time on forms themselves. Mark Rose sees fantasy, as generic form, "appearing" about the same time as science fiction, in the mid-nineteenth century.[1] And from this perspective, Rose warns against the anachronistic use of a term like *fantasy*, its application to forms that lie outside its historical range. I use this term, however, not as an anachronism but as a challenge to the hegemony of chronology as the means of defining such forms. I am not seeking the historical genesis for a form so much as the logic of a theme. I use the term *fantasy* to designate a certain moment (but not necessarily an evolutionary moment) of awareness—awareness of the *and*, of its coordinating function among fields of texts or forms. Through this I seek, on the part of literary forms, a new sense of configural relationship with other forms—a historical event insofar as it marks the end of the theme of isolation of forms.

The purpose of a basically thematic structure like medieval taxonomy ("chains" or "trees" of types) was to provide forms, here literary forms, with an immanent sense of their generic space: the forms "knew" where they were. But in a work like Cervantes' *Colloquio de los perros* something has changed. In this dialogue, two dogs embark upon a description of the habits and morals, from their point of view, of contemporary Spanish life. Were these creatures unaware of any anomaly in their situation, this would be simply be another animal fable, a satire content with its literary space because it knows no other. Cervantes however adds one all-important element: these dogs are aware that, in the "real" world (that is, the one they chronicle) they cannot and should not be talking.

Essentially these dogs realize that, if their narrative is to exist, they must create a new space for it. This space is not found in vertical taxonomies, for the forms designated there have no connection with (hence no awareness of) each other. The new axis formed by their generic "awakening" is horizontal, a connection between the dog's world and our world. The key to this axis, to such lateral generic awareness, is the *and*, the connection that permits interaction between worlds, and this story to be told. The dogs name their situation from within: it is a *"caso portentoso y jamás visto."* And the "case" they proclaim is actually a different literary shape, one that exists not by discriminating itself from, but by connecting itself with, other generic forms. Within their neatly separated boundaries these forms cannot discern such a connection; to them it remains *"jamás visto."* It is in this sense that Berganza, in the final episode, remains "unheard." In this scene Berganza, incensed with the social ills of *our* society, blurts them out to the mayor. This latter, however, does not hear words but barks, and has the dog soundly drubbed. Or so Berganza tells Cipión secondhand. In the firsthand world of the dialogue, however, we hear words as well as barks, we experience the dogs' world and our world simultaneously. Our talking dogs designate themselves here as binary entities. For if the world of human fiction, that of set generic boundaries, knows no connection with theirs, they literally know no separation from it. They are not simply talking about the "real" world, our world. They are talking, period; they share a discourse with that world, with us. Moreover, by sharing a discourse with us, they cause us to see our world's claim to sole "reality" as little more than the function of a generic identity that would justify itself by equating internal consistency with reality. By this act of sharing they designate all such claims for generic closure as problematic, contingent on the presence (implied or as here often suppressed) of a connective *and*.

Conversely, because the dogs continue to talk even though aware they should not be doing so, they signal a counterdesire to lift their discourse out of the human system of dialogue—in this case the generic category of the "colloquio"—it nominally claims to occupy. The content of their discourse appears both generically acceptable— it offers satirical portraits of contemporary morals—and acceptably mimetic, clearly referring to the "real" world. Yet as speakers their situation is binary. Their observations on our world are doubled throughout by discourse on an alternate fact: their ability (impossible in our world) to speak what we perceive to be human language.

Through this binary awareness the referential nature of this *colloquio*, assumed in our world, is gradually skewed, made oblique, finally "portentious." Coming as here from within the text, this sense of being double seems to bestow on that text what could be called a desire—born of the possibility of generic displacement—to place itself. And this is exactly what Cervantes' tale does: reposition itself as a binary form. The shared space of talking dog and talking man precipitates into a bipolar compound. The *and* is openly stated, and we are free, on either side of this fixed point, to designate forms. In this way, perhaps, the designations *fantasy* and *realism* are born. The dogs' world, in the final lines of the *Colloquio*, separates out, portentously claims, through a newfound ability to effect its own closure, a place on the literary map. For it is the dogs that, in the end, declare the existence of a diurnal rhythm: the alternation of day and night that will (beyond the confines of this text) provide topographical existence to the two forms that have emerged here from one. With tomorrow's daylight the dogs have agreed to be "normal," not to be able to speak. But when tomorrow night comes Cipión will, God willing, tell his tale.

For Mark Rose a genre "is not a pigeonhole, but a context for writing and reading, or in Claudio Guillén's suggestive phrase, an 'invitation to form'."[2] The "invitation" in Cervantes is more to an awareness of form, and beyond that, of a "context" determined less by external, historical factors than by internal, "topographical" ones. To Rose, genres are historical phenomena: they are "born" and they "die," they have primary, secondary and tertiary stages. They comprise therefore a measurable succession, an evolution, of forms whose placement depends then upon a quantitative logic of comparison. Their generic identity, insofar as it comprises a field, is governed by the comparative compound "more or less." What we saw in Cervantes' text, however, was an act of qualitative awareness: a sense of the "and" not as a generic but as a thematic marker, the point at which quantitative *or* entities accede to a qualitative field, a set of basic, perhaps "ideal" configurations that trace man's permanent interactive context, that with the natural world.

What I call *fantasy*, then, is what alerts me to the entry point into this topographical field, the place where generic forms make claim to thematic existence. They make this claim, as with Cervantes' dogs, by means of a logic. This logic of fantasy is a radical break with comparison and quantity. It occurs in the *Colloquio* when the principals in the generic game designate themselves not only other than their traditional roles but uniquely different. This violated traditional world, however, in the new sense of the topographical *and*, suddenly proves unstable. The dogs' logic, faced with this instability, is the logic of fantasy. It is a logic that seeks to redistribute the equation through a complementary gesture of closure. It is not a logic of exclusion—that is, in a generic world where dogs either can or cannot speak, when both occur, logic and genre are said to have broken down—but of inclusion. It is a literary world where talking dogs, conscious they should not be talking, still go on telling us about human virtue and vice. Doing so, they incorporate our world in theirs. Their telling, therefore, by virtue of this situation, is not direct address. The statements of fantasy do not perform, they inform, in the sense of inflecting, and finally rounding off, the statement structure shared with human discourse.

Fantasy refuses to be "invited," and may do so to the point of refusing both discourse and referentiality. Its system enfolds and frames generic "worlds" in its logic, as do Cervantes' dogs. There is, in extreme cases, no discourse with other worlds, no running back and forth (*dis-currere*). And, ideally, no referentiality, nothing taken out or brought back (*re-ferre*). Yet fantasy, because it is the means whereby we discover the *and* configuration (the "*portentoso y jamás visto*"), remains, even in its most radical logic of separation, connected by that *and* to a wider logical system. Critics may give fantasy a different moment of genesis, see it as a nineteenth-century reaction to a "crisis" in a realist or mimetic novel increasingly unable to "process" all the observable elements in its field of vision. Qualitatively speaking, however, here or in Cervantes, there is a similar manner of operation, a like awareness inside a given form of this correlative or *and* structure. Fantasy is not a traditional genre because it has no outside, no boundaries fixed by classification or evolution. It is instead literature's entry point into a binary field, where each form must lose its separate space so that all forms can operate within a same space.

The generic-evolutionary model insists on the order "realism >fantasy." I want to argue the opposite: that fantasy is the base element in my binary sets—the first term in the compounds "fantasy and realism," "fantasy and horror," and "fantasy and science fiction." It is so because it functions, in a fundamental manner, to inflect and define yet a broader field of balance, one implied in most human-generated binaries. We notice that our fantasy sets follow (instinctively perhaps) the same spatial logic as other prominent sets: realism and nominalism, or Roman Jakobson's metaphor and metonymy, or Northrop Frye's *dianoia* and *mythos*. Again, in this last case, the first term offers, as Paul Hernadi states it, the "simultaneous, quasi-spatial pattern of meaning" as opposed to "the temporal shape of a work."[3] What we seem to have here is an *Ur*-set: closure and openness (we remember that *realism* at its origin was a term of closure). And fantasy, more theme than form, marker of spatial rather than temporal distinctions (the talking dogs occupying our discourse space), is the entry point, not just to binary logic, but perhaps to the ultimate binary—the *and* that correlates, if you will, cosmos and mankind. If our *Ur*-set reflects the human desire for creative equilibrium, its reversal, as entropy and organization, makes *openness* the base term, provides an irreversible direction and terminal stability to the system. In light of this hyperset, literature's persistence in designating *closure* its base term is a sign (one fantastically futile perhaps, but now at least in its binary stage) of the human desire to stamp its order on the cosmos.

We have proof of the logic of fantasy investing genre thinking in a book like Käte Hamburger's *Logik der Dichtung*. Hamburger begins her study by noting her unorthodox use of the term *logic*: "Indeed, insofar as art is the object of inquiry of aesthetics and not of logic, and insofar as its province is the processes of shaping (*Gebiet des Gestaltens*), not those of thinking any talk of a logic of literature might seem superfluous, even confusing."[4] Yet she sees problems, both with literature's capacity to shape itself, and with the critic's ability to shape it into clear genres. She finds literature "an art form whose boundaries are drawn with difficulty," and quotes Hegel who calls it "that particular (*besondere*) art form in which art itself begins to dissolve (*sich aufzulösen*)." This is a binary perception, one that occurs (as was the "peculiar" case of Cervantes' dogs) inside the structure in question, where the single form, literature or the individual genres of literature, reveal their secret sharer, their *and* term. Literature discovers that, because it shares a common medium with other modes of discourse, what Hamburger calls the "processes of everyday speech and thought," its comfortable boundaries have become porous. Only logic then, as with Cervantes' logic of fantasy, can attest to this self-awakening, to the binary nature of literary forms, and in turn offer, now on a level of correlative elements, to reenact closure. This is what we see with Hamburger's ensuing attempt, the goal of her entire study, to designate *Dichtung* both as fiction and (much more radically) as *Nicht-Wirklichkeit*, nonreality. This designation, as we shall see, bears uncanny resemblance to definitions of fantasy given by recent critics.

Throughout her study, Hamburger's "logic" makes distinctions that are less exclusions than moments of binary awareness. Different generic forms, no longer allowed (as in a phrase like Frye's "novel proper") to claim their own space, are made, by virtue of this logic, to share a same space, a common ground upon which new, but this time interconnected, distinctions arise. Her first step, returning to the roots of the Aristotelian edifice, is to combine *mimesis* and *poesis*. But she does not say, as does Robert Scholes concerning "structural fabulation," that "there is no *mimesis*, only *poesis*. No recording, only constructing."[5] For that implies that *poesis* has displaced *mimesis*. On the contrary, she locates these two terms, coordinately, as parameters of a same space in order to take the next logical step: that of relocating literature, plotting its move toward closed structures in relation to the open systems of perception and statement.

We remember how Cervantes' dogs, suddenly aware within the mimetic and referential context of their discourse that their acts of speech are qualitatively different from those of other beings (that is, humans) occupying the same space, shift emphasis toward a discourse which, though it still may describe an outer world, no longer refers to it, but instead to itself. This is the same path followed by Hamburger's *Dichtung*. Speaking of epic, and dramatic "fiction," she would distinguish thereby two systems that share the common medium of language: the fictional-, and the statement-system. This latter system is open, along the subject-object axis, to concerns she calls historical, theoretical, and pragmatic. These are vectors, as Hegel sees it, of the disintegration of literary form. Fiction then, if it is to have its particular form, must set its utterances (for utterances there must be) rigorously apart from this statement system.

Hamburger's logic is clearly the logic of fantasy. Her lyrical "genre" is a case in point. The strong *I* subject of the lyric places it in the statement-, not the fictional-, system. But its awareness, within that system, that it is different, leads to its declaring itself a "noncommunicational" statement. In doing so, it relocates itself as a form analogous to fiction. For like fiction, its tactic is to place itself, finally, in the grammatical, not the epistemological or semantic, realm of discourse. Communication and reference are, Hamburger reasons, epistemological problems, and as such are of irresolvable complexity (such as that encountered by Cervantes' dogs when they seek to refer their world to that of their context). Fictional and lyrical statement, occurring within the grammatical realm, need not refer to any external reality. Not only that, within the grammatical system it would carve out its own, separate area of operation. There is, for Hamburger, one criterion that "establishes the reality [or referentiality] of the statement-subject: that we can ask about its placement in time." For the "designation of reality," she continues, "it is time and the temporal experience that are the decisive factors." *Dichtung*, however, does not present time in the normal grammatical sense. By logical analysis (brilliant here) she seeks to show that the tenses of *Dichtung*, despite the fact that they share the same grammatical space as tenses in the general statement-system, are actually atemporal, designating actions that bear no relation to the temporal experience of reader, author, narrator, or speaker outside their frame.

But to what extent is this, as W. R. Irwin, in his book on fantasy calls it, a "game of the impossible?" Irwin describes his form as a game, something that, if continuous and coherent, is still "an arbitrary construct of the mind with all under the control of logic and rhetoric."[6] In doing so he deprives his form of the rigor Hamburger uses to place her own fantastic construct, *Dichtung*. This is not something impossible. It is simply something never (before) seen. And it is not arbitrary, for that term implies comparison with a nonarbitrary (that is, real) world, outside the mind. Instead Hamburger wishes to give *Dichtung* a genuinely adjunctive existence. As separate world, or tense system, its status is less one one of analogy than of identity. It is not an *as if* structure so much as an *as* structure, one that allows the literary world, provided we "abide within" its logical system, to "appear *as* a world of reality."[7]

This *as*-existence of literature, however, depends on the rigor of its logic to locate its space, and in doing so designate the *and* that allows it to share, as equal, a common field with everyday semantics and grammar. There may be a sense, however, in which this game is impossible. Again, I use this word not to designate literature's *as if* nature, the relation of content to some standard of reality, but its *as* nature, the impossibility of affecting total closure within the *and* field. Cervantes' dogs, despite the logic of diurnality they proclaim, still fear that tomorrow night they may not, because of some catastrophic internal collapse, have the power of speech. Hamburger calls for a speakerless discourse, *dichtende Sprache* as *redende Sprache*. Even so, a speech act remains the common denominator. To Irwin fantasy, however tight its internal logic, cannot escape the context of speech, insofar as it remains "narrative sophistry conducted . . . to make non-fact appear as fact," sophistry requiring a "conspiratorial pact" with the reader. Hamburger, however, is more rigorous, and the *as* form she describes more rigorously fantasy in the deep sense of the term. For, doing away with Irwin's slavery to reference, where it is non-fact that must appear finally as fact, she inverts the proposition, seeing her general term *literature* possessed of a much more fundamental need to make fact seem as non-fact. Literature, in other words, takes refuge, finds its sole place of coherence and closure, in the realm she calls "non-reality."

At this point she returns to the etymological field to make another association: this time the historical shift from *poesis* to *fingere* (to feign). Fiction is traditionally feint, and as such places itself in Irwin's context of "narrative sophistry." To Hamburger, however, literature is a form of feint that now (and this is what has become fantasy) must proclaim itself non-feint. And it must do so to escape from an axis of discourse that can be deflected or distorted by a speaker's capacity to feint, by the discursive possibility of a conspiratorial pact of any sort. The question now remains: Why this *Logik der Dichtung*? Why should what is traditionally "dictated" suddenly strive to become the opposite, something that admits no speaker outside its own domain?

The Horror of Discourse

The answer lies in our perception of the nature of discourse itself. Increasingly, discourse is seen as the broad field of human activity, a vector of information encompassing all verbal constructs. Critics—and this is a modern awareness—see all literary forms and tenses as discourse: someone is always speaking. They no longer allow even such a minimal suspension of disbelief as Emile Benveniste's defense of the aorist past as the sole tense where "no one speaks."[8] It is significant that, to Hamburger, this same past is considered atemporal. For she is filled with Hegel's fear of the disintegration of literature. And that is, basically, a fear of noise: that the discourse field literature occupies is vectoring all sorts of uncontrollable elements. Discourse is an entropic medium, and its forms (as Norbert Wiener says) whirlpools in a stream of ever-flowing time. The struggle of discursive man, then, is to make these whirlpools increasingly resistent to the flow. And so arises a literature where, as with Cervantes' dogs, the speaking voice becomes aware, through a recurrent feedback loop, that it has neither origin nor destination outside its own speech. This is, as stated, a binary or *and* awareness. And becoming thus aware, it knows it is also discourse, hence contains the germ of its own disintegration. But this is a germ, in its deep embedding, that is highly compressed. The result is the trepidation of Cervantes' dogs: the more logic they use to close off their realm of discourse, the more that aspect of discourse that cannot be closed off (the fact that, to us readers, they speak the language of men) becomes portentous. We have the uncontrollable heightened, I will say horrifically, by an increased, and fantastic, desire to control.

Max Milner, in fact, separates fantasy from the "fantastic" by defining the latter as having a *surplus de sens*, leftover and unassimilable resonances.[9] It is just such a "surplus" that Hamburger sees the *I*, the first person narrator, introducing into the closed systems of her literary genres. She calls this (how rapidly her logic of genre reverts to epistemological concerns) a "feigned reality," duplicitous twists on the narrative thread by a speaker with positions in both "worlds" of discourse. This fantastic then, designating something unassimilable in the closed structure, indicates it cannot be closed. Doing so, it forces fantasy (or Hamburger's *Dichtung*) back into the stream of discourse: an awareness which, at this extremity, could bring catastrophic collapse to the structure itself.

Ordinary discourse is a compound field, there is a speaker and someone spoken to. But fantasy (and *Dichtung*) radically eschew the dual nature of the compound. Their discourse claims to have no object of address, only a speaking subject. It strives to be speech that is neither referential ("non-reality") nor, despite Irwin's claim, rhe-

146 GEORGE E. SLUSSER

torical. Literature, for Hamburger, has no designated addressee. In addition, it claims, as its speaking subject, the third-person. And less the *he* than the *they*, for its speakers are those collective "epic" patterns of myth—the timeless stories that lie beyond the more situation-bound discourse of first-or second-person speakers. This is an ideal, and it is an ideal that, by virtue of its need to cover the traditional field of genres, must at the limit, embrace a special "lyrical" *I*. For this speaker "we can no longer . . . determine whether the statement's content is true or false, objectively real or unreal—we are dealing only with subjective truth and reality . . . the experience field of the stating I itself." Yet this subject, excluded in some generic contexts, but admitted here, only brings binary ambiguity back into the logically closed system. More directly than the anonymous *they* of fable and legend, the *I* plants the seed of horror at the heart of fantasy.

Interestingly, Tzvetan Todorov, in his *Introduction à la littérature fantastique*, offers as the dominant themes of his genre two speaker-focused clusters; the *thèmes du je*, and the *thèmes du tu*. More interesting, Todorov presents his speaking subjects not as successive but as simultaneous determinants, as two speakers defining a single generic space, hence as a form of internal dialogue. He makes explicit what is implicit in Hamburger. For though she presents first the *they* forms (fiction), then the *I* forms (the lyric), it is soon clear from the logic of her argument that these do not mark separate genres but (as Todorov calls them) two variant themes that occupy the same thematic space of generic closure. This is the space of "non-reality," non-discourse. But bringing the *I* subject into this closed circle is dangerous, for, once closed in, this is the most discursive speaker of all—the soliloquist. The result of his activity is "special" forms (*Sonderformen*)—first-person narrative, the memoir novel—examples of general discourse eroding, in strange ways, the fictional space from within.

Todorov's description of the *thèmes du je* encompasses, if we look beneath the surface, the space of Hamburger's *Dichtung*. The narrative categories he cites—"suspended causality," "pandeterminism," metamorphosis, self-multiplication—seem traditionally nonfictional, examples of the *I* world encroaching on that of the epic *they*. The *they* mythos is sustained by such basic dichotomies as the mind/matter and subject/object distinctions. Todorov sees *I* encroachments like pandeterminism blurring these oppositions, breaking down their structure. By calling these categories the *thèmes du regard*—themes of onlooking rather than engagement, of reflexivity rather than reference—Todorov is making explicit what is implicit in Hamburger's logic. For here, in the context of these *I* themes, is not the act of turning *mimeis* into *poesis* the same as asking literature to create a world that is, of necessity, a mirror of itself? In such a world pandeterminism can exist because there is no connection with a single determined object-system, be it our consensus "reality" or some other form of "reality." Todorov, unflatteringly, sees these *I* themes as corresponding to the "world views" of such classes of people as drug addicts, psychotics, and children. But perhaps the formalist critic today has just this egocentric vision. Hamburger displays an extreme rage for generic logic. Its collapse from within, however, (and that of the formal limits she sets) shows us, as a form of literary psychosis, that such rigor is fantasy. It is so because it pursues the common (and self-destructive) desire of all such psychotic speech acts to deny its *and* connections: the binary field which is its creative extension.

But, to the psychotic, the possibility of self-extension may ultimately solidify as something menacing. Which brings us to Todorov's *thou* themes. These, which he identifies as: vampirism, incest, necrophilia and sadomasochism, he calls the "themes of discourse." *I* and *thou* may be, for Todorov, the two thematic areas that define the field of the fantastic. More important than a simple genre, however, is the problem of their connection. How does this connection create a "discourse"? And what kind of "discourse" can this be. In light of this connection, the *thou* themes listed appear as solid precipitates of the *I* themes, as if the closed mirror reflections on the observational world had taken flesh in some circular process of self-constructing perversion. *Thou* is the familiar you pronoun, and as such promises address that is personal, intimate, governed by emotion and even passion. But *thou*, like *I*, is a subject pronoun. The *I* can address it only in an indirect manner, laterally or paradigmatically, as one subject speaking to another. *I* speaks to *thou* then only insofar as it shifts its point of view from egocentrism to awareness of a potential, and potentially passionate, interlocutor. Discourse between two speaking subjects is, at best, virtual discourse. And in this state of virtuality the *I-thou* "discourse" acts very much like E. T. A. Hoffmann's Erasmus Spikher longingly addressing his mirror, watching his image willfully refuse to obey the figure before it. Hoffmann's perverse image finally steps out of the frame altogether, leaving the *I* staring at a menacing and horrific blankness. These *thou* themes, connected to the *I* themes by ties that are both oblique and passionate, tell us that statement, discourse, is not abolished by fantasy, but rather repressed. Indeed, as the *thou* subject overlays the *I*, both constrained by the fact that they are virtual, subjects without objects, something forms in the closed structures of fantasy: the perversion of statements promised and never made. This "discourse" is something trapped in the limbo between subject and object, where the act of looking becomes voyeurism, and the *I* what Baudelaire calls the "executioner of itself." Through this process, normal discourse has indeed become sadomasochism, and speaking subjects do feed vampirically on each other. If the *I* themes can be called the themes of fantasy, the *thou* themes then—and the Gothic nature of these themes as Todorov describes them more than attests to this—are themes of horror.

We should, however, I repeat, consider these terms not as designating singular forms, but in their conjunction, as fantasy *and* horror. Todorov, in fact, emphasizes the importance of the connective (if in a somewhat skewed and misleading fashion) when he calls the form defined by his *I-thou* themes "evanescent." The fantastic, for Todorov, operates between two generic forms—the uncanny and the marvelous. These are both forms that close upon themselves, that seek to define themselves by exclusion of the other. A story is uncanny for instance if its events, however "fantastic" they first seem, can be explained, in the end, by the laws of our world. A story is marvelous, however, when such an explanation can only occur under the laws of another world. Between these forms, the fantastic exists only as "hesitation," pure uncertainty as to which way to resolve. The fantastic therefore is less a genre in the classic sense than an indication of the elusive *and* that connects two forms that, in their radical need to claim their own space, could be called fantasy. But in the connection between *I* and *thou* we have more than "fantastic" hesitation at work. The *and* here is both unstable and explosive, the hesitation is such that it menaces the entire structure with collapse. Todorov gives us an example of this in Balzac's *Louis Lambert*. In this novel, the protagonist's *I*-world, an introspective state, bolstered by his "laws" of monistic materialism, that leads eventually to complete solipsism, is overlaid with a *thou*-world: Louis meets a beautiful girl, she becomes his fiancée, and marriage, the consummation of his growing desire, approaches. The result of this conjuncture is a violent hesitation, one that precipitates Louis into catatonic shock. This is discourse that collapses into total noncommunication.

The German word for genre, *gattung*, at its root, suggests both joining, and matrimonial joining, *gatten*. Todorov intuits this when he locates his fantastic at the junction between *I* and *thou*. But he does not develop this insight in terms of his generic system as a whole. For the other forms he mentions also bear the mark of a speaker. These speakers are not (as Todorov suggests) formal or grammatical entities so much as thematic loci: the "attitude" of a text as it were toward conjunction, or discourse, with some other speaker-directed text. For example the "uncanny" and the "marvellous" could both be said to have the *I* speaker. These forms, Todorov tells us, are generically opposed to each other. And to justify this opposition, he relates each, in parallel fashion, to a "neighboring" genre: the uncanny with poetry, the marvellous with allegory. But poetry and allegory, he qualifies, are not so much opposed to each other as both opposed to something else: to those literary forms that are "transitive," referential. Poetry is an intransitive statement, one read on the "pure level of the verbal chain that constitutes it." Allegory is a statement where the literal sense is entirely subsumed, "effaced," by the figurative sense. The latter then is wholly figurative, the former wholly literal. As such, both deny connection, the joining possibility of generic discourse. In doing so, both reveal they have the same speaking subject: the *I*, the subject that (Todorov tells us) does not desire to speak to other speech worlds, but merely to look to its own.

In all of this the fantastic is not just an evanescent presence: it is a superfluous one. For its "hesitation" is simply the denial of the *and* that joins generic forms, and as such is already implicit in the *I* speaker that governs the uncanny and the marvellous. Both of these forms however (and Todorov's *I*-themes suggest it) are examples of what I call fantasy. Fantasy is a solid term, and I use it here to bring to light (what Todorov's evasive "fantastic" does not do) a central fact of the system: in this case the strong pull this *I* speaker exerts on the connective of generic discourse. Fantasy is the form in which a speaker tells us there is no speaker, hence no need for discourse. This is the *as*-logic that seeks to transform the discursive *I* of normal statement into the involutive *I* of the fictional (that is, fantasy) enterprise. The *as*, however, cannot function except as equal sign. This logic does not abolish the connective so much as underscore its presence.

We saw in Cervantes fantasy's resistance to the "married land" of genre. This text, as a "colloquio," assumed a generic field where the connection is between the declared *I*-speaker and the collective speaker, the *they*. This is the same nexus that generates the themes of discourse for the field we call realism. The *I* can consort with the *they* if the latter is accepted as the consensus speaker: that is, the mimetic speaker who by means of this consensus (the *I-they* link) is empowered to re-present fictional worlds. Fantasy's reaction is described by Hamburger: it is the equation of *mimesis* with *poesis*, declaring the power of the nonconsensus speaker to make a world of fictional speech that is equal to the consensus world. Fantasy does not represent, it presents. In doing so, it places itself on the *I* side of the connection, as if that connection were an equation. It pulls then on the *and*, and this tension causes the *they*-subject to modulate toward a middle position: that of Todorov's second-person speaker. This speaker, in reaction to the egocentric logic of the *I*, increasingly desires to couple, to draw the fantasy structures back into contact. But contact with what? *I*-speech is speech that uses language as an instrument of logic, hence of closure. *Thou*-speech, however, rediscovers that language is also a medium: in this case the conduit whereby logic encounters passion, and closure issues into entropy. This is why the *I-thou* link is one of horror, because it draws fantasy to become the executioner of itself.

The Catastrophe Nexus

The *and* is the mark of conjunction and coordination. But it is also the mark of intersection. As such it determines a geometry of forms, a field of intersecting shapes. We have seen that this *and*, in governing a field of literary forms, does not function as a neutral equal sign. It is the same in this literary geometry. For here shapes are controlled, their configurations inflected, by thematic motivations. Curves are plotted on coordinates of logic and desire. With her *as*-logic, Hamburger (in a graphic sense) is forcing the curve of fiction to form a steeper and steeper vertical slope in relation to the horizontal axis of discourse. Todorov's *I* themes do the same in relation to the *thou* axis. The result of both is instability of the vertical structure, and its inevitable collapse. If we are dealing with geometry here, it is a geometry of catastrophe.

Samuel R. Delany, in his novel *The Einstein Intersection*, offers a geometrical description for what is clearly our fantasy-horror conjunction: "Einstein defined the extent of the rational. Goedel stuck a pin into the irrational and fixed it to the wall of the universe so that it held still long enough for people to know it was there. And the world and humanity began to change. And from the other side of the universe we were drawn slowly here. The visible effects of Einstein's theory leaped up on a convex curve, its production huge in the first century after its discovery, then leveling off. The production of Goedel's law crept up on a concave curve, microscopic at first, then leaping to equal the Einsteinian curve, cross it, outstrip it."[10] The steep fall of the Einstein curve summons a correspondingly steep rise of the Goedel line to its unstable maximum, which (it is implied) must in turn fall and resummon the Einsteinian. In this wave-like process equilibrium is a line drawn through the points of intersection. To wish to define "the extent of the rational," and in doing so impose maximum logical control over any limited system, is what I call fantasy. The sharpness of the crest however opens a correspondingly deep trough, marking instances of irrationality which, in mirror fashion, plunge to the point of maximum instability. At this point the negative curve places itself, pins itself violently to the "walls" of the closed, fantasy "universe," and doing so takes tangible shape and direction, begins its sharp rise to closure and fall in turn. This negative line, by virtue of the imagery it commands, is horror. Delany's speaker, Spider, emphasizes this when he calls for a "Goedelian answer" to our Einsteinian questions: "I don't want to know what's inside the myths, nor how they clang and set one another ringing, their glittering focuses, their limits and genesis. I want their shape, their texture, how they feel when you brush by them on a dark road, when you see them receding into the fog, their weight as they leap your shoulder from behind" (p. 130). Again, our most radical closures, the "glittering focuses" of fantasy, precipitate a resurgence of open concourse, but as it were compressed by this process into perverse and horrific shapes, into violent physical contact, aggression.

Asking for a Goedelian answer might seem to imply there is a Goedelian form—a fictional world equally coherent as the Einsteinian, but where uncertainty is now the norm, the rule that governs its "logic." Critics have come up with genre designations for such a form, calling it "experimental" or, more accurately, "deconstructive" fiction. Delany's own novel has been placed in such a category. Indeed, the author seems to encourage us to do so, for he prefaces the novel with fragments from an "author's notebook" that tell us deconstructive things, such as that endings, to be useful, must be inconclusive. Intersection, however, is a trans-formal category. Einstein and Goedel, in light of their intersection, are not "ideas" in the sense of something that reinforces a preexistent formal entity. Delany's Spider calls them "theories." They are more theorems (*theorema*—a sight): visible lines of thought that, intersecting, form different spatial configurations. Intersection, because it focuses or locates these configurations, is the theme. Einstein and Goedel are the vectors shaped by this theme. The result is configurations that are characterized less by formal categories than by dynamic ones such as stability and instability. We can have a steady rhythm, alternating curves of maximum Einstein and maximum Goedel. Or we can have the process Spider describes: one line or curve "eagling over" the other, a rhythm of violent rise and collapse. Fantasy and horror then, doubled by these Einsteinian and Goedelian vectors, have become intersectional terms. Delany's theoretical geometry reveals, in its literary interface, its human face.

Putting a human face on geometry is, in a sense, what recent "catastrophe theory" attempts to do. Mathematicians, scientists, and social scientists have developed "catastrophic" models to deal with sudden shifts in equilibrium in given systems, shifts that lead to "catastrophic" collapse of curves toward radically different states of balance. This topological plotting—a multidimensional version of Delany's "Goedelian" geometry—is being used in widely varying situations. One of the most interesting uses (in terms of a fantasy-horror nexus) is the treatment of the psycho-physiological "catastrophe" anorexia nervosa, where increasingly wide metabolic swings, from starvation to gluttony, have replaced the more moderate body rhythms of eating and digesting. Fantasy and horror, it could be said, represents a like "metabolic" imbalance in the fictional system. If we think of current distinction, or rather conjunction, between story and narrative (*histoire/récit*), we see it also headed for catastrophe. On one hand we have narrative, through the structural logic of theoreticians and new novelists, claiming autonomy to the point that the counterclaims of story line have virtually disappeared. This radical stance has, in turn, summoned an equally radical "Goedelian" reaction. And in a series of horrific texts issuing from a seminal work like E. T. A. Hoffmann's "Sandman," we have the dominance of a story line so arbitrary and unpredictable that narrative, despite all its powers to close, can no longer shape coherent characters or plots.

The *and* then, in fantasy and horror, has become a catastrophic cusp. But if stories are to be narrated again—if discourse, story and world are to find once more, in this field of catastrophe, a smooth continuous relationship—this *and* must somehow take a different fold. One that allows the literary system to recover an equilibrium. What I call science fiction may be the result of such a fold, one which allows potential catastrophe to issue into a new shape, "complementarity," where the *and* has become, at one and the same time, a mark of catastrophe and continuity. In itself the binary "science-fiction," as term, is a structure of complementarity: a compound of fiction and science, in other words of fantasy and something that confronts and enfolds horror, inflects the "I-thou" nexus toward one better described as "I-you," discourse that has circumvented desire, made the *and* once more a neutral, informational connective. Delany's Spider asks this question of his Einstein intersection: "I want to know how you take to the idea of carrying three when you already bear two?" (p. 130). This question demands, beyond a Goedelian answer, a science-fictional one. For if fantasy would be no discourse, and horror, in catastrophic response, what Plato calls "dead discourse," then might not SF designate a breakthrough beyond breakdown, a fold that returns us to the living discourse of human inquiry?

Fantasy, horror, SF: all then are topologically determined designations. As such they are less forms than themes, locatable in an *and* field capable of carrying two, three, *n*-dimensions perhaps. Hamburger gropes toward such a topological sense of genre with her division between temporal and spatial modalities of language. Temporal aspects, present everywhere in the grammatical structure of this medium, can determine order and degree (and hence value in the quantitative sense of more or less), but cannot determine shapes. Time, in fact, is seen to transform shape. Therefore, because she seeks to place fiction or literature as something qualitatively different within this general statement system, she must empty it of time, prove its tenses are atemporal. And Todorov redefines the subject function of two statement-subjects from this same system of general discourse by declaring them to be themes. He thus displaces them from the statement vector of grammatical time or tense, and gives them a synchronic function: that of governing speech configurations in a same interconnected space. Theme is traditionally *topos*, a designation of place. And catastrophe theory offers a tool for analyzing more complex designations, the configurational fields generated by the *and*. For what it focuses on are the "themes of and" themselves—the themes of connection, catastrophe, and complementarity. In our case, each of these governs a thematic set. These are, respectively: fantasy and realism; fantasy and horror; and fantasy and science fiction.

The Field of Texts

As we have seen, sophisticated critics have difficulty in setting boundaries between genres such as fantasy and science fiction. Yet the most unsophisticated consumer recognizes instinctively the shape of that field of texts he calls "fantasy and science fiction." Critics, publishers and booksellers seem to be afraid of the *and*; they prefer to place books in neat niches. But our consumer is not afraid. Nor does he hesitate to join other forms—horror and, via mystery, even realism—to this field. His perception is a valid starting point for mapping this field of texts, for at least he has a sense of the shape of forms to come. But we must see their connections, the function of the *and* in organizing the shapes. The territory defies the generic map-maker. It calls instead for the topographer.

First of all there are, in this field, texts that seem to link on the vector of "fantasy and realism." One class of these are works that extrapolate a future world from a clearly historical base. Classic examples are Isaac Asimov's *Foundation* and Frank Herbert's *Dune*. By calling themselves "future histories," however, these works invert the extrapolative vector. For that vector runs from past to future, whereas this formula places the future *before* the past. This future then is a world that does not prolong history but sets itself against it. And Hamburger's "logic" may suggest the reason why. For Hamburger the reality of a statement does not depend on the reality of the object "imitated" or spoken, but on that of the speaking subject. Though she does not specify, her historical statement-subject must be a *they*. For in order to utter with any mimetic assurance the statement: "it happened," there must be a consensus that it did happen, several speakers present at the same moment in time who agree it did. Hamburger's speaker-centered logic, however, makes the process of *mimesis* problematic. How reliable is this consensus subject? With the subject in question, the conduit of representation becomes unsure; problems of referentiality, now "metaphysical," insoluble in terms of statement alone, invade the text. Given this crisis in mimetic statement, a "future history" is the next logical step. For by locating the historical statement in the future, it turns away from problems of consensus and referentiality. To Hamburger, the historical is measured in time that is structured by chronology not topography. These statement-futures, in terms of chronology, do not exist. Even the *yet*, that marks the possibility they may someday exist, is at best a designation of place. A place out of time, this future world is striving not to refer to anything, nor to depend for its existence, as statement, on a consensus subject.

This "future history" then is history as *I*-pronouncement. Its speaker pulls back from the *they* connection that constitutes mimetic speech. He would sever the individual from the collective speaker, and by doing so disconnect history from time, locate it in the personal space of what is a fantasy construct. In the light of fantasy, the reason for this shift is clear. Consensus is the search for a temporal anchor. But as the basis for historical statement, it can lead to a fascination with chronology. And in the "realist" statement this fascination yields to a tyranny: that of reference. As, in realism, the relation of speaker to world becomes the increasingly problematic one of consensus to *mimesis*, that speaker's control of his speech world succumbs to the singularities of chronology. Thus dominated by this external sense of time, the mimetic speech-world is an *as-if* world. Reacting to this, "future history" seeks to be an *as* world. For the act of equating history and futurity is, in a very real sense, one of conflating *mimesis* and *poesis*. The speaking subject of "future history" is withdrawing from the problems of conjunction itself: the problems of the *and*. In doing so, he asserts the freedom, beyond the tyranny of time-links and referents, to locate his own world. The *and*, therefore, that joins future and history, fantasy and realism, could be said (on the metaphysical level) to mark an interaction between free will and determinism.

Foundation offers a case in point. Its field of activity includes both determinism and free will. But the former is the function of a referentiality that exists here only outside the fictional frame. Asimov can make the statement that history repeats itself because he can compare acts inside the frame with a set outside that frame. In other words, he can determine that there is determinism. But no character inside the fictional world is allowed to make such a reference. They all believe, on the contrary, that their history is governed by "laws" they formulate, those of "psychohistory." History is relocated here, from some external temporal theater to the space of the human mind. In these characters' view, repetition is not the mark of a "higher" determinism, but of the mind's control over historical processes.

To resolve the conflict between author's and character's views of history, James Gunn invokes the Judeo-Christian model.[11] This, however, only subordinates one view to the other. For it places a predetermined "reality" around a fictional world where the actors have "free will" only to the extent that they can ignore the outer frame. The logic of fantasy would say that they are thus free not to refer. For by choosing not to refer, they become free to speak themselves into existence, and to govern that existence by "laws" that are formulated internally. To Gunn's Judeo-Christian model, however, this freedom is not fantasy but illusion. The *and* here is not neutral. But it must be made so if fantasy is to have equal status in the equation. For only the neutral *and* will allow the reversal of polarity that lets free will challenge determinism, and fantasy realism. What occurs in *Foundation* is a new foundation, fantasy investing the role of *poesis*, making its own laws.

Foundation is an *I*-fantasy that not only invests the consensus world of history, but challenges the determinism of God's (and the author's) *they*. Herbert's *Dune* is an outright *I*-fantasy. The future world of *Dune* is a reprojection of our past: this time not of the Roman Empire, but of the history and culture of desert peoples, of

Islam. "The true test of prescience," Herbert's narrator tells us, "[is] to see the past in the future." But what character, inside the fiction, has such prescience? We, the readers, along with the author, see the Islamic signifiers, and others that indicate a determined past. So do the official "historian" Princess Irulan, and the compiler of the glossary. But these are frame figures. The protagonist Paul Atreides, however, does not see the past in the future; he does not recognize the fatal lineage his name indicates. Instead Paul places the past in the future, and he does so by literally encompassing it in his single, personal, visionary speech act. Equating foresight and memory, Paul causes the entire historical universe to collapse within the confines of his vision: "Paul felt himself at the center, at the pivot where the whole structure turned." He is simultaneously center and circumference, engendering world as his word, and enfolding it in that word. By substituting his timeless *logos* for the temporal discourse of history, Paul claims freedom. It is freedom, however, itself determined by the limits of a speech-act: a self-created world.

There is a third fantasy structure born of this retreat from the *and*. This is where the text offers, not a personal *logos*, but an alien one. Such texts claim to present the alien through alien speech, so that it locates its own linguistic space, an *as* world, within our common system of statement. In the literal sense such location is not possible. If it were, it would not be detectable, for no message would pass. It is possible figuratively however. Fiction has a capacity to designate itself as alien discourse, and we have an example in James Tiptree, Jr.'s story "Love Is the Plan, the Plan Is Death." As its chiastic title suggests, this story seeks to create, within the open and referentially diffuse field of common discourse, a world of sound chains, of alliterative relationships that turn upon themselves, striving as they do so to erase the semantics of shared words, the statement dimension of common syntax. These word-structures strive to be purely ornamental in nature, to refer in circular manner only to their own stylistic form, as we see in Tiptree's title, or in the nonsensical sound-circle "grendalgren" that organizes the vast, apparently chaotic, cityscape of Samuel R. Delany's novel *Dhalgren*. In these works, the common meanings of words, and the shared events and emotions they traditionally convey in fiction, are converted into something self-contained: the *I* speaker posing as an *it*.

The more extreme the fantasy plan, however, the more unstable it becomes. If Delany's word-chain joins the beginning and the end of his novel, the going in and coming out of the city, the chain itself retains a point of connection. This is the hobbling figure of the protagonist, with his one shod and one bare foot, who is increasingly, in the larger harmonies of verbal sound, a point of stress, a false note. And Tiptree's plan is no simple balance. For the opposites it would contain are not the classic ones of life and death, but a more explosive pair: love and death. We see here the familiar process. In its denial of reference, fantasy is denying the connective, the *and*. It is then (suicidally we might say) denying the very field that engendered it. And which, despite this denial, continues to sustain it. For Tiptree's "plan" is more than a stylistic counter, the central term in a chiasmus upon which a self-contained, hence nonconnected, structure pivots. Like Delany's hero, the "plan" remains a connective: the link between realms of statement and of style, reference and closure. But like that hero, because of the stress placed on it by the fantasy denial, that connective is defective. Paul Atreides, as he describes himself, is such an unstable *and*: "I need time now to consider the future that is a past within my mind. The turmoil comes, and if I'm not where I can unravel it, the thing will run wild." This extreme fantasy, no less than the continuous logical attempt to contain all the enharmonics of language, has so stressed the field of forms the language medium would normally sustain that it has brought about catastrophic collapse. Or brought us to the verge of it. Take *Dune* for example. If the disorderly sequels are an indication, the structure of its fictional world, as it is increasingly circumscribed by Paul's *I* fantasy, has collapsed. This same instability may be the reason why in film, a visual medium whose overtones are even harder to control than those of words, fantasy structures regularly collapse into horror.

This is the fantasy-horror nexus, and there are many texts in our common field that operate here. These are, despite their apparent generic disparity, easily identifiable by a similar topography. Stanislaw Lem offers works like *The Investigation* (a mystery story?) and *Solaris* (a satire or "anatomy"?). Or there is Philip K. Dick's unclassifiable *Ubik*, where the characters' private worlds begin, literally, and with the passionate intimacy I have described, to devour each other, precipitating a complete collapse of fantasy or fiction. A less obvious example, however, is Brian Aldiss's novel *Cryptozoic!* (British title *An Age*). Aldiss's characters use mind travel to range across the whole span of geological time. Mind travel is a perfect metaphor for the fantasy enterprise as I have described it. By means of the mind these travelers can detach themselves from all historical determinants; what they dramatize, passing unattached through all eras of time, is fantasy's search to be free of the tyranny of the referent. They observe the ages they pass through, but in no way can those ages act upon them, or they upon them. These travelers also, especially the protagonist Edward Bush, have cut loose in order (as with fantasy) to relocate at a position which is absolutely self-contained. This is the "cryptozoic," the hidden fantasy key to all ages. It is the single, and impossible, fiction that would encompass the multiple statements of evolutionary time.

But mind travel and the cryptozoic contain as well the deep contradictions of the fantasy enterprise. For though the travelers operate like transparent eyeballs, passing unobstructed through the ages just as Bush passes through the petticoats of Queen Victoria, they remain nonetheless attached (as per the British title) to *an* age. The connection is physical: the individual body must remain in suspended animation. But there is also, and despite the mind's claim to freedom, a mental connection as well. For Bush, the motivation for mind travel, we discover, is something deeply rooted in his personal psyche. He draws the parameters of his own world only to discover that the things that connected him to other worlds—the worlds of his mother, biology and history—are still operative inside the mindspace that constitutes that private world. The word "repressed" is perfect to describe the nature of this hidden *and*. And its repression, by these fantasies of mind travel, render it highly unstable.

What reveals the presence of this hidden *and* is the fact that Bush's personal search triggers a general catastrophe: that fantasy precipitates horror. Bush's quest for the cryptozoic begins as a private fantasy. But it soon encounters a collective version of that fantasy: the apparent consensus that forms, among a band of such traveling shades, around Silverstone's theory of reversed temporality. Silverstone proclaims the future to be our past. But by doing so he is, at the same time, saying that our past is our future. This is the same gambit we saw with "future history": where the individual fantasy is generalized into a sweeping collective vision. Here time moves in reverse, bullets leap out of bodies and return to the barrels of guns. But this cosmos, however marvelous for collective man, is ironically a dangerously collapsing one for the individual. Here is how Silverstone describes the "future": "Gradually, over countless forgotten eons, it had drawn in upon itself, like a large family returning to the same roof in the afternoon, when work is done."[12] Like a balloon stuck with a pin, Silverstone's sweeping vision suddenly shrinks to a monologue, and its collective future seen for what it is: a fantastically inflated version of the individual past. Indeed, it is just such a family past, in this case a mother-fixation, that has driven the protagonist, Bush, on his mind travels, toward that catastrophic moment when, in this insane circular logic, past and future collide.

Pursuing a future that is in reality his own hidden past, Bush is like the speaker in Keats's "Ode to a Nightingale," whose fantasies, his *I* structures, harbor a secret, and treacherous, addressee: the *thou* which is his incestuous love of death. The situation is quite analogous: there is the flight of freedom, the fantastic discourse of disconnection, which only reinforces the pull of the connective, present in the very need of this speaker to address someone, until that connective finally "tolls" him back to his sole self, to his physical situation. For Bush however, the tolling back is a catastrophe. His physical situation can no longer be resolved by a simple choice like: do I wake or sleep?, because both have now become nightmares. The eagling curve of Silverstone's fantasy world collapses, in the last chapter of the novel, into a brave new world: a dystopia as absolutely impermeable to human needs as the mind travelers' utopia was permeable to them. Speakers like Silverstone and Bush, by placing their futures in the past, the *I* in the *thou*, actually create their present. For what precipitates from this conjuncture is something like a chain of chance, disorder that now affirms itself *as* order. The only fixity, in the landscape of things and events Bush encounters upon his return to body-reality, is a chain of alliterative and onomatopoeic associations—an age, Ann, Annivale, anomia, amniotic. Such a sequence, in the fantasy mode, is said to operate parallel to human design. Here, however, it has, somehow relevant but inscrutable, usurped that design: it is an organizing force operating, in terrifying fashion, beyond our understanding. In this meaningless, and fatally binding, subtext we experience nonreferentiality with a vengeance—a "horrifizing" of that same closure system by which Tiptree hoped, fantastic paradox, to create the controllable linguistic alien.

Todorov has a quote from Martin Buber that is quite relevant here: "Quand l'homme dit Je, il veut dire l'un ou l'autre, Tu ou Cela."[13] For Buber there are but two addressees for the *I* or fantasy speaker: the *Thou* or the *That*. Both addressees, probably, are God, and we must choose between them: choose a personal or an impersonal relationship. In the catastrophic world of *Cryptozoic!* however, there is neither God nor choice. To address the *thou* is, invariably it seems, to encounter the inhuman order of the *that*. But must *invariably* be the word? Buber gives us only an *or* choice, and thus seems to lock God into this catastrophic nexus. This is to forget, however, the presence of the *and*, that tenacious presence that neither our fantasies nor (as it proves) our nightmares can efface. For the *and* allows that between the desire of *thou* and the determinism of *that* falls a shadow. By its logic (one it seems that even God ignores) the *and* has to offer an alternative, the possibility of some other discourse vector. This, I argue, is fantasy and science fiction. The term "science" does more than merely signal a return to rational discourse in a postrational context. The term here does not designate chronological advance (or return) so much as a topological reconfiguration of catastrophic space. The addressor remains the fantasy *I*. But the addressee changes. "Science fiction" exerts a pull on the connective, slight but enough to divert the curve of discourse from *thou*, the subject of desire, to *you*. This addressee is "scientific" precisely because it is universal: it designates subject and object, singular and plural. It is, in the broad sense of the word, participatory. And for the *I* to address it, to link its fictions to it, is to swerve from catastrophe to complementarity.

Fantasy and science fiction is the configuration that, at the point of connection where literary forms could be said to "discourse," allows discontinuity (the *thou* is everpresent as option) to seek more continuous paths. The *I* speaker, at the horror nexus, casts up structures that, like Spikher's shadow, not only break from their source but turn on it destructively. The science fiction nexus, however, offers the possibility, beyond the catastrophic breakaway, of renewed discourse. Through this connection fantasy gains new freedom, even if only the very limited freedom promised by the second-person universal status of the addressee: a status that allows human reason to coexist with inhuman monstrosity. Many works of fiction, in fact, are expanded forms of address, their titles vocatives: *Madame*

Bovary, Anna Karenina. The first is a formal family name, the second a first name and a matronymic. We could say that as address becomes more passionate, the result is more catastrophic: in the case of these two addressees increasingly violent suicide. And in novels like *Cryptozoic!* the addressee (the exclamation point is a mark of address) is not a person but a passionately personified thing. The *they* becomes a *Them!*, and as this happens the act of naming, the invitation to discourse, itself becomes a vehicle of horror. What about a title like *Dhalgren* however? It is a section of a chain of syllables composed from the name, a name precipitated by the terrible tyranny of this loop, of the monster Grendal. But how did the *h* get into this sequence? It is superfluous, not there in the monster's name. Putting it there however, in the vocative act which is the novel's title, opens a small space, in this case the space of human whimsy, in a closed structure. The *h* signifies, within the oversimplified geometry of literary catastrophe, the possibility of other configurations, new curves and shapes of continuity. It is the minimal mark of SF: the *you* added to the *thou*, the locus of complementarity, the redesignation of the *and* as a sign of integration, the meeting point of parallel lines short of infinity.

This fantasy and science fiction connection, as I call it, informs many texts in our field. Often, because of the overlay of genre categories, the functioning of this connection is unnoticed, as is that of the fantasy-horror nexus. My choice of texts to analyze can only be random. But in order to show how widespread fantasy and science fiction have become, I compare two examples from the nonverbal narrative of film. Both films are variations on the theme of evolution, hence on that nonteleological process that our catastrophe fictions have rendered deterministic, Calvinistic even. For, caught at the nexus of fantasy and horror, evolution becomes more than cycles that repeat. Our evolutionary fantasies, in which the human form seeks to hold its invarying place as the form of order, actually trace a vortex, where man and nature inexorably collapse in some cataclysmic Fall.

Our first example is the Bolero sequence from the Italian animated film *Allegro non troppo*. In the opening frames, a spaceship leaves a deserted planet. A Coke bottle is tossed to the ground, and out of this act of interstellar littering organic life stirs. Protoplasmic shapes leave the bottle, and evolution begins. At this point, there are several options: first, alien evolution can replay ours; second, it can appear to follow a different path; third, it can follow a consciously concerted different path, be "really" alien, as far as our imagination allows. The first is the *I* fantasy, where all evolutions, because they are recognizably calqued on ours, come full circle in the human form. The second, less obvious, is the *it* fantasy. Here the external forms of evolution seem "alien." But this is merely cosmetic, a façade that conceals the ultimately human logic that governs the superficially strange biosphere. The third is the extreme autistic fantasy that precipitates collapse into horror: Aldiss's cryptozoic, or the fall of the Invincible in Stanislaw Lem's novel of the same name.

Visibly, *Allegro non troppo* cannot make a choice between these evolutionary fantasies. Or should I say, visually. For working within the shared medium of the image, each choice seeks to impart its direction to the visual landscape. The medium itself is the *and* here, and concurring fantasies place terrible stress on it. The forms that first leave the Coke bottle are perceptibly alien, and at first appear to evolve in nonhuman manner. But as soon as they are given vector, we begin to notice, beneath the wildly proliferating forms, a gradual (and increasingly familiar) process of ascent. The creatures pass through shapes that are vaguely reptilian, then less vaguely mammalian, finally to affirm themselves as quite recognizable *homo sapiens*. There is a similar process at work in Ridley Scott's *Alien*. Great pains are taken here to make the emergent creature, visually, a non-human alien. But the creature, despite itself, begins to evolve. And in its evolution moves, in visually confused manner but inexorably nonetheless, toward the humanoid, as if gradually captured by the fantasies and myths of the life form it visually is meant to oppose. In a sense, the *it* world is summoning its *I* origin. Drawn back from its alien musings, that self emerges with the passionate desire to address its alien double as *thou*. This emergence, at that intersection which is the image world they share, acts to destabilize the fantasy construct. For instance, the discourse between man and alien in Scott's film is clearly catastrophic. On one curve the alien, within the metallic order of the spaceship artifact, evolves toward human form. But on another, inversely corresponding curve that order itself is devolving, metal lines becoming organic chaos, incarnate mind visually grounded in bowel-like tunnels. The collapse of fantasy again generates horror.

Ravel's music acts as an ordering device for the animation in this film. But here, as well, order is an ambiguous, destabilizing, mixture of *I* and *it*. At first glance, this music seems the perfect vehicle for the *I*-fantasy. For *Bolero* is a single melody line, one that advances by repetition and accretion, but that undergoes no syntactic change in the process. It is, therefore, a marvelous vehicle for simulating ascent, for disguising the everpresent form that orchestrates the evolutionary fantasy. The monotony of this device, however, reveals, increasingly, an alien logic at its illusory core. This, as opposed to the human syntax of evolution, is paratax: in this case the vertical process that increasingly alienates the single line by passing it through different instrument groups and dynamic levels, subjecting (on the metaphorical level) human destiny to the inhuman logic of a prefixed system of categories.

It is the tensions of Ravel's music that orchestrate the evolution of images in this film. And that evolution comes to rest on a huge statue of a man standing astride the apogee of his technology—the city. As end product, however, this is a vessel that would contain endless repetitions of the single melody line of human fanasy. Scott's spaceship world, we remember, closed upon a computer named "mother" at its functional core, hoping to trap the generative source of evolution in its metal casing. In like manner, the metal statue of man is both the shape behind the fantasy and the device by which it perpetuates itself. Suddenly, however, the head of the statue cracks open. A leering ape peers out, and the entire edifice, city and statue, collapses. This ape is a paratactic figure in the evolutionary syntax of this fantasy. He pops up anachronistically throughout the ages, accompanying the journey as a malicious and destructive secret sharer in the ascent of man. He is the *thou* addressee our *I* speaker represses by transferring his form and logic to mechanical surrogates. In terms of true evolutionary discourse, the ape is but a step, as is man. His passing is a sign that we too must pass, must connect or communicate with something else. To deny this connection is to perpetuate the ape: to generalize what was a term in a process into a product of that process—the organic force of evolution now cast (like the statue) as man's eternal nemesis, his catastrophic double. Through the sensuous replay of *Bolero*, the *I* finally addresses the *thou*, the crafty and passionate ape that haunts his evolutionary fantasies. The ensuing collapse reveals the *That*: the iron determinism of the replay, Bolero as broken record, each turn reinscribing more and more deeply the horror of the Fall.

The statue falls here; there is catastrophe. That fall is diverted, however, in another film with similar evolutionary premises: Stanley Kubrick's *2001: A Space Odyssey*. This film modulates the horrific juxtaposition of man and ape. It springs the trap, and in doing so creates the configurational opening I call science fiction.

The initial inspiration for *2001* comes from Arthur C. Clarke. Clarke's version of the story though, presented in final form only in a novel written after the film, remains a classic replay fantasy. In the novel, for instance, the room at the end of Bowman's infinity voyage is not an evolutionary way station. It is a projection of his mind: "There being no further use for it, the furniture of the suite dissolved back into the mind of its creator."[14] And Bowman's transformation, supposedly an evolutionary move to the next step, is curiously described, not as a line or even a spiral, but in terms of arcs and cycles: "Time flowed more and more sluggishly, approaching a moment of stasis—as a swinging pendulum, at the limit of its arc, seems frozen for one eternal instant, before the next cycle begins" (p. 217). What is more, the amplitude of this cosmic pendulum is governed by human norms of balance. And once the "next" cycle begins, we realize just how homocentric it is. The supermind is still a star *child*; the discorporate being is inexorably drawn back, not just to human form, but to mother earth. Here the creation of a new cycle of history can only be human history all over again.

Like Hamburger, Clarke does not seem to see the fantasy nature of his fiction. He does not see that the claim to uniqueness or "newness" is based not on opening the system but on closing it. The system can be that of discourse as statement or (in this case) as evolutionary interaction. It can be closed in relation to reference or (in this case again) to time, to any irreversible vector of change. What Kubrick does, in his film, is to push Clarke's *I* fantasy toward the *thou* connection, to activate the catastrophe nexus. In a sense he does this, as in *Allegro non troppo*, by creating a visual subtext to the evolutionary journey: a copresence that, like the leering ape in the animated film, is a permanent sharer in man's ascent. The coexistence of these texts marks the *and* as a point of stress. But is it a sign of advancement, of sequency of forms?, or is it a sign of stasis, of simultaneity, hence equality, of forms? Caught at this nexus, man cannot surpass his origins; origins and ends, in fact, close on themselves, only to collapse inward. Accompanying Bowman's evolutionary destiny in Kubrick's film is a double more catastrophically problematic than either Clarke's star child or the leering ape. That double is biology itself: those biological links that Clarke's man, though he cannot break them, represses, apocalyptically, at the center of his fictions of transcendence. For the star child conceals a superweapon; and the statue to be smashed here is all men's earth.

In Kubrick's film, intersecting the curve of man's evolutionary rise, is a plunging curve. This latter traces a fall somehow inexorably rooted in his biological origin and condition. How steep the slopes of these curves is measured by the famous bone, tossed high in the air to become, as it begins its sharp descent, a spaceship. The bone functions, visually, as an ambiguous connective. For the act of throwing it in the air literally effects the *I-Thou* nexus. A link is made between disparate image-worlds, between past and future. Abolished by this link, man is rendered at the same time a catastrophic presence because of it. In the prehistoric world, man's relation to nature is one of passive observation. In the future, the observer has not become an actor. Instead he creates nature, as machine, in his own image, and engages it in passionate, and destructive, discourse. As the bone moves from past to future, it forms a connecting point that is catastrophically unstable. For what is elided, erased by the toss, is no less than all of human history, and the human present itself. The compounds this connection forges reflect this instability: the bone is both tool and weapon, the emblem and means of life and death; the spaceships conceal, in their elegant waltzings, the terrible force of doomsday destruction.

Clarke's fantasy then, in the film, is made to discourse with horror. Kubrick, however, does not stop here. To do so would be merely to cultivate curves of ascent and catastrophic collapse, to stress the connective with cataclysmic oxymorons such as the cut from bone to waltzing spaceship. For Clarke, man's expansion into space is never more than the projection of his own form as model for order: evolution as mindscape. Man here remains that *I* observer: the fulcrum upon whch the pendulum swings. Kubrick decenters that observer. He is denied any fixed, or edenic point. In the film, the apes do not begin their odyssey, even from a Coke bottle. They are found in the middle of things, sitting in a landscape of dust and hunger. From this post-Lapsarian beginning, there can be no replay, only a playing out. They seek to disconnect from their grim origins. And this they do by transferring their biological drives to metal surrogates. Their *as* fictions take form as copulating machines however; once again it is the act of uncoupling that couples, forces more terrifying discourse. Spaceships have portholes like red eyes. They seem to carry an organic sharer, and are heavy with menace. HAL, the machine with a human name and voice, but no human form, obliges his creators to renew discourse by literally attacking them. HAL is all eye, emblem of the connective our observational fantasies have effaced: a connective that has now become a void. And that void now summons something menacing to fill it, to reconnect catastrophically with its maker. What is summoned is what has been repressed in this fantasy transfer: biology.

In HAL, the fantasy curve seems stretched to the breaking point. For forced on the machine, along with its surrogate human existence, is the human capacity to fall. And HAL's is a fall into biology. The computer has, as man forces humanity on it, taken on a "female" personality: the classic one, duplicitous and vengeful, of the temptress. HAL's subsequent attack on Bowman is often seen as awakening biology, in the form of the will to survive, in the eunuch astronaut. It seems rather, in the manner of an Eve, to precipitate a further fall. Wearing a helmet decorated with sperm-like markings, Bowman enters the computer to find himself less in a womb than in a reddish hell where he is at the even more passive mercy of forces that carry him wide-eyed into horror. But not to the true infinite. Mankind, for Kubrick, is by his lack of actions engaged on a journey that is a return, not necessarily to his sources, but to the connective that his initial fantasy transfer sought to deny. The observer is brought to the discourse of passion, the *I* to the *thou*.

Man, going to the future and the stars, clearly does not escape his biological past. For, in sheer visual terms, the voyage to the infinite takes him through a landscape that can only be described as amniotic. Throughout this voyage, Bowman remains a passive observer, first a face, then an eye that reacts to a barrage of images. The point, however, is not that, by this fantasy, he summons biology, but that he summons it with such conjunctive violence. This perhaps explains what happens in the famous white room at the end of his voyage. The room is a visual representation of Western man's ultimate fantasy of closure: eighteenth-century decor wholly organized by the elegant logic of reason. Quintessential "enlightenment" space, the room is hermetic and sterile; there are no shadows or dark corners. All objects seems to emit their own light; the area admits no "noise" and no statement, is perfectly nonreferential. Yet in its metallized perfection this space, like the de-organicized ship in *Alien*, seems to call forth increasingly violent conjunctions of destiny and biology. Bowman is in his space capsule; suddenly, without transition, he is standing outside in a space suit; he turns his gaze and, as if in a mirror of devolution this time, sees himself standing unadorned. The sole tool he now has, the cup, is for nourishing the organic body. Misusing it, knocking it from the table, he glances over to see himself old and dying on a bed. Biology works in continuous cycles, death moving to rebirth. But here we have separate frames violently thrown together, a series of calques. On top of the dying old man is superimposed a child. That same child, transposed to a mandala-like enclosure in the final frames, is in turn superimposed on the landscape of the film's beginning: superman calqued on ape. Clarke speaks of cycles; these connections mark points of maximum instability: catastrophic oxymorons.

But unlike the statue in *Allegro non troppo*, Kubrick's room does not collapse. For into his set of intersecting vectors he introduces an element, a visual space, that like Delany's *h* causes their catastrophic potential to inflect toward a geometry of continuity. That element, allowing the iron loop of destiny and biology to twist into a moebius structure, the scant space between right-hand and left-hand recurring forms, is the black slab. Clarke, recasting this slab as a transparent "teaching machine," makes it merely another fantasy mirror. But Kubrick, visually, insists on its opacity, and on its appearance at the catastrophic intersections of his film. It is there at what are the crucial moments of address, of attempted discourse, in the film. And what it offers, at those moments, is a sign: that of the n-dimensional possibility of human discourse. Throughout Kubrick's film the slab is visually associated with scientific advancement. In relation to it, however, the pursuit of science is revealed, for ape and man alike, to be an archetypal *I-thou* discourse: that between destiny and biology. The slab does not just mirror our aspirations. By not reflecting faces and wishes, it draws the seeker into passionate con-

tact with it. Both the ape in the "dawn of man" scene, and Floyd on
the moon caress it. Bowman pursues it beyond the infinite, and on his
deathbed still reaches yearningly for it. Man, it seems, conquers the
stars only to remain trapped, catastrophically, by his biological fall.
Yet in this final scene, Bowman does not caress the slab. It floats just
out of reach of his yearning arms. Something has fallen here between
the shadow and the act, the slightest space, but enough to mark a shift
from *thou* to *you*. The slab, positioned just out of reach, acts to create
a spiral out of a circle, to redirect the unstable structure of horror
toward at least the possibility of continuity.

The discourse of Kubrick's film, finally, is one of complementarity. Its field, however, is one of extreme tension, and its swerve from
horror to SF so slight, yet so fundamental, as to make it a *locus
classicus* in today's topology of fictional forms. By the same token,
2001 has proven a work supremely resistant to placement in a single
generic category. I have been using genre terms—realism, fantasy,
SF. But I use them to designate vectors in relation to the *and* that
shapes them into interconnecting forms, and thus regulates the field
of fictional activity. In the "grammar" of fiction, this lowly conjunction is in reality the key part of speech. For it is the one that makes the
field (as Todorov suggests and I argue) one of discourse. Because of
the *and* no form can stand alone; each addresses another, and in
doing so, whether by stressing the *and* or refusing it, shapes a field.
And that field, it seems, can be infinitely plastic. For the *and*, by
guaranteeing two, can guarantee three, n-curvatures to its fictional
space.

But there are, it appears, basic vectors in relation to the *and*:
those of connection and disconnection (or at that place where form
and idea intersect, openness and closure). Realism, *mimesis*, the *they*
themes, are forms of radical connection, so radical that they repress
the *and* by ignoring all counterneed to disconnect. *They* ignores *I*,
and fantasy in turn, developing its *I* themes, radically represses
connection: that of reference and, finally, that of discourse itself.
This pull back and forth on the *and* generates shapes both variant and
different: the *thou* connection of horror, the *you* of SF. But is not SF,
by imposing the pull of reason on the catastrophic *and*, moving again
in the direction of disconnection? Kubrick offers us the nexus; out of
it comes the spiraling possibility of transcendence that (in the minds
of many) most characterizes what is called science fiction. Here the

question of the field again arises: as SF places new tension on the *and*, what shape results? Would mystery be a good term? And would it designate *we* themes? For in response to the increasing tendency of *you* to become a singular (transcendent) addressee, the *I* modulates toward a position of deferred closure: that of mystery, represented by the collective, intermediary speaker *we*.

We can have fun naming points on the literary map. And to continue doing so, we will have to invent new speakers and addressees, create new pronouns for our n-dimensional grammar. But that is just the point. We can do so if we understand the basic topology of the field, the role of the *and*. To René Thom, the most striking feature of all systems and processes is not their quantitative complexity but their qualitative stability.[15] Fantasy then is not the shape of things that never were, nor SF the shape of things to come. Used by themselves, these terms can be historical, counters in the *or* process of quantitative analysis. Linked with the *and* however, they are no longer historical markers, but are free to designate basic configurations: the qualities of the field. Delany's Spider offers us, in our search to define forms, alternate visions: we can seek their limits and genesis; or we can feel them as they brush by us on the dark road. A genre theory based in historical processes seeks primary and secondary phases, the birth and death of functions and forms. The only alternative it allows is that of darkness and confusion: the chaos of formlessness. All we need do, however, is replace Spider's *or* with an *and*. Doing this we establish a complex place. And one that is stable because it locates both catastrophe and continuity. Compounds are emerging that display their *and*. Only by understanding the qualitative nature of this connective, present whether visible or invisible as that which gives structure to change, can we as literary critics deal with them.

Homecomings: Fantasy and Horror

Celeste Pernicone

A prominent member of my household recently bullied me into making an on-the-spot distinction between fantasy and science fiction. Off the top of my head, I said that fantasy is what my seven-year-old would enjoy, and science fiction, well, that's the stuff grown-up dreams are supposed to be made of. I meant this to be a flippant response. But then I began to think. The "grown-up dreams" of SF are, largely, those of the explorer, of the person who leaves home to find new worlds. The generic mark of SF is adolescence, and its generic space that of transit. Fantasy, on the other hand, is by and large the world of the child. It is the static world of the home, not as a place where we grow up, but something we grow into or out of. Fantasy is a world of dreams; of confinements and flights of imagination; of absent parents and imaginary friends. But, it struck me, the concept of fantasy alone, as it is usually thought of, is not large enough to encompass this rhythm of inside and outside, this world of the home. I am looking for the form or mode that interacts with fantasy, and must conclude that science fiction, with its sequential patterns of growing up, of leaving home, is not it. That form is rather horror, the nightside to our homecomings. I do not want to discuss fantasy and science fiction, then, but fantasy and horror. The child and the home comprise their joint generic space. And as we see from examples of literature and film, the relationship of fantasy to horror is complex and interactive. For in these works we see our child surrogates grow in and out of their acts of closure: we see how dreams of home, becoming still lifes, shade in and out of nightmare.

Fantasy encompasses all that is childish, not in its sophistication of lack thereof, but in its perception of the world before it. It's a children's world, and we see it through their eyes: upward, outward,

certainly too much for one to grasp. Perhaps that is why so often our
fantasy stories concern themselves with tiny creatures: hobbits, water rats, munchkins, skeksies: even a favorite of mine, the unlikely
pairing of a piglet and a spider. Since the environment is too great for
the little creatures to grasp fully, they inevitably struggle simply to
make do in it, the most poignant example being the lab rats in the
film, *The Secret of NIMH*.

The child grows up into the world about him. Life becomes a
constant struggle not just to make one's peace with the world—can
we survive the end of the month without a bounced check?—but to
control as absolutely as possible our hold on our particular position—
pay off the American Express card bill, finish an essay before dead-
line. All that *The Secret of NIMH*'s heroine, Mrs. Brisbee, is really
concerned with is moving her home, and she, a field mouse, never
even attempts to do anything about, or even begins to question why
NIMH, the National Institute for Mental Health which conducts
experiments on lab rats, should exist so near her field. How different
from the classic SF film *Them*. The film begins as several random
murders are committed in the desert outside the Los Angeles basin,
and it is only later that we discover who, or rather what, the culprits
are: giant mutated ants. The story enjoys all the elements of good
detective fiction. Two peace officers investigate the scene of what
appears to be a brutal crime, without the corpses. The only witness is
a child survivor who repeats over and over the single word, "them."
The child's perspective, that of fantasy, knows only that ants have
destroyed her family. As soon as the authorities arrive—police,
scientists, army—the film shifts to vintage 1950s science fiction. The
story becomes a series of questions and answers, some wrong, some
eventually right (the children are saved and with that, ultimately,
mankind), and the film ends with a final question: "What about the
hundreds of other atomic tests?"

At issue here is our relationship to the cosmos, the ecology, call
it what you will: I call it home. Do we build the home about us, or
does it build us? A chicken and egg question to be sure, but one that
is, if not answerable, at least understandable through our individual
perceptions of the world we first see before us and only later abstract-
ly grasp our own placement within.

The first book that my son and I shared was a picture book.
Think back to those childhood years, and imagine a book without any

words. Simply a series of crudely drawn images: a boat, an airplane, a god, a red ball. My child's earliest world, the world of colors and blurred shapes, sharpened into recurring images: the airplane mobile above his head and the German Shepherd who nuzzled his toes. Language for my infant son held no more than a secondary position to the things which he saw both in his world and in his cloth book. Not until after he connected those real things, the red ball to his bathtub toy, did he begin to attempt speech. And those first utterances were attempts to communicate things that already held meaning for him.

I don't pretend to explain Man in the Cosmos. No one can. Primarily, I don't believe we share a relationship. I'm as much an accident of nature as nature itself is a series of accidents. Stories, on the other hand, bring meaning to life, because myths are the metaphors we make for the greater world. The environment we create, we also control. Our world is the home.

If your home is a metaphor for the world, then it ought to follow that representations of the visual world—paintings and photographs for the home—are extended metaphors that simultaneously encompass the home and the world. On my living-room wall is a grouping of two numbered bird-of-prey lithographs, two silk flower paintings, and a framed print of a Toulouse Lautrec poster, each an item that I consciously chose and thoughtfully arranged. They soothe me, and therefore tell you a great deal about my perception of reality; that is, if you care to know. Pictures are another person's interpretation of the world, the artist's, whom we have designated to interpret our own preconceived notions of the world. We choose paintings because they not only please us, they satisfy us. They are literally a sunshiny day.

I display but one photograph on our dining-room bookcase, taken of my three-year old. Even though it's a charming photograph, I display it only because I feel constrained to. One must arrange one's children on bookcases and end tables and do so prominently. But unlike my soothing living-room pictures, this one always unsettles me. You see, that little boy doesn't exist. The blond kid in Oshkosh jeans is now the family chess champ. Photographs, the past preserved, is our world as we would wish it, but as it never really was. A posed picture is simply that, a pose. The framed 8-by-10 is more than a loss, a Barthian perception; it was never really there to begin with. How much more disturbing then, the photograph sent me by my husband's two dear old aunts: their nephew at age sixteen months in September 1943. It is a past I never shared, a world I was not yet part of. Forty years separate the two of us: the photo of a toddler wearing his uncle's army hat and me, here, now.

There we have it: the two worlds, one of the fantastic, the artistic, the world we can make peace with; the other the science-fictional, the filmic world, a document of that which we reject and are rejected by. Fantasy beckons; science fiction teases, dances before us and then suddenly jumps back as we reach out to touch it.

It's perhaps why the best of our children's writers, Dr. Seuss, is as successful at storytelling as he is. His is the fantasy world; he transforms childish nightmares into monsters of delight. The Cat in the Hat and his cronies, Thing One and Thing Two, are grotesque tricksters. They invade the children's house while Mother is gone and destroy everything, down to Mother's polka-dot dress. But where is the terror? Does the Cat threaten these children? Or rather is it Mother's wrath that they, and in turn, we, fear? Consider the closing lines:

> Should we tell her about it?
> Now what SHOULD WE do?
> Well . . . .
> What would YOU do
> If your mother asked YOU?

In this passage three words are emphasized: that most hateful and Freudian of words, *should* (all tragic heroes suffer from a case of *shouldn't have*), and the words, *we* and *you*. Sally's brother and Sally both make peace with their world, a place that extends no further outward than the living room door. Seemingly because of the weather, they are constrained to stay in the house—an unnatural place for children, at least in Dr. Seuss's world. The comfortingly familiar opening reads:

> The sun did not shine.
> It was too wet to play.
> So we sat in the house
> All that cold, cold, wet day.

A home cannot be played in. It is, to paraphrase the good doctor, a place to sit and sit and sit. Along comes the cat, the cat in the hat who performs "new tricks," the cat in the hat who wears a red bow tie and carries an umbrella.

The cat who compensates for what Sally and her brother do not have: the hat and bow tie and umbrella that Father, whom we never see, must certainly wear (we do see Mother's legs, recalling that as children all that we can hope to see of her are her legs), Father who is never even mentioned. He is our own lost Father, the father of the 1950s whom we seldom saw because we lived in the house in the suburbs, a two-hour commute from the city where he worked. The Cat in the Hat reconciles; he is what our Father was not; he is there.

But the nameless hero of Dr. Seuss never admits that he does indeed suffer from his father's absence. Literally, the two children never admit the great Cat into their house; the Cat knocks and then steps in uninvited. The entire story could be read as a series of unsuccessful attempts to rid the house of the Cat and of Things One and Two. (It was kindly pointed out that Things One and Two are alter egos for the children. They fly kites in the house and go through Mother's things: forbidden fruit to Sally and her brother.) The narrator and his sister Sally, through him, appreciate the day's adventures only in retrospect.

Let us now consider Val Lewton's 1944 film, *The Curse of the Cat People*. This sequel to *Cat People* bears little resemblance to its precursors in storyline, although the two films share Lewton's continuous theme, that of the line between reality and imagination, or rather, cinematically, what the eye sees and what the eye believes that it sees. Interestingly, *Cat People* ends in marital estrangement and death. *Curse* sings an optimistic tune: a family is united and in turn joins the larger community of a New England township.

The plot is simple enough. The conflict is that of a child's world of inner fantasy—imaginary friends—and the adult's world of visible, real fantasies—playmates, hula hoops, model ships. Amy Reed, a friendless six-year-old, lives in a world where old trees are magical mailboxes, where rings grant wishes, where loneliness vanishes the moment she names, and in naming beckons, a secret friend, Irena, into her garden world. Curiously, Amy's town, Terrytown, is itself a crossroads to the two worlds she inhabits: Terrytown, the home of the Sleepy Hollow legend.

And unlike Dr. Seuss' young narrator, Amy feels the emptiness in her life. She repeats again and again, "I want a friend," this child whose very name means friend. She is terrifyingly sensitive to her father's growing estrangement, and is helpless to breach the gap. Not until the film's climax do the parent and child both learn that the friend she has longed for is actually her father.

The film begins on Amy's birthday—her sixth—and ends, fittingly, several months later on Christmas Day. Christmas: the most fantastic of Western celebrations, at once a day of giving and of receiving. The day on which history—the birth in Bethlehem—is reconciled with miracle—the myth behind the birth. On this day Amy can finally call out to her father, "Come here, Daddy, come here," and the father can tell his child that he too sees the secret friend in the garden, even as Irena, the one who brings peace, now transparent, fades before our eyes.

Significantly, the film ends with an embrace; the father carries his child back into the house and, with those final steps, into the family and into a greater sphere: the real world. How unlike the ending of *The Cat in the Hat!* If there is a union in Dr. Seuss, it can exist only between the two children within the story and the reading audience, children themselves. Everything else in the book—the rainy day, Mother, the Cat—these, at best, coexist with the children.

But how do we distinguish Dr. Seuss' world from Val Lewton's? The children in both tales share a common dilemma: boredom, loneliness, isolation from the very space they inhabit. However, recall that *The Cat in the Hat* is an adventure remembered. In fact, unlike the reader, the young narrator can only enjoy that day as he retells the story, never when he is a character within the tale itself. We know that there will be other rainy days, and that the memory of that one special day will suffice for the storyteller as it does for his audience. In other words, Sally's brother's experience is remembered as though it were a series of related photographs. What happens and what is recalled are identical incidents—he never lies to us—and what changes are his feelings about what happened.

I am reminded of my bridesmaid years, from age nineteen to twenty-two, and that endless barrage of August weddings, the most dreadful being family weddings, of course. I would argue that the most important person at a wedding is not the beautiful bride, nor Aunt Dot's caterer, nor the priest; it is the photographer, the one who creates more than captures the fantasy of that special day. How many receptions are nothing more than a series of stills that we seem to cherish more than the vows themselves?

And perhaps, there lies the distinction between Dr. Seuss' children's story and Val Lewton's fantasy film. Pleasure, for Dr. Seuss, is shared communally between the two main characters and the readers, and is shared as memory. In fact, the conspiratorial "Would you tell your mother?" binds them together. The Cat belongs to us all.

It is just the reverse in *Curse of the Cat People*. Amy, as Irena had foretold, quickly forgets her secret friend. But she forgets Irena in the same way that we lose our dreams: we experience them as we sleep, but upon awakening, they recede into our psyche and allow us to function as a consolidated personality. Amy doesn't have to live on memories. She returns home, comfortable in her world as it is given to her, within her father's embrace.

None of our homes look like Frankenstein's castle, nor like Norman Bates's Victorian Gothic, except perhaps on Saturday mornings. These we relegate to the classic horror story. But the homes in the two fantasy stories I've thus far discussed, and in a third, Steven Spielberg's *Poltergeist*, are normal homes: they're our homes, which is why they are all the more horrific. Homes are the trustworthy refuge of constancy in a chaotic world, aren't they? I should think they'd be that faded blue corduroy jacket or, in my case, a Wallace Stevens poem like "Sunday Morning." But the jacket and the poem share something very few homes have: they are complete in themselves, and homes always lack something. Most often, they lack money. Recall D. H. Lawrence's child, madly riding his rocking horse in order to quiet the home's incessant moans for "money, money, we must have more money." Mystery in the horror or fantasy story need not be a tangible presence. Absence and loss form the heart of all horror stories. And what fascinates me is that in nearly every case, the loss is defined in terms of a single parent and is usually replaced by a single individual. We could caption all these stories, "Where have all the fathers gone?" Master Paul, in "The Rocking Horse Winner," lacks not so much money as he lacks a strong father to overcome the castrating mother. The Cat in the Hat, threatened by Mother, temporarily replaces Father who is never acknowledged by anybody but me. Amy Reed has a mother—a good one—but she is shunted aside in the storyline. She, Alice, is as receptive to Amy's imagination as is the ghostfriend, Irena. But Alice lives in a home brooded over by the father's sense of order. Irena takes Amy into the garden—in every sense. The Cat brings the garden—chaos and, with that, the potential for tragedy—into the home. The home is monstrous because we see it that way, we see ourselves reflected in it. And in those two stories, when the people get right, the home gets right. Fantasy stories summon up friends, good friends: fairy godmothers and cats who clean up their toys. Horror stories summon fiends. In Stephen King's *Carrie*, Amy Gone Wrong, the mother, fatally stabs her child, and in turn, Carrie turns on her mother, crucifying her with kitchen cutlery. The house, engulfed in flames, crashes down over them.

There is only one horror story I know of in which it is important that the entire family—mother, father, and all three children—consolidate themselves as a family: *Poltergeist*. Their dream home, a tract house, is built on top of a cemetary, unbeknownst to the living occupants. When the Freeling family contract a swimming pool to be dug in their yard, the youngest child, Carol Ann, is spirited away by ghosts who upon death had lost their way to the light and now require someone, Carol Ann, to guide them. As Dr. Lesh, the film's parapsychologist, explains, "They just hang around. Watch TV. Watch their friends grow up." To balance these middle-American ghosts is a racier phantom: "The Beast," who lies to Carol Ann.

Carol Ann focuses the story, but she shares the focus with the house itself. The real world is the world that the Freelings inhabit in their home: a world of accumulated things. The surreal is the world within the home, that can only be entered through Carol Ann's closet, the second most frightening place in any house, the first being, naturally, under the bed.

The *Poltergeist* house ought to be the stereotypical suburban home, and would be, if we were still good 1960s liberals. We know better now. It truly is the home that you and I live in, that is, if you were lucky enough to buy before 1974. Cul-de-sacs, greenhouse windows, remote controls, jacuzzied home featured of *Home and Garden* (always a selling point for your own home) and a sleepy Spanish name, Cuesta Verde.

That's just how we like to see our home, painted over with things and with a sense of belonging to the community. Horror, unlike fantasy, tells us otherwise. The film opens into a home in which the occupants are segregated not only into separate bedrooms but into distinctive lifestyles. There is the upwardly mobile father who ought to be there—he is the tract realtor—but seldom is, because he lives on the unrequited promise of a company partnership. And sixteen-year-old Dana, too aware of her own sexuality and aware of little else. And the mother, Diane, who after sixteen years of marriage believes that she has realized her dream house, or has she; there is after all the new swimming pool to be dug. And there is Carol Ann, the youngest, the child who has been born into that house and is reclaimed by it when the closet opens and sucks her into its throbbing tissuelike womb.

The film could have ended when Diane successfully retrieves Carol Ann from the home's heart. That is how *Curse of the Cat People* ends. In both films, the key parent retraces the child's steps— a quest into chaos and ultimately up to Death's doorstep—and in so doing, can reclaim the child. But *Poltergeist* doubles back and the ultimate violation occurs the next day when the graves are desecrated and seen by Diane and the two youngest children. Trapped, her home collapsing about them, Diane calls out for help: "Help me somebody . . . God—help me . . . Steven, help us." With that final plea, Diane, Robby, Carol Ann, even Ivan, the family dog, break loose and run into Steven's arms. It is an echo of Amy's plea to her father. And both fathers are there, at the last, to embrace.

And here we have this family, a perfect family with no money problems, no marital discord, fleeing its home with nothing saved but the clothes on their backs. They drive off, huddled together in the car, as the home collapses behind them.

The film doesn't end there. It ends in precisely the same way this paper chooses to end: homeless. The Freelings drive to a Holiday Inn, your home away from home, your most impersonal of homes. We see the family walk, one by one, into a single motel room. Steven Freeling, the last to enter, turns to the camera, gives us a final defiant look, steps into the room, closes the curtain, slams the door shut, then after a moment or two, opens the door and wheels the television out, facing the camera. It is the last thing we see, the television. A warning to us; or the final locking out, that of the voyeur who has peered into this family's lives, perhaps too intimately. A deconstructionist's delight, this ending. Steven has retrieved his family and given them—what? A bed, toilet facilities, one another. He has returned them to the primordial cave.

A Holiday Inn is something else besides. Dana alludes to it earlier when she accidentally confesses to her mother that she is familiar with the motel's locale. Motels, those most impersonal of places, are also the most illicit: where lovers meet and live out their private fantasies in a world that can never be hoped for, nor looked back upon: a timeless magic, whether it be Dick and Liz or a prostitute and her John, a magic wholly dependent upon the imaginations of the persons involved: the possibility of a home, and of a home within.

A couple of years ago I heard a story about a middle-aged man who left his family for a time. And during that period he felt freedom and peace, not so much with the new world about him—there was another woman—but with himself. He happened to return to his home one day (his wife was gone for a weekend) and as he stood in his living room, he gazed about him and looked at all the things he had left behind, the things that he had missed during those intervening months. He stood in that room for quite a while, and then he decided to return "home." When I heard that story, it sent a shiver up my spine.

Science Fantasy and Myth

Brian Attebery

Among works that mingle elements of science fiction with those of fantasy, a surprising number incorporate story lines and characters from traditional myths. Roger Zelazny, for instance, whose stories frequently straddle the border between science and magic, has reworked Greek, Egyptian, Hindu, and an invented alien mythology with great success. Why is this hybrid form so hospitable to demons and demigods?

One answer is suggested by examining the linguistic and psychological resources science fantasy draws on. Before doing so, however, we need a clearer sense of what science fantasy is. I am using the term to mean fiction that makes use of the conventions of science fiction and those of genre fantasy (in the tradition of Tolkien, Lewis, or E. R. Eddison) to comment on one another and on the world view implied by each mode.

Science fiction in its pure form is extrapolative and analogical. Starting from our current state of knowledge of the universe, it projects new developments in both understanding and technological application. Alternatively, it isolates some factor in our lives, such as the division into two sexes, and builds up a world in which that factor, with all of its ramifications, is expressed differently or not at all. At its best, it then enters into the extrapolated world, so that we see how individual human lives are improved, worsened, or merely altered by the changes.

No other popular literary form is so dependent on ideas, and no other mode, popular or otherwise, has proven so hospitable to new ideas. Science fiction has developed a vocabulary—consisting of robots, spaceships, time machines, and the like—in which meaning-

ful statements about quarks or clones may be composed as soon as
those concepts become available.

I know of no examples of undiluted science fiction, but there are
works that come close to the hypothetical pure strain, such as
Clarke's *Rendezvous with Rama*, Le Guin's *Dispossessed*, or Benford's *Timescape*. These works are primarily extroverted: interested
in behavior, physical environment, and the mechanisms of society.
Science fiction shares this interest in observables with another self-
consciously "scientific" literary mode, naturalism. The main difference between the two is that naturalism is concerned with
documenting the present, while science fiction characteristically
looks to the future. It is Promethean, appropriately enough for a
genre that began with "The Modern Prometheus."

Fantasy is Epimethean. If science fiction's gaze is outward and
ahead, fantasy's is inward and into the past. Fantasy is bound by
tradition: its structure and motifs are drawn from folk literatures,
including European fairy tales, Celtic legendry, Norse epic, and
various bodies of myth. Science fiction chooses manmade objects for
its icons, but the apparatus of fantasy consists of things found in
nature, though perhaps shaped and used by humans: trees, jewels,
caverns, springs.

The landscape and characters of fantasy are defined partly by
their physical attributes and behavior, but more fundamentally by
their roles in a symbolic drama. Here I am talking about a capacity of
fantasy, not always realized. Even in some lesser fantasies, however,
the entire fantasy world becomes a map of the mind, and the conflict
that takes place there is like a medieval psychomachia, a contest
between personified virtues and vices, or in more modern terms
between integrative and destructive forces within the personality.

A vital element in fantasy is a sense of the connectedness of
things: invisible chains link a ring and a dark fortress, or a star-shaped
birthmark and the stars inlaid on a harp. In a fantasy, these intangible
connections are called magic; in a visionary poem they may be called
correspondences. Fantasy at its best has little in common with natu-
ralistic narrative, but much in common with the work of Blake or
Rimbaud or Roethke.

In their pure forms these two kinds of narrative seem to have
little to do with one another, and indeed, a common critical judgment

says that they should not be mixed. Ursula Le Guin is reflecting this judgment when she criticizes her own early novel, *Rocannon's World*:

> There is a lot of promiscuous mixing going on in *Rocannon's World*. We have NAFAL and FTL spaceships, we also have Brisinga-men's necklace, windsteeds, and some imbecilic angels. We have an extremely useful garment called an impermasuit, resistant to "foreign elements, extreme temperatures, radioactivity, shocks, and blows of moderate velocity and weight such as swordstrokes or bullets," and inside which the wearer would die of suffocation within five minutes. The impermasuit is a good example of where fantasy and science fiction *don't* shade gracefully into one another. A symbol from collective fantasy—the Cloak of Protection (invisibility, etc.)—is decked out with some pseudoscientific verbiage and a bit of vivid description, and passed off as a marvel of Future Technology. This can be done triumphantly if the symbol goes deep enough (Wells's Time Machine), but if it's merely decorative or convenient, it's cheating. It degrades both symbol and science.[1]

It is true that many writers of science fiction seem perfectly willing to cheat. A typical novel by Jack Chalker, Marion Zimmer Bradley, or Piers Anthony is rife with short cuts and easy answers. The science is bogus; the fantasy insincere. But these writers, when they are not trying to outproduce the Stratemeyer syndicate, have also produced works of considerable interest blending elements of science fiction with fantasy. So have critically acclaimed writers like Roger Zelazny, Samuel Delany, and Gene Wolfe. What leads these people to mix their modes?

One answer to the popularity of science fantasy among both writers and readers may be found in Maud Bodkin's classic *Archetypal Patterns in Poetry*. This 1934 study was one of the first works of myth-symbol criticism, and Bodkin's psychological training and critical acuity set it apart from its many successors. Setting out to test Jung's thesis that the greatest poetry owes its emotional significance to the presence of "primordial images," she examines her own response to particular works and correlates this intuitive response with psychological studies and the testimony of readers like Coleridge, I. A. Richards, and John Middleton Murry. Among her findings, the one most relevant to the subject of science fantasy is that human beings seem to see the world simultaneously from two perspectives, one emotional and the other rational. Both derive from everyday experience:

> The beliefs that fire burns us, that water drowns and cleanses, and will quench our thirst, that earth yields crops for food, and sustains our dwellings, and will hide our bodies at the last, have all a twofold aspect, emotional as well as intellectual. We can extend their content by abstract but sensibly verifiable relations till they make up a large part of our scientific knowledge. Or we can transform them into poetry by using them to satisfy our need for emotional expression; as when, with Prometheus, we call upon Earth, the mighty mother, or, with St. Francis, praise God for the many services of Sister Water. In these instances the very intimacy and range of our practical knowledge of earth and water adds power to the ideas as instruments of emotional expression.[2]

A poem like "The Ancient Mariner" moves us, says Bodkin, because it calls on the latter kind of knowledge. The relationships among the images within the poem constitute its meaning. They are a kind of truth apart from science, but, like scientific truth, grounded in everyday perception: "not as extended and ordered in its objective aspect by physical science, but true as belonging to that tradition, also collectively sustained, which orders the emotional aspect of experience" (p. 81).

Bodkin's ideas transplant readily to the ground of our discussion. Science fiction bases its claim to our attention on its use of scientific insights. Fantasy, like poetry, is more concerned with archetype and emotion. Also, like poetry, its patterns of organization are traditional and "collectively sustained."

One of the images Bodkin pursues is that of water. Characteristic of the way water is treated in fantasy is the phial of Galadriel in *The Lord of the Rings*. This small bottle holds water from Galadriel's Mirror, a silver basin with prophetic powers. In it is trapped the light of a star, a very special star because it was once of the Silmarils, jewels of great beauty and potency. The phial glows in the dark, it helps Frodo and Sam escape the guardians at the gate of Mordor, and it bolsters their spirits in the midst of desolation. These properties are clearly magical: there is no rational explanation for them. Yet they are also clearly derived from our everyday experience of water. Water cleanses and refreshes, as Bodkin points out. It refracts sunlight or starlight in such a way that it seems to glow from within. Its surface can startle us with images of faraway things, although we know scientifically that those things must be directly in line with the water at an angle to the surface equal to that of the viewer. Tolkien builds his magical portrayal from these commonly observed properties, exaggerating them in a way we find emotionally, if not scientifically valid.

A similar vessel of water in a work of science fiction, Vonnegut's *Cat's Cradle*, has a very different significance. The thermos of ice nine represents the ultimate scientific manipulation of water, turning ordinary H_2O into a catalyst for the destruction of all life on earth. Ice nine functions as a symbol within the novel, and it certainly carries an emotional significance, but its symbolic and emotional weight are dependent on our intellectual understanding of the processes by which it was produced and by which it may lead to disaster. The more we know of chemistry and physics—for instance, the fact that carbon can crystalize into forms as different as coal and diamond—the more fully we appreciate the significance of a sample of water that remains solid at room temperature and that triggers adjacent water to take the same form.

What science fantasy might be able to accomplish is the reintegration of these two perspectives: to show water as both molecule and miracle. However, the two viewpoints are not easy to reconcile. The split is a fundamental one, making its mark on the very language we use to describe reality. Owen Barfield's *Poetic Diction*, published six years before Bodkin's book, follows a philological trail to similar ends.

The further back we trace the history of any word, says Barfield, the more concrete the meaning of that word seems to be. Thus, the ancestor of *spirit* was not an abstract essence or soul but a puff of wind. However, according to Barfield, it is a mistake to suppose that at some point the Indo-European-speaking tribesman decided to apply the concrete term metaphorically to some principle of life within himself. Instead, the older term meant something that was not exactly "wind" and not exactly "life" or "spirit" but a more inclusive category incorporating all of these. At some time in the past, there were no pure abstractions, as we can determine by finding the goad in *centrifugal* or the twist in *wrong*. Likewise, there were no purely concrete words. The words for "flame" or "seed" included in their meaning both the perceptible objects and the perceiver's subjective response.

Only later, as language and thought developed, did "these single meanings split up into contrasted pairs—the abstract and the concrete, particular and general, objective and subjective."[3] Until that time, natural symbol and spiritual significance were one and the same, and from that unity came myth: "The naturalist is right when he connects the myth with the phenomena of nature, but wrong if he deduces it solely from these. The psychoanalyst is right when he connects the myth with 'inner' (as we now call them) experiences, but wrong if he deduces it solely from these. Mythology is the ghost of concrete meaning. Connections between discrete phenomena, connections which are now apprehended as metaphor, were once perceived as immediate realities" (pp. 91–92).

In *Splintered Light: Logos and Language in Tolkien's World*, Verlyn Flieger points out that J. R. R. Tolkien was an admirer of Barfield's work and aimed in his own writing at recapturing the undivided perception from which myth emerged.[4] He certainly brought together the physical and the spiritual, but only by limiting his treatment of physical reality to a prescientific conception of the world. What the serious writer of science fantasy is attempting to do is not to recapture an older worldview but to forge a new one from elements that have long been developing in isolation.

The first task the science fantasist faces is introducing two perspectives in a single story; hence the frequent appearance of traditional gods and heroes. Then he must bridge them. There have been many ingenious solutions to the former problem; far fewer for the latter.

In *Rocannon's World*, Le Guin posits two cultures, one a space-going technocracy and the other a feudal society with a belief in magic. In her prologue, a woman from the feudal society visits the world of the scientists, and in the novel proper the anthropologist Rocannon returns the favor. Both times, events are perceived according to the biases of the onlooker either as straightforward cause and effect or as the working-out of legend. The mix is largely successful and would be more so if, as Le Guin says, she had kept her science more rigorously scientific and her magic less eclectic. By the novel's end, Rocannon has come to view the natives' outlook as no less valid than his own: what he has been calling telepathy and coincidence might with equal justice be called magic and fate.

Roger Zelazny's science fantasies constitute a series of variations on the theme of technological advancement so great that men and women can become the gods they have always imagined. In *Lord of Light* the Hindu pantheon has been recreated on a colony planet, and in *Creatures of Light and Darkness* a more loosely interpreted Egyptian pantheon rules the entire universe. This formula serves Zelazny very well, allowing him to suggest that at the end of the road of scientific discovery lie the same problems dreamed of by our ancestors. He implies that it is easier to acquire godhood than enlightment.

Andre Norton has explored nearly the whole spectrum from science fiction to fantasy. She characteristically shows a misfit from a technological society seeking refuge on some less developed world and discovering there an ancient and sympathetic magic. When, as in *Beast Master* or the early Witch World novels, she shows science and magic in conflict, magic nearly always proves superior. An interesting exception is *Judgment on Janus*, in which the hero must, like the two-faced god for which his planet is named, look both ways, making use of both magic and machinery, to defend himself and his world.

John Crowley's *Deep* portrays a fantasy world as artificial creation within a larger science fictional universe. In his novel, the world of magic is a closed one, eternally repeating the same archetypal pattern until a visitor from outside—an android, a being created not by magic but by science—breaks the pattern. *The Deep* might almost be a science fiction writer's comment on the limitations of fantasy, with its reliance on a few inherited models.

A particularly ingenious way of juxtaposing the rational and emotional, or scientific and magical perspectives is that used by Samuel Delany in *The Einstein Intersection*. In this novel, Delany finds the justification for looking beyond science within science itself. Citing Goedel as a sort of patron saint of improbability, he constructs a world in which nothing is what it seems, and the old Einsteinian limits on perception and movement are bypassed. The characters in his novel, who seem to be mutated humans, are not; rather, they are, as the computer PHAEDRA says to one, "a bunch of psychic manifestations, multi-sexed and incorporeal . . . trying to put on the limiting mask of humanity."[5] The ways these beings find order in their irrational world is to re-enact human myths, from Orpheus to Billy the Kid.

One of the most elegant practitioners of science fantasy is

Richard Cowper (John Middleton Murry, Jr.). In *The Road to Corlay* he provides alternate perspectives on a number of phenomena. Water, for instance, plays a key role in the story, not a small container of it this time but a flood that has turned Great Britain into an archipelago.

In the quasi-medieval future of Cowper's story, a few people remember the scientific explanation for the flooding: "The Drowning was the direct result of humanity's corporate failure to see beyond the end of its own nose. By 1985 it was already quite obvious that the global climate had been modified to the point where the polar ice caps were affected."[6] However, to most people it was the Third Coming, a scourge sent by God to prepare the way for a spiritual rebirth at the beginning of the third millennium A.D. Like the atomic holocaust in *A Canticle for Leibowitz*, it has its material cause in man's technological overreaching, but it may also represent divine intercession. In the latter view, it fits into a prophetic sequence: "The first coming was the man; the second was fire to burn him; the third was water to drown the fire, and the fourth is the Bird of Dawning" (p. 38). After Christ comes Pentecost, then floods, and finally, at the time of the story, the White Bird.

By overlapping the two kinds of narrative, Cowper may be attempting to reconcile scientific and religious world views, thus following up on some of his father's ideas. Alternatively, he may be examining the nature of other kinds of nonmaterial entities—beliefs, ideas, perceptions—and showing how they impinge on the physical world in ways not yet predictable by science. His choice of images supports this reading: the rush of invisible wings, a story that changes lives, and a tune that can heal or kill and overload a circuit a thousand years before it is played.

Barfield and Bodkin offer useful techniques for judging individual works: following their lead we can examine how aware the writer seems to be of the twofold implications of words and images. In the best of these works, archetypes are subjected to the same scrutiny that a writer of conventional science fiction will give to the paradoxes of time travel or the ecological implications of terraforming new worlds. The test of good science fantasy is that it generate patterns we can respond to as we do to well-made fantasy without losing the cognitive dimension of good science fiction. This is not a simple requirement to fulfill, but then, one would not expect the making of contemporary myth to be an easy task.

This bird is another key image connecting the scientific and supernatural viewpoints. There is no visible, tangible bird in the story. It first appears as a vision, perhaps a mass hallucination, on New Year's Eve of the year 2999. The source of the vision is a tune played by a young piper, who is martyred immediately after. Thereafter, the White Bird is considered to manifest itself in various forms: in the pipes, in the tune the boy played, in the saint's legend, in certain followers of the new faith, and in their developing psychic powers.

To the faithful, the bird is real and capable of miracles. However, Cowper is careful always to provide alternate explanations. The maker of the pipes, though he is called the Wizard of Bowness, may have performed his wizardry through rediscovered technology: "in Kendal the folk used to whisper that he'd stored up a treasurehouse of wisdom from the Old Times" (p. 28). The pipes' magic could be explained as sonic manipulation of emotions. Other seemingly magical phenomena might be the result of a mutation for extrasensory perception and psi powers.

Reinforcing this view of events is a second plot concerning a man from our own time who, as a reslt of an experiment with "compound neurodrugs," finds himself inhabiting the body of a man a thousand years in the future. His experiences are witnessed by his coworkers on a sort of super electroencephalograph hooked up to his unconscious body. He and the research team monitoring him interpret events scientifically, while the characters in the future see them from a religious or magical perspective. The former view assumes a rationally explainable, mechanistic universe, while the latter sees the world as a moral battleground in which immaterial forces may be embodied temporarily, as the White Bird is embodied in the piper and his tune.

Does Cowper reconcile the two views? His plot is so engineered that its resolution depends on both. The twentieth-century research team sends a man into the future. There he meets and falls in love with a woman who thus becomes the foretold Bride of Time; their child will carry on the work of the White Bird. Each event is both natural and magical, both wave and particle, as it were.

Gravity's Rainbow: Science Fiction, Fantasy, and Mythology

Kathryn Hume

Gravity's Rainbow has been hailed by John Brunner as an "incontestably science-fictional retrospective parallel world," (that is, an alternate wartime London); also, by Geoffrey Cocks as the Miltonic epic of science fiction that "has taken science/speculative fiction beyond the genre's limits into metaphysics, metapsychology, and cosmology."[1] It has also been identified as gothic, as encyclopedic, and as various kinds of satire or anatomy.[2] I am particularly sympathetic to the desire of some critics to claim *Gravity's Rainbow* for science fiction, because so little mainstream fiction engages with science in any significant way, and because the identification would perhaps attract more attention from the academy for that uncanonical literature. However, the problems of defining science fiction complicate the ascription, and any single label blinds us to the generic interactions within this maverick work. I would prefer to work with a broader palette of terms when trying to describe the experience that is *Gravity's Rainbow*, and would like to focus on the interrelationships between three: science fiction, fantasy, and mythology. (In no way do these three exhaust the generic possibilities.)

I am going to argue that Pynchon draws on science and contributes to science fiction by creating a fictive analogue to the post-Newtonian universe, and he forces us to consider probabilistic and uncertain realities in a way that we normally avoid, even if we are aware of the implications of contemporary science. However, it is not science, but rather his arsenal of fantasy techniques that allows him to create this fictive analogue to scientific reality—each one of those techniques flagrantly nonrational and nonrealistic. Counterpointing the fantasy and science fiction is a traditional yet technological mythology, through whose repetitions, oppositions, and mediations we can find some of Pynchon's values, including a modified hero monomyth. Let me fill in this picture—the three generic forces interacting—and then consider briefly the implications to questions of definition and canon.

Since our society is fundamentally technological rather than scientific, contemporary non-Newtonian science has had remarkably little effect on our everyday thinking about life. The ten or eleven dimensions now favored by cosmologists rarely impinge on our consciousness. Reality, for us, is the stone that hurts our foot when we kick it; our assumptions do not reach to empty space, interrupted here and there by atoms, let alone to the energies which make up those atoms. All our normal assumptions about what is real are, as Rosemary Jackson puts it, bourgeois categories of the real.[3] They assert the nature of reality in terms of practical material concerns, quite regardless of any insight or contradictory evidence available through science or philosophy.

Science fiction has done relatively little with the implications of non-Newtonian science in everyday life. When black holes turn up as grist for the story mill, they are often hunted down and captured for commercial purposes; the unimaginable is thus domesticated and made normal. Uncertainty in most science fiction is usually confined to our not knowing in detail how the story will come out. Unknowability does appear in Lem's *Solaris*, for instance, but most science fiction is predicated on the mysteries of the physical universe proving knowable. As Gary K. Wolfe puts it, these stories celebrate our turning chaos into cosmos by means of scientific method.[4] Uncertainty, unknowability, and other aspects of nonmechanical physics are usually ornamental, if present at all, in much science fiction.

Pynchon creates a world in which some subatomic characteristics of reality are dealt with at the level of everyday life. Pseudo-Heisenbergian uncertainty bedevils the main characters, but even more important, it constrains the readers. We cannot know some things. Contradictory evidence is given, and at best we can work out some sort of probabilistic and nonvalidatable answer. Slothrop is convinced that he was conditioned to the smell of Imipolex G, though he and we know that it was not invented, or at least not patented, until 1939. Gottfried, too, impossibly knows that smell from his childhood. Slothrop's sexual adventures at sites soon to be blasted by V-2s cannot be explained by normal science, and we are left wondering just what, if any, is the relationship between these parallel series displayed on identical maps. The existence of "Them" is undeterminable. The novel's many paranoids detect multitudinous plots, but readers cannot verify the reality of those conspiracies.

What Pynchon creates is a fictional analogue to the post-Newtonian universe. We and his characters have to operate in his world as if such subatomic constraints as uncertainty and complementarity could operate at the quotidian level.[5] If we really worried about the implications of the new science or philosophy, we might not make many casual assumptions about reality, such as the existence of cause and effect, or the communicability of anything. Pynchon helps us experience a world in which it is a survival factor to be aware of such unsettling possibilities and shape one's actions to this new, nonbourgeois reality.

Contrary to the assumptions of some literary critics, however, his is not scientifically a non-Newtonian world. There is no way that even his characters worry about determining the momentum and location of an electron at the same time for everyday living. One might call Pynchon's a parallel universe in which subatomic irrationalities become quotidian, rather than a direct translation of science into life; more accurately, however, I think one can say that his is a philosophical universe, and that he is using science as a structural metaphor to embody and reinforce the philosophical principles. I would argue that Pynchon's cosmos is not intended as an alternative to wartime London (in a Moorcock sense—as Brunner claims), nor as an alternate reality based directly on scientific theory. Rather *Gravity's Rainbow* is science fiction in the metaphorical manner of "Heat Death of the Universe," and as a celebration of technology, however ambivalent that celebration may be.

In order to create this fictive analogue to the universe that science gives us, Pynchon relies on fantasy techniques. To create a world scientifically and philosophically more real than our bourgeois reality, he resorts to what we would usually call the nonreal and nonrational, elements we would normally label fantastic.

To begin with, Pynchon establishes that his is a pluriverse, a realm of multiple realities which cannot be put in a hierarchy from the more to the less believable or real. Until physicists arrive at a satisfactory Grand Unification Theory, we are in approximately that position of being unable to unify multiple realities, but we don't worry because it doesn't affect our getting three square meals a day. Pynchon presents us with multiple realities that one does have to deal with, and leaves us to cope with the influx of data rendered nonclassifiable by such plurality.

One of his realities is that generated by dream: the book starts with an imagistic but apparently realistic sequence during the Blitz in London, only to be relabeled as Pirate Prentice's dream after we have oriented ourselves in this carefully-visualized reality, which includes such loving detail as the old-fashioned style of pulley wheel with S-shaped spokes.

Drugs also blur the lines we normally maintain between reality and fantasy. Parts of Slothrop's sodium amytal vision are documentable (indeed, the details come from Malcolm X's autobiography). But Slothrop's malaise with blacks becomes a fantasy of sodomy, and he struggles to elude this fate by diving down the toilet bowl. His subsequent trip down the sewer never explicitly ends. Both Pirate's dream and Slothrop's drug-vision are openended, thus erasing our guidelines to reality and making a statement about what comes afterward. The rest of the novel is in a sense an extension of the V-2 bombings, and Slothrop's excremental vision is symbolically the future his Harvard classmates will have to face, in which their WASP reality is shattered and they will be known not by family names or money, but by the kind of shit they produce.

Pynchon also destabilizes our novelistic ontology through a technique that Brian McHale calls attention to.[6] Many characters map onto each other, and most map onto Slothrop at some point. A vivid example of such peculiar cross-overs occurs between Slothrop and Gottfried. Gottfried ends up riding in the V-2, which we might have expected to be Slothrop's fate, given his "precognitive" attraction to these rockets and his quest for their secrets. As Gottfried snuggles down in his Imipolex G insulation, the narrative voice remarks: "The soft smell of Imipolex, wrapping him absolutely, is a smell he knows. It doesn't frighten him. It was in the room when he fell asleep so long ago, so deep in sweet paralyzed childhood."[7] But it is Slothrop who was apparently exposed in infancy to Imipolex G by its creator, Laszlo Jamf. As if this exchange of childhoods weren't enough, Slothrop experiences Gottfried's take-off in the rocket. When making love to Bianca, he starts to experience his own orgasm as if he were within his own cock, about to be launched: "his sperm roaring louder and louder, getting ready to erupt, somewhere below his feet [. . . .] an extraordinary sense of *waiting to rise* [. . . .] their own flood taking him up then out of his expectancy, out the eye at the tower's summit and into her with a singular detonation of touch. Announcing the void, what could it be but the kingly voice of the Aggregat [that is, the V-2] itself" (p. 470). Thus, in fantasy, the two men exchange places, and destroy our readerly assumptions about individuals as entities with well-defined limits.

Pynchon also creates fantastic vantage points to disorient us. We see a Pavlovian lab, and suddenly find ourselves in among the rats, who are grown to human size and who sing a beguine (p. 230). At another point, we overhear skin cells in our own bodies parodying World War I heroics as they talk of "going epidermal," and facing the deadly ultraviolet radiation. Or we find ourselves in a future where men with machines can monitor stray thoughts of members of a crowd.

All of these manifestations of the fantastic reinforce messages Pynchon gives us at other levels. The world he describes is the world of modern science, philosophy, and language theory—the world of Heisenberg, Nietzsche, and Saussure. This fashionable negativity is what has most attracted the attention of critics.[8] Indeed, they focus so exclusively on this void containing both nothingness and infinite possibility that they have almost entirely overlooked Pynchon's stabilizing mythology, so let me turn to it next.

"A mythological universe," remarks Northrop Frye, "is a vision of reality in terms of human concerns and anxieties."[9] He points out the tendency of myths to aggregate into mythological universes, and offers the Bible as the prime Western example. Pynchon's mythological universe certainly takes some of its form from the biblical prototype. The paradise is America as virgin continent; the fall is the inability of the settlers to live within the cycles of nature, their choice of what became technology and capitalism; Gottfried's ascent in the rocket corresponds to the crucifixion as central symbol of violence; and there are allusions to several possible futures, all apocalyptic in the sense of being both destructive and revelatory. With appropriate modifications, Pynchon tells this linear tale of origins-to-apocalypse at four levels: for Western technological civilization; for Tyrone Slothrop; for the V-2; and for the history of technology.

I believe this can be called mythographic writing: first, because it works to fill the ontological gap between event and meaning, between our absent origin and the meaning of our place in the world; second, because it explains the world in human terms, measures it in human values (Northrop Frye); third, because of the archetypal nature of the major units of this symbolic history; and fourth, because it both shows us the shortcomings of the myths of our culture and manages to suggest the values that will have to supervene if we are to survive in a post-Newtonian, post-Darwinian world.[10] Pynchon's four strands of story add up to a complex account of Western civilization and the danger it is approaching, namely *immachination*, or marriage between man and the machine. (Let me remind you that Pynchon explores a related theme in his first novel, *V.*, namely, the process by which animate flesh and spirit become inanimate, a process he represents symbolically by having V replace more and more parts of her body with mechanical prostheses.)

The mythology is not just a symbolic story line; it embraces Pynchon's entire cosmos. His world is mythic: directions like south and north have meanings. Illuminations and breakthroughs, partial though they usually are, take place in high places, or in the depths, or in wastelands. The Other Side, a pastiche of otherworlds from several traditions—insists not so much on the reality of its own details as on the existence of something beyond material reality. Pynchon's world is inhabited by more entities than is ours—the omnipresent Them; angels (Moslem, Rilkean, Kabbalistic, and the Angel of Death); the Titans; Pan. It lacks a benevolent deity and exhibits a bias toward the demonic, but is quite as much a mythological world as that in the Bible.

Let me sketch briefly the contents of Pynchon's mythology, and then sum up what Edmund Leach's structuralist approach to myth can tell us about this literary mythology. Then we will be in a position to see how this stabilizing pattern interacts with all of Pynchon's aggressively destabilizing strategies linked to science and fantasy mentioned above.

The early stages involve America as a potential paradise for the death-oriented European cultures. The settlers fail to realize this potential, and Slothrop's ancestors, the patriarchs of this new world, decline from God-smitten Puritans to Yankee materialists dealing in paper—the medium for shit, money, and the Word. Parallels to this Europeanization of the American continent are alluded to in stories

about Katje's ancestor on Mauretius, in tales of Tchitcherine's litera-
cy campaign in the Russian steppes, and in references to Weiss-
mann's colonialist exploits in Southwest Africa. As these cultures
stamped from the European matrix develop, we also watch the
development of various technologies—dyes and plastics and rocketry
in particular. Franz Pökler sees the early firings of the *Verein für
Raumschiffahrt*, and takes part in the failures and advances of the
A-2 and A-3 rockets. That the plastics and the V-2 take on mythic
values is obvious in the way that the rocket draws first blood, lives on
the lives of those dedicated to it. Similarly, the plastic Imipolex G is
semialive, erectile.

World War II coincides with the New Testament of this mythology. In a heavily mythological passage reeking of ritual sacrifice, we
see Gottfried's wedding to the rocket, his immachination, which is
made literally a wedding, with "bridal costume," "white satin slip-
pers," "white stockings" a "bridal" room, careful physical mating, a
pressure switch that is the clitoris of the V-2. When Pynchon used the
term immachination earlier (p. 297), he shows us another form of the
hybridization of man and machine, a futuristic space helmet: "The
eye-sockets are fitted with quartz lenses. Filters may be slipped in.
Nasal bone and upper teeth have been replaced by a metal breathing
apparatus, full of slots and grating. Corresponding to the jaw is a
built-up section, almost a facial codpiece, of iron and ebonite,
perhaps housing a radio unit, thrusting forward in black fatality."
Such Darth Vader suits will be worn in the high tech future in a
society governed by the "Articles of Immachination." The rocket
limericks that follow this future fantasy celebrate man's mating with
machines in yet another mode. The theme surfaces in another strand
of the plot, for Enzian supposedly had "a wet dream where he
coupled with a slender white rocket" (p. 297). Plasticman, the hero
of the comic Slothrop enjoys, and Rocketman, the persona he
adopts, also embody variants of man united with technology. Whereas the central death in Christianity supposedly promises an end to
death, immachination ultimately promises an end to life as we know
it. Human life will depend on the machine for continuance, as happens in space, for instance, where one must abide by the rules and
limitations of the machine or die. Or man and machine will perish
together in the Liebestod of rocket falls.

The apocalyptic ends are only alluded to, but Pynchon does
sketch four, all sharing the feature that man lives and dies by his

technology; he is no longer separate or separable. Immachination in space is one. Rocket-borne war is another. The future (almost our present) of multinational corporations and of Them might be called the *1984*-version of our future, with its elite and its helpless preterite. The web of control exercised by I. G. Farben and its present-day counterparts, is real enough. A minor figure suggests that "Once the technological means of control have reached a certain size, a certain degree of *being connected* one to another, the chances for freedom are over for good" (p. 539). Pynchon also alludes in passing to what might be called a *Brave New World*-form of the future. The City, as it is called, is a living complex based on verticality, with elevators whose interiors are more like courtyards, with their flowersellers and fountains. There, uniformed, good-looking young women, "well-tutored in all kinds of elevator lore" (p. 735), refuse to answer questions about such taboo subjects as the Rocket, and the narrative voice alludes to social repression. This vision of the future is followed by a description of a Hitler Youth Glee Club, reminding us of the polished orderliness that was one of the Hitlerian ideals, and which is a powerful force in this City of the future, and in *Brave New World*. Other writers to explore this kind of dystopian future include Zamiatin, *We*; Vonnegut, *Player Piano*; and Levin, *This Perfect Day*. All show worlds in which poverty and material suffering have been reduced to negligible levels, only to leave other, more hopeless suffering, the more complete damnation of the preterite because they are inferior to machines. Such worlds find humanity acceptable only to the degree that it can become machine-like.

Turning from general history to an individual, we see the origins-to-apocalypse of Tyrone Slothrop. His ancestors, the patriarchs of the new era, fill us in on the development of Yankee know-how, capitalism, and the exploitation of the new continent. Slothrop himself is conditioned as a baby to respond sexually to a mystery stimulus (that he later concludes must have been Imipolex G). Sexual conditioning to a product of technology puts in symbolic terms Western man's fascination and obsession with his own technological creations. Slothrop is later crammed with rocket information, and goes in quest of V-2s. In the course of his search, he does indeed find the Mittelwerke where they were assembled, and Peenemünde, the "Holy Center" of rocket technology, but like Parsifal, he fails to ask the right questions, and does not reach true insight at the birthplace of the rocket. As Technological Man, or even The American,

Slothrop's end is particularly interesting, for Pynchon imagines him as becoming briefly a vatic harmonica-Orpheus in the Zone, who ultimately disintegrates.[11] His sparagmos is appropriately orphic, but this loss of identity and then of substance for Technological Man seems to suggest either that man as individual will similarly disintegrate when wedded to the machine, or that the only escape from immachination will be such total dismantling of the ego, or both. Whether you cooperate with the machine and power structure or oppose it, the end is the same. Life as we know it will disappear.

When we look at this mythological history, using Edmund Leach's basic characteristics of myth—redundancy, binary organization, and mediation—we find that they effectively point to the values the myth inculcates, and they show us how the myth works as a stabilizing structure amidst the uncertainty and unknowability set up by the fantasy and science. The process of applying Leach is long, so I can only summarize here a few of the results relating to redundancy.[12]

Redundancies are seen most clearly when characters map onto each other, for they undergo the same experiences, share the same insights, and—usually—fail the same tests. Slothrop is the most heavily redundant character, in this sense; his actions help alert us to what to look for in the others. Among those shared experiences or characteristics most frequently found in the redundancies are:

(a) the shock of discovering a They-reality superimposed on our quotidian, material reality;
(b) the tantalizing awareness that higher illumination is possible, coupled with the failure to achieve the breakthrough;
(c) the desirability of becoming open to the Other Side;
(d) the development of a kind of flexibility to meet whatever improbability next appears;
(e) acceptance both of one's own preterition and one's death;
(f) the importance of kindness to ameliorate our preterite lot, and indeed a general shift from eros toward kindness;
(g) the need to avoid exerting control over others;
(h) the necessity of imposing some limits on one's own freedom in order to survive and be part of a social complex, but the desirability of not letting these limits multiply and become tyrannic bonds; and
(i) the need to recognize that we have fallen into time and cannot go back to living within a totally renewable cycle of nature, and must therefore make intelligent choices when we reach the cusps that history offers us.

What emerges from looking at the myth in modified structuralist ways is, in part, a new hero monomyth, or new concept of the individual and that individual's pattern of development. Given Western assumptions—including our rather inflamed egos and romantic concepts of the individual—we are likely to find Pynchon's alternative pattern spineless and shiftless. Within the new pattern, there is none of the respect which we shower on certain obsessions (for knowledge, money, material possessions, power, persuasiveness, competitiveness, and the like). They belong to the elect, not the preterite. In essence, Pynchon seems to be arguing that even survival values are changing, that flexibility and openness are more valuable than aggressive self-interest if the species (as opposed to the individual) is to survive; that whatever nature may be, man had better not be red in tooth and claw, or the result will be the stockpiling of means of death, the ICBMs of today, made possible by the V-2s.

Without wishing to belittle Pynchon in the least, I think him more traditional and less deconstructive than do most other critics. All the fantastic effects that destabilize novelistic ontology are there to create the fictive embodiment of the new cosmos we must face, the cosmos of modern science, philosophy, and language theory; of uncertainty, unknowability, of arbitrary relationships, and ultimate incommunicability.

Generically, we have the interplay of one kind of science fiction (science as metaphor) with fantasy. The technologically oriented mythology is another kind of science fiction, however, that functions to give warning, and to suggest possible ways of changing so that we could survive in the new cosmos. Particularly in its apocalyptic arguments, it reflects the dystopian strain in science fiction. We also have the science-fictional theme of man's relationship to the machine. The celebration of technology reflects yet another branch of science fiction. And some of the values that emerge from the mythology are the values Pynchon seems to feel we need to live in a post-Newtonian, post-Darwinian world, which amounts to a kind of moral-scientific speculation.

In conclusion, I'm not sure that in most literary analyses we should even think of reducing any complex work to a single generic label. Yes, *Gravity's Rainbow* is science fiction—by several definitions if not by all—but to have called it science fiction, or fantasy, or mythological literature, and to have limited oneself to the insights available through one of those perspectives, would have distorted our understanding of what it achieves. Even limiting the discussion to these three genres is unwarrantable. In addition to casting doubt on the wisdom of such labels (except to use them as a temporary tool or starting point), this experience with *Gravity's Rainbow* suggests the usefulness of our defining science fiction as a family of related but competing literary strains, (as Michael McClintock argues elsewhere in this volume) rather than our trying to create a single exclusive definition.[13] We can define science fiction in an exclusive and limiting fashion—be it as cognitive novum, or as informed extrapolation based on firm knowledge of science, or celebration of ritual transformation of chaos into cosmos via scientific ritual, or as investigation of human interaction with technology. But any such unitary definition is likely to distort our reading of any one work—if we try to apply the definition with any seriousness.

Science Fiction: Going Around in Generic Circles

David Clayton

> The fundamental levels of experience which motivate art are related to
> the objective world they draw back from. The unresolved antagonisms
> of reality return in works of art as the immanent problems of their form.
> —Theodore W. Adorno, *Ästhetische Theorie*

I

What is the relevance of genre for the study of science fiction?[1] I
often have the impression that when teachers of literature discuss
science fiction the term *genre* must appear without fail, as if it were
only possible to speak of some entity called "the science fiction
genre." Is this simply a maneuver aimed at divesting science fiction of
some of the disreputable associations that still cling to it in the
academic mind owing to its long sojourn in the wasteland of pulp
magazines and cheap pocketbooks? Does adding the word *genre*
have the effect of bringing together the highly diverse works produced by science fiction writers? Should the reader or critic assume
the concept of genre as a permanent context for the analysis of any
science fiction work? Do generic conventions function as a code that
the reader has to decipher, consciously or not, in order to make sense
out of the text? In other words, in what way can genre help us to
meaningfully define the science fiction enterprise? To answer this
question, we should begin by setting aside the specific problems
entailed in the writing of science fiction and restrict our attention to
the concept of genre itself.

Even a brief glance in that direction shows how little hope we
have of finding an answer to our problem. A survey of the critical
writings that attempt to define the meaning and scope of genre itself

gives one the impression of an unresolved crisis dating from at least the early decades of this century. In 1924, Boris Eichenbaum lamented that: "Our literature suffers from the lack of genres and from the search after them."[2] Over forty years later, Rene Wellek, assessing the current status of genre, could hardly record any progress but had to admit "that in the practice of almost all writers of our time genre distinctions matter little; boundaries are being constantly transgressed, genres combined or fused, old genres discarded or transformed, new genres created, to such an extent that the very concept has been called in doubt."[3] While "Modern genre theory is, clearly, descriptive" and "doesn't limit the number of possible kinds and doesn't prescribe rules to authors,"[4] genre's abdication of prescriptive authority documents its most serious weakness: the absence of any certain basis for its classifications.

Traditional—most notoriously, neoclassical—theories of genre imagined they possessed such a foundation in some absolute, extraliterary system of values. Without prejudice, we can characterize such theories as dogmatic, in the sense that they appeal to a standard outside literature that is not usually called into question, whether that standard is the belief, partly theological, partly rationalistic, in an unvarying order of nature that underlay neoclassicism, or the rhetorical distinction proposed by Plato and revived by Northrop Frye between types of discourse.[5] Such standards, however interesting or valuable they might be in themselves, evidently raise questions outside the competency of a theory which "classifies literature and literary history . . . by specifically literary types of organization or structure."[6]

The alternative strategy for dealing with genre, adopted by many present-day critics, we can label by way of contrast pragmatic. The goal of this theory had already been concisely formulated in the 1920s by Boris Tomachevskii who declared it "necessary to achieve a descriptive approach to the study of genres and to replace the logical classification with a pragmatic and utilitarian one, only taking account of the distribution of material in the defined framework."[7] While Tomachevskii's programmatic thesis remained without effect outside of Slavic speaking countries, Mario Fubini independently developed the salient points of such a theory in an essay that appeared some twenty years later. In Fubini's opinion, the use of genre is: "Legitimate, if the genre is not considered as more than a means or instrument, whose function exhausts itself in recalling to the mind the notions that are necessary to determine and fix our judgment; and if it is required by the development of the critical discourse and responds to the critic's need to deal with a given work in particular historical conditions—thus to result from the discourse itself, even if it is one of the traditional genres.[8] Genre ceases to perform this useful auxiliary role when "forgetting its instrumental character, [it] sets itself up as a criterion of judgment," and this happens whenever "genres attribute to themselves an inappropriate substantiality."[9]

But the pragmatic approach itself involves difficulties that clearly emerge in the most ambitious treatment of science fiction literature produced so far, Darko Suvin's *Metamorphoses of Science Fiction*, whose subtitle, *On the Poetics and History of a Literary Genre*, brings the question into the foreground. Seeking to avoid the improper hypostasis of generic categories denounced by Fubini, Suvin defines genres as "socioaesthetic and not metaphysical entities" which "have an inner life and logic of their own"[10] and defends their value as "heuristic models" akin to those employed in the natural sciences:

> A heuristic model is a theoretical structure based on analogy, which does not claim to be transcendentally or illusionistically "real" in the sense of mystically representing a palpable material entity, but whose use is scientifically and scholarly permissable, desirable, and necessary because of its practical results . . . . An acceptable heuristic model or set of models for a literary genre is as necessary for its understanding, for the setting up of standards pertaining to it, as the theory of ideal gases was for its time and discipline.[11]

Although one might sympathize with the usefulness of such a procedure, which enables Suvin to get on with his discussion of the history of science fiction, one must still question the adequacy of his analogy. The relation of genre to a literary text is not that of a scientific concept to a body of data but that of one kind of discourse to another—of one conceptually mediated object to another; such a relation requires *prima facie* a different methodology for its interpretation than that used in the sciences, though not a less stringent one. In the first place, one might well ask: What sort of rules govern the construction of genres in this way? Can a critic simply conjure up as many genres as he or she wants? If Suvin recognizes Ockham's razor as one of the hallmarks of the scientific method, why should he allow genres to be multiplied beyond necessity?[12] If the critic is to be able to cut through what Suvin calls the "genological jungle" shouldn't the former have some guarantee that the models being used are well-constituted and logically motivated? These are, after all, exactly the requirements that would apply to the use of heuristic models in the sciences.

Indeed, the very appeal to a classificatory concept such as genre presents logical difficulties which cannot be written off as a metaphysical will-o'-the-wisp, unless one intends to apply the same judgment to many of the questions which have occupied modern mathematics and logic. The history of set theory, to cite only one example, demonstrates how *"contradictions and antinomies* of various kinds" could "directly or indirectly *originate from the notion of set*, that is, from collecting individuals to a unit."[13] One might, of course, accuse me here of making use of the same type of false analogy for which I earlier reproached Suvin, but the desiderata of logical consistency and coherence which the example brings out— and to which I think Suvin would subscribe—owe nothing to the specifically mathematical content of set theory. To the contrary, the example furnishes a striking parallel to the question posed in an earlier paragraph, that of the adequate constitution of genres. With his statement that: "The concept of SF cannot be extracted intuitively or empirically from the work called thus,"[14] Suvin wisely rejects the fallacy of basing generic definitions upon inductive generalizations— the latter all too often based, in turn, upon surface features. Since he does not explain how he arrived at his own definition of science fiction as "cognitive estrangement," however, in what way does Suvin's "heuristic model" practically differ from such a generalization?

While Suvin might remedy these shortcomings by a more astute discussion of the properties of his heuristic model than the one he supplies, he must still answer a more fundamental question: Why does a critic who makes no bones about his adherence to Marxism want to utilize a model so eminently incompatible with the dialectical ends he has in view? In good Marxist fashion, Suvin polemicizes against "positivism" but he raises his theoretical edifice by means of a positivistic device par excellence, sanctioned by the practice of

philosophers such as Carnap or Popper hardly more favorably dis-
posed to dialectics than to "metaphysics."[15] Having eviscerated the
concept of genre by this summary treatment, Suvin further weakens
his argument by cutting off the concept from its historically problematic context, reduced to the terms of trivial scholastic disputes:
"It seems therefore unnecessary to reopen the debates of the medieval nominalists and realists about the 'real' existence of entities such
as SF or any other genre; such debates hinge on a pseudoquestion."[16]
One need not be an unreconstructed idealist to accord concepts an
objective status different in nature from that of material objects; to
refuse to do so makes it impossible to give a satisfactory account of
genre, which "puts, in a specifically literary context, the philosophical questions concerning the relation of the class and the individuals
composing it, the one and the many, the nature of universals."[17]

Bearing in mind that "The generic classifications of neoclassicism," as Claudio Guillén notes, "showed no sense of history,"[18] a
nondogmatic genre theorist must begin by imposing the requirement
of historical self-reflection on the concept itself. This history, as we
previously saw, has been marked by an ongoing crisis, centering
upon what Karl Viëtor called *"the* dilemma of genre history": *How is
it possible to write genre history when there is no previously ascertain-
able norm*, when this norm must be established on the basis of a
survey of the mass of historical, individual works?"[19] What underlies
Viëtor's dilemma, nevertheless, is clearly the "philosophical questions" mentioned by Warren above, because "Following the distin-
tegration of the medieval *ordo*, art has been assimilated to the total
process of advancing nominalism. No universal is permitted to art as
a type and the older types are sucked up by the vortex."[20]

The most notorious attack upon genre dates from the publication in 1902 of Benedetto Croce's *Estetica*, but the problem that
Croce dismisses rather than resolves had been anticipated in a far
more penetrating and less sensational way over a century before by
Friedrich Schlegel in a number of writings, many of them no more
than fragments. While Schlegel did not succeed in bringing these
speculations together into a new theory of genre, he found an appropriate form for presenting many of them in his "Dialogue on
Poetry," in which he could allot conflicting ideas—to each of which
he in some degree assented—to different speakers. Here, as in a

Platonic dialogue, philosophical debate becomes drama. To Amalia's opening sally, "I always shudder when I open a book in which the imagination and its works are topically classified,"[21] Marcus retorts: "No one would ask you to read such detestable books. But a theory of poetic kinds is just what we lack. And what can it be but a classification which would also be a history and theory of poetic art?"[22]

It is not hard to see how the differing attitudes toward genre set forth by the participants in the "Dialogue" anticipate, sometimes almost word-for-word, those of twentieth-century critics such as Croce, Tomachevskii, or Viëtor; with Marcus' complaint that "a theory of poetic kinds is just what we lack" Schlegel had already confronted "*the* dilemma of genre history" in his own way. Yet the metaphorically charged language of the feud between Marcus and Amalia suggests that Schlegel had taken a step further in recognizing how little the dilemma has to do with the collapse of binding aesthetic norms. Marcus' assertion that "Without abstraction no creation takes place"[23] implies an aesthetic analogy to the processes of birth and death, to which Amalia responds when she claims that the artistic means become "a detour, which too frequently kills the sense for the highest before the goal is reached."[24] In effect, by translating the concept of genre back into its archaic, biological terms, the "Dialogue" potentially transcends its own limits and reveals how "all concepts . . . derive from the nonconceptual, since they are themselves components of reality, required for its development—primarily for the sake of controlling nature."[25]

Thus the "Dialogue" tacitly exposes the real sore spot of genre theory: the antagonism between the claims of the individual and those of the class to which it belongs. Moreover, as Peter Szondi demonstrated in an illuminating essay, supported by entries from the posthumously published notebooks, this unsolved problem provided the ultimate focus for Schlegel's reflections on genre, contemporary with the writing of the "Dialogue." Starting by distinguishing the historically determinate "spirit" of genre from its transhistorical "form," Schlegel radically historicized the three traditional genres of epic, dramatic, and lyric poetry, a change marked by his shift from the substantives *Epik*, *Lyrik*, and *Drama* to the corresponding adjectives *episch*, *lyrisch*, *dramatisch*. According to Szondi, this "adjectivization:"

and the resulting relativization of generic differences indicate for Schlegel's poetic genre conception their reduction to differences within a combinatory system, ultimately the elimination—or at least, eliminability—of the generic division of poetry. It remains open whether this is a logical consequence or a realization of the intention to overcome genre. Then the question whether kinds of poetry exist at all is already posed with the critical question of the condition of their possibility. A statement such as the following from the year 1797: *"It is not true that the individuals have more reality than the genres,"* shows, to the extent it can be related to poetic genres, that Schlegel did not have the answer from the beginning. However, other statements contrast with this apology for the concept of genre—for example, *"One can just as well say there are infinitely many as that there is only one progressive kind of poetry. But then there is none at all, since species cannot be conceived without co-species."* Or: *"There is only one of the modern kinds of poetry or infinitely many. Each work of literature a genre for itself."*[26]

If Schlegel's investigations abortively culminated in a series of brilliant paradoxes, one cannot reproach him for having tried to cover over the difficulty with a specious resolution; by pushing his inquiry a step beyond this point, he might have seen how such paradoxes arise from the marrow of conceptual thinking itself and not just from the concept of genre.[27]

2

Commenting on Schlegel's notion of a unique poetic genre, Szondi remarks that it: "is limited to modern poetry. In the second fragment, this postulate—in which *one* is only another word for *infinitely many*—leads to the thesis that every work of literature is a genre for itself. But in this context work of literature means *progressive, modern* work—that is, the novel."[28] On this point, Schlegel turned out to be genuinely prophetic, though not in a way he could have foreseen or probably wished. More than any other variety of imaginative literature, the novel illustrates the simultaneous merging of generic boundaries and proliferation of new genres noted by Wellek. This process reveals the significant role played by an extra-literary force in the breakup of traditional generic categories and constraints: the influence exercised by the demands of the market-place upon literary creation, most strongly evident in the production of novels. "With the vast widening of the audience in the nineteenth century," Austin Warren points out, "there are more genres; and, with the more rapid diffusion through cheap printing, they are shorter-lived or pass through more rapid transitions."[29]

A perception of the radical changes brought about by the commercialization of literary production may well have provided the impetus for some of the key doctrines of the first truly modern school of literary criticism, Russian formalism, which flourished from the opening years of this century until being suppressed by the Soviet authorities around 1930. The formalist emphasis upon how a work of literature is made and the effect it produces upon its recipient rather than what it means shows a remarkable sensitivity to the values of industrial mass production, an affinity that becomes even more obvious in the formalist approach to genre expounded by Yuri Tynyanov in his essay "The Literary Fact." Tynyanov proposes as a fundamental mechanism of literary history that "In the epoch of its decay, any genre moves from the center to the periphery, but a new shape emerges in the center from the trivia of literature, from its back alleys and lower orders."[30] The essay dates from 1924, making it more or less contemporaneous with the flowering of modernist experimentation in both Western Europe and the USSR, and Tynyanov undoubtedly drew upon his own experience of the artistic events taking place around him to formulate a generally valid law of literary change, yet he also acknowledged, as previous critics had not, the extent of the commercial revolution which had radically altered the status of the text. No longer a gift offered to a wealthy patron, the literary work of art had become a commodity subject to the law of supply and demand—registered in part by the rise and fall of genres. Intentionally or not, Tynyanov had put into critical language one of the basic assumptions of capitalist economics, that "Value in exchange, when left to itself, arises spontaneously in the market as the result of competition."[31]

The generic crisis thus exhibits a process of double erosion, within and without: as a result of the advancing nominalism that undermines traditional artistic standards, and as a result of the commercial expansion of literary production, the equivalent in the material sphere of nominalism in the conceptual. Faced with such a prospect, the critic has no choice but to start from scratch. Yet how to do so? If Suvin's unsatisfying treatment of genre points up the risks of ignoring the historical problem raised by generic classifications, even such a superficial consideration of the problem as we have engaged in here establishes the futility of seeking to rehabilitate the traditional categories. To commit either error exposes one to the risk of historical amnesia. At the same time, the critic must beware of falling prey to the danger, rightly denounced by Suvin, of substituting a mere inductive generalization for a generic definition. "One who searches for structures at the level of observable images," Todorov cautions in his critique of Frye, "simultaneously refuses any certain knowledge."[32]

If we hope to arrive at any "certain knowledge" about the science fiction genre, our only point of departure can be the text itself. Structuralism, which in practice often gives the impression of processing texts rather than interpreting them, a bad example avidly pursued by semiology, supplies a valuable theoretical justification for such a procedure. The structural properties of language guarantee that "every manifestation is iterative, that the discourse quickly tends to close on itself—in other words, that the mode of being of the discourse contains in itself the conditions of its representativeness."[33] One need not amass a quantitatively large number of science fiction texts in the hope of extracting a generic essence from them; one must instead strive for a strong reading of the individual text that would allow its generic dimension to appear. More importantly, focusing upon an individual text opens up the possibility of exposing the unresolved tension which underlies genre as concept. When "conceptual order complacently inserts itself before what thinking wants to comprehend,"[34] it blocks the dialectical process, as does Suvin's heuristic model, which amputates "*the* dilemma of genre history" before it can even come to light. Such a reading, responsive to the intrinsic alterity of the text, gives itself over to the text in the hope that if "Thought really alienated itself in the object, addressed itself to the latter instead of its categories, then the object, under the lingering gaze of thought, would itself begin to speak."[35]

Let us take as a prospective object a text that would seem to be an indubitable example of the science fiction genre: Robert Heinlein's *Starship Troopers*. Yet in what sense is this a work of science fiction? It neither presents a scientific theory—as does LeGuin's *The Dispossessed*—nor does it, like *The Mote in God's Eye*, deal with scientific research. Is it only science fiction then because it takes place

in the future? Is it no more than an embarassing vestigal survival of
that perennial staple of the pulp-publishing industry, the science
fiction cum adventure tale? Our difficulty in responding to the question illustrates one of the real problems in defining the genre: the gap
that exists between science fiction as it is perceived by its consumers—few of whom would hesitate to classify Heinlein's book as
science fiction—and as it is studied by literary scholars concerned
with locating the genre within the larger context of literary and
cultural history—a context that plays little direct role in determining
the buying habits of the consumers. Forced to choose between imposing a standard that would eliminate the majority of what is sold as
science fiction from our definition of the genre or accepting the
opinion of the consumers, we can only opt for the latter. If literary
theory has any hopes of one day changing that opinion, it must begin
by critically examining the "facts" in order to understand their mode
of existence.

Viewed in this way, *Starship Troopers*, one of Heinlein's most
well known novels, offers a strategically valuable opportunity for an
inquiry into the nature of the science fiction genre. Rather than
comparing it to some *a priori* definition, however flexible, to see
whether the book conforms to it or not, I propose to concentrate
upon a microtext that clearly belongs to the science fictional dimension of the narrative: the description of the "powered armor" that
Johnny Rico uses as a member of the Mobile Infantry. Heinlein
lavishes several pages in recounting the advantages and operation of
this piece of gear; the main points can be resumed as follows: made of
steel, weighing two thousand pounds, "The suit has feedback which
causes it to match *any* motion you make, exactly—but with great
force."[36] In addition, the suit has jet propulsion, carries rocket
launchers, is fitted with elaborate audio and visual circuits, sensors,
radar, all of which serve one purpose: "to leave you free to follow
your trade, slaughter."[37] According to Johnny, "the beauty of a
powered suit" is that "You don't have to think about it. You don't
have to drive it, fly it, conn it, operate it; you just wear it and it takes
orders directly from your muscles and does for you what your muscles are trying to do. This leaves you with your whole mind free to
handle your weapons and notice what is going on around you . . .
which is *supremely* important to an infantryman who wants to die in
bed."[38] Structurally, the role played by the suit in the text corre-

sponds to what Roland Barthes called an index, a basic narrative unit that he distinguished from a function, which "correlates to uni-ties of the same level."[39] While functions provide a system of relays which organize the action, indices refer to "a concept more or less diffuse, although necessary to the meaning of the story . . . the relation of the unit and its correlative is no longer distributional . . . but integrative; to understand what an indicial notation is 'good for' it is necessary to move to a higher level."[40] What then does the suit index? To what concept does it refer? Certainly not to science in the first place. To be sure, Johnny Rico provides a certain amount of scientific discourse— "The secret lies in negative feedback and amplification"—to differentiate the device from the magically powered gadgets that show up in sword and sorcery novels or cheap science fiction.[41] This discourse, however, does not provide the focus of the passage; it only supplies a scientifically credible premise for the existence and operation of the suit.

Technology, not science, occupies the foreground in this description. Read out of context, it could easily give the impression of a purely accidental subordination of technology to destructive ends for which twentieth-century history could provide more than enough parallels. The reader might imagine that the emphasis falls so heavily upon technology's potential for destruction just because Heinlein has chosen a time of war as his setting; perhaps, in a more peaceful era, technology would serve to improve human life rather than to eliminate it. By no means: as Heinlein makes clear elsewhere in *Starship Troopers*, technology itself functions as a weapon in the struggle for survival in a hostile universe. To the question "Does Man have any 'right' to spread through the universe?" Johnny replies: "Man is what he is, a wild animal with the will to survive, and (so far) the ability, against all competition . . . . The universe will let us know—later— whether or not Man has any "right" to expand through it. In the meantime the M.I. will be in there, on the bounce and swinging, on the side of our own race."[42]

The war that Heinlein presents in the novel, far from being a passing episode after which humankind could settle down to forging swords into ploughshares, constitutes a permanent state of affairs. Still, to maintain, as H. Bruce Franklin does, that "militarism— together with imperialism—is the novel's explicit message" does not seem an adequate formulation.[43] Militarism and imperialism imply a subordination of technological, as well as other means to ends of national policy, especially for the sake of economic advantage in the form of increased profits to concerned enterprises; wars waged for such goals stand in the same relation to what Heinlein envisions, the total expropriation of the universe by the human race, as the medieval crusades do to the imperialist conflicts of the nineteenth or our own century. The technological subjugation of nature, symbolized in its crudest form in the novel by the adversary aliens, the Bugs or Pseudo-Arachnids, furnishes the *causus belli* and war becomes the fulfillment of human progress.

At this point, one must raise the question: need the expansion of technology necessarily imply a total conquest of nature? Certainly, other conceptions of the social role of technology exist than the one Heinlein presents; to argue otherwise means accepting precisely the same fatalistic view of history that Heinlein himself tries to force upon his audience. What Heinlein seeks to pass off as "science," mainly expounded in the novel by Johnny's mentor Dubois, ideologically subverts technology, mobilizing it for the sake of a survival-of-the-fittest ethos transparent in the passage cited above and that I have discussed in another essay.[44] The powered armor indexes a conceptual complex in which technology dominates science but is in turn dominated by ideology camouflaged as science. Like any piece of ideology, this one has its origins in objective social relationships—specifically in the "dialectic of the enlightenment"—and not in the mind of the writer, who only dramatizes it; like any piece of ideology, however, it fundamentally distorts what it presents.

Up to this point, we have only dealt with one structural axis of the powered armor, the metaphorical; as Barthes observes, "indices [imply] metaphorical relata."[45] However, this is not the only way the object functions in the story; Johnny introduces his description with the words: "But I do want to mention a little about powered suits, partly because I was fascinated by them and also because that was what led me into trouble."[46] A nodal point that synthesizes several major themes of *Starship Troopers*, the suit also enters the story as the cause of a chain of events, a micronarrative that makes up one unit of the book. What events does the suit precipitate? Owing to his infatuation with the suit, Johnny fails to take proper safety precautions during an exercise and must undergo flogging as punishment for this infraction. This episode, whose narration takes up chapter 7, could almost be read as a short story and exhibits the characteristic features of a minimal narrative: Johnny's acquisition of the suit creates a disturbance of equilibrium culminating in an act of self-betrayal; this peripety leads to his punishment, which in turn brings about his reintegration with the community.

If this analysis elucidates the narrative structure of the sequence, it hardly explains the bizarre discrepancy between the initial event and its outcome, however well this discrepancy harmonizes with the manic-depressive tenor of the narrative. Why should Johnny Rico suffer because he "was fascinated by" powered suits? Is this only an example of the illusionism of narrative technique, "that which comes *after* being read in the narration as *caused by*?"[47] An apparently minor detail suggests looking at the incident from a somewhat different point of view: recording his impressions before his flogging, Johnny exclaims, "The nightmare hallucination—."[48] In psychoanalytic terms, this phrase in which the semantic unit *dream* occurs pleonastically can only indicate a wish fulfillment, disfigured by the nightmare and censored by the final dash. Moreover, the illusion, mentioned above, that what "comes *after*" in the text is read "*as caused by*," is the same means the dream uses to signify causality. Of the two methods by which the dream can express a causal relation, consecution or transformation of one image into another, Freud tells us that "in both cases, *causality* is represented by a *succession*."[49]

The intrusion of desire into the text causes us to radically alter our first reading: instead of saying that Johnny suffers as a result of acquiring the suit, as if he were a child punished for wrecking an expensive toy, we must describe the punishment as the fulfillment of a promise latent in the act of gaining the suit. But why should desire manifest itself in such a strange way? To answer this question, let us return to the suit. A. J. Greimas calls such narrative constituents "actants"—which can be translated as "narrative agents"—and classifies them into six basic categories: subject, object, auxiliary, antagonist, sender, and receiver.[50] If we keep in mind the analysis sketched above, then powered armor, as a kind of tool, should play the role of auxiliary, and nature that of object/antagonist, with Johnny as subject. Yet the mere physical facts contradict this hypothesis; the suit dominates its wearer and "The means are fetichized: they absorb pleasure."[51] Deviated object more than tool, the actant here also has a sphere of action—of functions, in Greimas' terminology that consists, in this case, in bringing about the hero's punishment.[52] In this way, agent and function show themselves well attuned to one another: the fetishistic object perfectly complements the masochistic mode of gratification, since what both share in common is the inversion of desire.

Making use of a famous Freudian distinction, we can readily discern the latent fantasmatic scenario which supports the manifest narrative events of this episode. Since, as Johnny admits, "I fell in love with powered armor," the sequence, in a malicious parody of the scheme outlined by Propp for analyzing the Russian folk tale, must conclude with a marriage ceremony; the flogging signifies Johnny's defloration, performed as in a primitive society, by a tribal elder.[53] This reading poses a crucial question: what forces drive the hero on to act out such a painful and repressive fantasy? Why does he ally himself with an inanimate object and then sanctify this union with a rite which requires his subjection to corporal punishment? The traditional psychoanalytic explanation would relate his submission to "primary masochism," itself the vehicle of the death instinct, although the former can only intervene in the subject's life modulated by the figures of the Oedipus complex. We would then have to explain Johnny's desire to be punished as the symptom of an inadequately resolved fear of castration: seeking to circumvent the authority of the Father by a culpable—in this case, fetishistic—form of pleasure, he simultaneously tries to cancel out this guilty act by offering himself up for punishment, gaining a perverse masochistic surplus pleasure which compensates him for his sacrifice. In effect, he voluntarily undergoes castration, while nullifying its signification by appropriating the symbolic value to his own benefit.

Wherever we choose to place the emphasis—on masochism or castration—we reduce the fantasy to an emanation of forces operating within Johnny's own psyche. The text, however, which blatantly insists upon the libidinal investment at work here, only weakly supports such a reading. To the contrary, the fantasy we encounter in this episode corresponds exactly to what Gilles Deleuze and Felix Guattari have called a group fantasy, which is "Laid out, machined on the social body. To be fucked by the social body, to desire to be fucked by the social body, does not derive from mother and father, although they have their role there as subaltern agents of transmission and execution."[54] It is no subjective perversion of desire, attributable to some disorder in the personality of the individual, that erupts here; both narrative agent and function bear witness to the profound social mediation of desire. The suit is a technological artifact and an economic object of exchange; the punishment is a public act, sanctioned elsewhere in the novel by Dubois.[55] The pathology belongs to the society, not just its members.

Extrapolating from the results of our narrative analysis, we can infer that the inversion of desire patent in the events of this chapter must pervade the entire world of *Starship Troopers*. What kind of inversion? The two elements, the suit and the flogging, designate two quite different forms of inversion, fetishism and masochism, each having its own etiology and thus causal significance. Since acquisition of the powered armor leads to the punishment, however, the text indicates a repression of fetishistic pleasure for the sake of masochistic submission; only after having undergone the flogging can Johnny enjoy a certain residual pleasure in possessing the suit. Inversion in the case of masochism, Freud argues in his essay "Triebe and Trieb-schicksale," includes two components: the redirection of instinctual gratification to one's self and the transformation of activity into passivity.[56] As we will see in a moment, the first component, which entails a gain of narcissistic gratification for the subject, has its own role to play in the scenario; the second, which constitutes masochism properly speaking, comes to the fore with Johnny's admission that "A flogging isn't as hard to *take* as it is to *watch*."[57] Passivity typifies the status quo of desire in this society, a passivity we have previously observed in the subordination of technology to ideology indexed by the powered armor.

Should we then interpret the punishment as an example of regression to barbarism? A primitive rite, as I have sarcastically proposed above, anachronistically surviving in an advanced society? *Starship Troopers* certainly does supply such instances of archaic behavior subsisting in a future state, the Mobile Infantry being a case in point; nevertheless, the intrinsic content of such archaisms radically changes when prolonged into a qualitatively different social formation. In so-called primitive societies, Deleuze and Guattari state: "The recipient in the rituals of affliction does not speak, but receives the word. He does not act, but is passive under the graphic action; he receives the stamp of the sign. And what is his pain but a pleasure for the eye which regards it? The collective or divine eye which is not animated by any idea of vengeance, but only ready to seize the subtle relation between the sign graven in the flesh and the voice coming out of a face—between the mark and the mask."[58] To the contrary, the ritual depicted by Heinlein has a fundamentally passive quality for both recipient and spectators, as Johnny's remark makes clear; nothing in this scene suggests active pleasure on the part of any of the participants.

To the question: Who enjoys this spectacle, if not the onlookers? We can reply: the social body or *socius*, in Deleuze and Guattari's terms. Does this mean that the society as a whole, in some abstract sense, enjoys the spectacle? No—the *socius* functions as an element in the social process of production, an analogue to what the authors call the "body without organs" in the libidinal process of production. A reaction to this process, which momentarily calls it to a halt, "The full body without organs is the improductive, the sterile, the unengendered, the unconsummable."[59] But once we move out of the individual into the social process, the picture inevitably changes:

> If we want to have an idea of the subsequent forces of the body without organs in the uninterrupted process, we must draw a parallel between production by desire (*production desirante*) and social production. Such a parallel is only phenomenological; it does not prejudge in any way the nature of the relation between the two productions, nor even the question of knowing whether there are really *two* productions. Simply, the forms of social production also imply an unengendered, unproductive stage, an element of anti-production coupled with the process, a full body determined as *socius* . . . . In short, the *socius* as body forms a surface on which all the production inscribes itself and appears to emanate from the surface of inscription.[60]

In a primitive society land plays the role of *socius*; in a despotic social formation—for example, imperial Rome or the Byzantine empire— the despot's own body "immobile, monumental, unmoveable, appropriates all the forces and agents of production . . . ."[61] In the world presented in *Starship Troopers*, however, this role falls to capital which "is certainly the body without organs of the capitalist, or rather capitalist being . . . . It produces surplus value, just as the body without organs reproduces itself, burgeoning and extending itself to the limits of the universe."[62]

If we accept Deleuze and Guattari's fundamental thesis that "the social domain is immediately traversed by desire, that it is the historically determined product, and that the libido has no need of mediation or sublimation, of any psychic operation, or of any transformation, in order to invest productive forces to relations of production," we can combine the two apparently divergent readings the text has so far yielded.[63] At first, using the suit as a semantic index, we inferred a domination of technology by ideology; now, desire appears as submission to the *socius*—in effect, Johnny's desire to succeed by totally integrating himself into the Mobile Infantry. In either reading, the central theme which orients all the other themes is that of productive forces. On the one hand, technology, metaphorically symbolized by the powered armor presupposes a certain level of productive forces—which thus dominate it. We can then put our earlier formulation into a conceptually more accurate form: strictly speaking, ideology does not dominate technology but functions as an operator which distorts the socially objective perception of productive forces embodied as technology. (Technology exists only for the sake of conquering nature.) At the same time, the libidinal investment of technology sustains the social process of production by channeling into it the productive forces, the desires of the collectivity.

Instead of two readings, one socioeconomic and objective, the other psychoanalytic and subjective, we have a thematic network we can look at from two points of view. Ideology legitimates Johnny's punishment, but since society and individual dialectically imply one another, ideology itself feeds upon the libidinal investment of the individual. Remembering that "the transformation of sadism into masochism," according to Freud, "signifies a return to the narcissistic object, since . . . the narcissistic subject is exchanged through identification with another, alien ego,"[64] we can see how identity, "the proto-form of ideology,"[65] supplies the link which binds individual subject and social object together—the place of the "alien ego" being filled by the *socius*. The principle of exchange, which governs the economic life of the social organism in which the individual must survive, "is primordially related to the principle of identification," whose "extension keeps the whole world in the bounds of the identical, totality."[66] At the same time, the individual registers its success in adapting to this organization through recognition by society of its narcissistically invested identity.

In discussing the scene of Johnny's flogging, we argued that it must designate the enactment of a group fantasy, not the fulfillment of a fantasy existing only in Johnny's mind. By taking into account the role of identity in the formation of ideology, however, we can demonstrate how Johnny's own fantasy, that of becoming a hero in the Mobile Infantry, serves the ideological purposes of the social institution. "When the notion of group fantasy was elaborated in the perspective of institutional analysis," Deleuze and Guattari relate:

> The first task was to mark its difference in nature from the individual fantasy. It appeared that the group fantasy was inseparable from "symbolic" articulations which define a social domain insofar as it is real, while the individual fantasy reduces the extent of that domain to "imaginary" [that is, narcissistic, D.C.] givens. If one prolongs that initial distinction, one sees that the individual fantasy is itself laid out on the existing social domain, but perceives it through imaginary qualities which confer on it a kind of transcendence or immortality under whose protection the individual, the self, plays out its pseudo-destiny. What does it matter if I die, says the general, since the army is immortal! The imaginary dimension of the individual fantasy has a decisive importance for the death instinct, since the immortality conferred on the existing social order entails in the self all the investments of repression, the phenomena of identification, of "super-egoization," and of castration, all the resigned desires . . . including the resignation of dying in the service of that order, while the instinct itself is projected without and turned against the others (death to the foreigner, death to those who are not like us.)[67]

Isn't this precisely the drama we see unfolding in *Starship Troopers*? The masochistic submission to authority doubled by the desire to preserve "our race"? Identical units interchangeable with one another, the characters of Heinlein's novel lead a cellular existence indistinguishable from the "ultimate dictatorship of the hive" Johnny attributes to the Bugs. His exclamation "The nightmare hallucination—" takes on added significance in this light as the recognition that the worst of all fantasies, the regression to a state of nature, is becoming a reality; calling it a nightmare attempts to disavow its reality—to no avail.

3

Arrived at a point seemingly far removed from the question of genre, we find ourselves looking at it again from a new, but illuminating perspective. Paradoxically, the world of *Starship Troopers*, a hell for human beings, represents a generic paradise whose particulars are all on the way to total assimilation by the universal: the primordial machinery of identification guarantees both the subordination of the individual to society and that of the literary work to the genre. *Starship Troopers* exhibits each of these aspects to such a high degree that one could with equal right describe the narrative action as an allegory of the triumph of genre or the book's generic saturation as an allegory of the ideology of power it celebrates. The biological categories lurking behind the discussion of genre in Schlegel's "Dialogue," Amalia's defense of the work of art's right to self-determination and Marcus' demand for its subjection to generic laws, manifest themselves in Heinlein's novel on an interplanetary scale as the human race's quest for empire over nature.

Hence we can also read this loony epic as one of the struggle for survival of science fiction itself as genre. Even Suvin, maintaining an ideological position diametrically opposed to Heinlein's, assumes a nearly chauvinistic tone when he speaks of the "genological jungle" and science fiction's need for "generic affirmation"—as if he were Johnny obediently conning one of Dubois' lessons.[68] In this way the past history of genre which Suvin disregards takes its revenge on the unwary critic. Clearly, however, science fiction does not contend with nature for its survival; it fights with other genres in the literary marketplace. In other words, it seeks to assert itself in a world of uncontrolled productive forces dominated by the regime of exchange value just as do the characters in *Starship Troopers*. As we could have already inferred, in the novel productive forces and not nature function as the real adversary, productive forces which impose themselves with the fatality of natural disasters. The infernal machinery of the "dialectic of the enlightenment" dictates that "The curse of unchecked progress is unchecked regression."[69] While in *Starship Troopers*, this regression means the accelerated transformation of human society into that of the hated Bugs, in literary terms it means total absorption by the conditions of production: the more science fiction succumbs to generic constraints, the more it forfeits what makes it valuable as literature and turns into a mere consumer artifact.

In no way does the important role we have allotted productive forces reflect a peculiarity of Heinlein's text. Just as in *Starship*

Troopers, in most science fiction writing productive forces do not appear explicitly; technology indexes and to a certain extent masks them. Nevertheless, the existing level of technology in a science fictional world always supplies a clue to the implicit question: What productive forces are capable of generating the technology we see? Technology only superficially figures as the subject of science fiction; in reality, it serves as a question mark that brings to the fore the relation between productive forces and the forms of social organization. This question forces itself upon the Time Traveller immediately with his arrival in the future: the absence of disease and the plenitude of vital resources among the Eloi indicate a high level of civilization and thus of technological progress. But how can he reconcile this state of prosperity with the Eloi's nearly primitive social organization? The answer to the question lies, then as in Wells's own time, underground with the real source of productive power.

By embodying the same productive forces which determine its own sociohistorical existence in narrative form, science fiction paradoxically converges with an important current in twentieth-century experimental art that seeks to confront audiences with its conditions of production at the expense of a spurious organicity. While in the works of such innovators as Picasso, Stein, Cage, Pollock, or Kerouac, this confrontation might wrongly seem no more than a pretext for scandalizing the public, in Brecht's analogous use of estrangement in theatrical production, it takes on a consciously emancipatory function: to force the passive spectator to take account of the production of the work of art implies the possibility of requiring him or her to come to terms with the productive forces—social, economic, political, or even libidinal—that have shaped his or her life. Yet does not science fiction, even in such a wrong-headed and retrogressive work as *Starship Troopers*, share the same goal? Distant relatives who can trace their common ancestry back to Poe, science fiction and experimental art stand equally at odds with traditional art in their refusal to ignore the impact of technologically mediated productive forces upon society; the difference lies in their historical development, not in their origins.

Such an hypothesis enables us to look at the problem of genre in a completely different way, by realizing that what counts is not what genre is but what it does. Owing to science fiction's long and hardly ended subjection to the conditions of mass production, genre has constantly acted as an inertial force on the writing of science fiction. In all likelihood, genre has played a similar role throughout literary history. In traditional literature, genre translated into aesthetic theory the need of the species to organize itself—at the cost of the individual, if necessary—for the sake of preserving itself, a bondage to the struggle for survival which reproduced within society the very natural conditions it sought to escape as a human collectivity; as we have seen, this insight glimmers from afar in the strife of Marcus and Amalia. Nevertheless, genre forfeits this validity the moment society possesses technological means sufficient to guarantee the health and well-being of its citizens. Arrived at this point in its history, genre can only play two roles: either that of a classificatory system for literary scholars along the lines envisioned by Tomachevskii or Fubini, or that of a blueprint for success for aspiring writers. In the latter case, the influence genre continues to exert over literary production, rather than being that of an "invitation to form,"[71] mimics in literary terms the fallacious "struggle for survival" portrayed in *Starship Troopers*.[70]

Following Adorno's profound observation that "Social productive forces . . . return in their naked form, stripped of their facticity, in works of art, since artistic labor is social labor,"[71] we can momentarily return to Heinlein's text to answer a question we had left open. When we asked: Why does Johnny submit without protest to his assimilation by a totalitarian state? We replied that he did so for the sake of affirming his identity. But what larger forces guide the behavior of the society as a whole? If "nature" is not, as Heinlein pretends, the real enemy of the World Federation, who or what is it? Is there some conspiracy operating behind the scenes that Heinlein doesn't let us in on? Nothing in the book hints at such a possibility; what the book does reveal, as our reading of the powered armor episode suggests, is a central contradiction in capitalist production itself which must simultaneously develop new and more powerful productive forces in order to maintain its profit margin and try to keep these same forces from rendering it obsolete. It can only do so by means of archaic social institutions such as the Mobile Infantry which serve both as an instrument of social control and as an important reserve for the investment of surplus capital. "The social axiomatic of modern societies is torn between two poles and doesn't cease to oscillate from one pole to another," Deleuze and Guattari argue: "Born out of decoding and deterritorialization, on the ruins of the despotic machine, these societies are torn between the *Urstaat* that they want to revive as a hypercoding and reterritorializing unity and the unchained flux which drags them towards an absolute threshold."[72]

This formulation perfectly describes the double movement of *Starship Troopers*, the expansion to the limits of space and the regression to a barbaric form of social organization; at the same time, because of the crucial way productive forces enter into both the narrative and the production of the book as commodity, it specifies the function of genres: as an element of antiproduction that "insinuates itself everywhere into the productive machine and combines with it in order to control productivity and realize surplus value."[73] Just as the World Federation tries to protect its own survival by projecting the forces it has unleashed into space and displacing their threat onto a false, "natural" adversary, generic conventions hold in check the disturbing potential for social criticism latent in science fiction narrative by imposing on it a network of imaginary identifications which structure the act of reading and thus distort its role as group fantasy: positive identification with the "hero," negative with the "aliens." But doesn't the suit already manifest this tension in a local form, within the field of antagonistic forces that compose the text? As the embodiment of productive forces the suit's existence marks the possibility of overthrowing an oppressive and stupid system of social relationships instead of spreading them throughout the universe; as the locus of a group fantasy, it could serve to ignite a conflagration of desire instead of extinguishing it in a degrading social ritual.

Since Heinlein informs us that those who refuse to enlist face disenfranchisement, we could glimpse in their fate that of texts that abandon the generic fold: ostracism. But the science fiction writer does not face so grim a choice as do the characters of *Starship Troopers*, between submission and isolation. True, he or she cannot give up generic conventions altogether, with the risk of forfeiting his or her identity as a producer of science fiction; in fact, to the extent these conventions represent not only the sedimented past of science fiction but in a larger sense our own past from which we have not escaped, our inability to control the powerful forces we conjured up in the form of technology, the writer has no choice except to come to terms with them. One possibility is to violate the conventions, as Jerry Pournelle and Larry Niven do in *The Mote in God's Eye*, to refuse to make aliens into enemies—indeed, to make them, like the Houyhnhnms, the point of departure for reflections upon our own situation. Another, and even more powerful alternative would be to incorporate the conventions in the text in such a way as to bring the ideologically specious role of genre into full view, as Joanna Russ has done in the austerely beautiful short novel *We Who Are about to* . . . . Starting from a situation which could otherwise serve to initiate a Heinleinian epic of space pioneering, Russ unmasks the reactionary appeal of such a fantasy and chooses suicide for her heroine after the latter firsts deserts and then kills the other characters. Better death than more empire building à la *Starship Troopers*.

It hardly seems an accident that genre has consistently found its elective metaphor in the circle, from the medieval wheel of Virgil down through the goofy circular diagram of Julius Peterson to Hans Robert Jauss's promotion of Dilthey's "hermeneutic circle" as the universal panacea for all generic woes.[74] Apart from the imaginary allure that this figure exercises, shrewdly discerned by Jacques Lacan, what it most evidently designates is the element of repetition intrinsic to genre.[75] While that element rightly corresponded to the inability to overcome natural constraints at one time, today it simply means the stagnation of productive forces inhibited by inadequate forms of social organization, forced to go around in circles literally and figuratively. Jauss assures his readers that when:

> One puts the historical concept of a continuity "in which each antecedent expands and enlarges itself through its successor," . . . in place of the natural genre concept (genre as idea which appears in every individual being, only repeats itself as genre), then the relation of individual text to genre forming text series presents itself as a process of continued creation and change of horizon. The new text evokes for the reader the horizon of expectations and conventions, familiar from earlier texts, which can then be varied, expanded, corrected, but also reshaped, crossed out, or only reproduced.[76]

What do we gain by exchanging the old, "natural" circle for the new, improved hermeneutic one? Only the image of the functioning of the culture industry, which, as Horkheimer and Adorno point out in their penetrating analysis in *Dialectic of Enlightenment*, "consists in repetition."[77] Science fiction, the prisoner of genre, has the honesty to expose this horizon for what it is: the shadow of our own limitations. The intensity with which it proves to us that we can only go on repeating the circle as long as we accept this horizon as the edge of the world derives from the faith it has never completely lost—Heinlein is the most striking example of it—in that other place, outside, which bears the name Utopia.

Notes

Biographical Notes

Index

Notes

Parallel Universes: Fantasy or Science Fiction?

1. Martin Rees, as cited in *Black Holes and the Universe* (New York: Halsted Pr., 1981), 188.
2. Robert L. Forward, "A Taste of Dragon's Egg," *Analog Science Fiction/Science Fact* 100 (1980):64–74.
3. Michael Moorcock, *Behold The Man* (New York: Avon, 1970).
4. Gregory Benford, *Timescape* (New York: Pocket Books, 1981).
5. Isaac Asimov, *The End of Eternity* (New York: Lancer, 1963).
6. Frank Tipler, "Rotating cylinders and the possibility of global causality violation," *Physical Review* 90 (1974):2203.
7. Philip K. Dick, *The Man in the High Castle* (New York: Putnam, 1962).
8. Harry Harrison, *West of Eden* (New York: Bantam, 1984).
9. Mark Twain, *A Connecticut Yankee in King Arthur's Court.* (New York: Harper, 1917).
10. Keith Laumer, *Worlds of the Imperium* (New York: Ziff-Davis, 1961).
11. L. Sprague deCamp and Fletcher Pratt, *The Incomplete Enchanter* (New York: Pyramid, 1962).
12. Philip Jose Farmer, *Behind the Walls of Terra* (New York: Ace, 1977).
13. Robert A. Heinlein, *Glory Road* (New York: Berkley, 1970).
14. Robert A. Heinlein, *The Number of the Beast* (New York: Fawcett Columbine, 1980).
15. Roger Zelazny, *Nine Princes in Amber* (New York: Avon, 1972).
16. J. R. R. Tolkien, *The Lord of the Rings* (New York: Ballantine, 1966).
17. Isaac Newton, *Philosophiae naturalis principia mathematica* (London: W. Dawson, 1960).
18. J. G. Frazer, *The Golden Bough* (New York: Macmillan, 1935).

High Tech and High Sorcery: Some Discriminations Between Science and Fantasy

1. Arthur C. Clarke, *The Lost Worlds of 2001* (New York: Signet, 1972), 189.

2. See for example, Kingsley Amis, *New Maps of Hell* (New York: Harcourt, 1960), 17–19; J. O. Bailey, *Pilgrims Through Space and Time* (Westport, CT: Greenwood, 1973), 10–12; Mark R. Hillegas, "Introduction" *Shadows of Imagination: The Fantasies of C. S. Lewis, J. R. R. Tolkien, and Charles Williams*, ed. Mark R. Hillegas (Carbondale: Southern Illinois Univ. Pr., 1969), 2; Robert M. Philmus, *Into the unknown: The Evolution of Science Fiction from Francis Godwin to H. G. Wells* (Berkeley: Univ. of California Pr., 1970), 2–3.

3. Quoted in Peter Nicholls, ed. *The Science Fiction Encyclopedia* (Garden City, NY: Doubleday, 1979), 160.

4. *Alternate Worlds: The Illustrated History of Science Fiction* (Englewood Cliffs, NJ: Prentice-Hall, 1975), 32.

5. Cited in Brian Aldiss, *Billion Year Spree: The True History of Science Fiction* (Garden City, NY: Doubleday, 1973), 8–9.

6. See Malzberg, *The Engines of the Night: Science Fiction in the Eighties* (Garden City, NY: Doubleday, 1972), passim; and Delany, *The Jewel-Hinged Jaw: Notes on the Language of Science Fiction* (New York: Berkley Books, 1978), 4–18.

7. *Kinds of Literature: An Introduction to the Theory of Genres and Modes* (Cambridge, MA: Harvard Univ. Pr., 1982), 46. Further references will be given in parentheses in the text.

8. *In Search of Wonder*, 2d ed. (Chicago: Advent Publishers, 1977), 1.

Filling the Niche: Fantasy and Science Fiction in Contemporary Horror

1. Paul Gagne, "The Shadow's Edge—Interview with Whitley Strieber," *Whispers*, ed. Stuart David Schiff (Oct. 1983), 20.

2. For further discussion of genre in *The Stand*, see my "Science Fiction into Fantasy: Stephen King's *The Stand*" (Fifth International Conference on the Fantastic in the Arts: Florida Atlantic Univ., March 23, 1984).

3. The Xanth novels are, in order of appearance: *A Spell for Chameleon* (New York: Ballantine, 1977), *The Source of Magic* (New York: Ballantine, 1979); *Castle Roogna* (New York: Ballantine, 1979); *Centaur Aisle* (New York: Ballantine, 1981); *Ogre, Ogre* (New York: Ballantine, 1982); *Night Mare* (New York: Ballantine, 1983); *Dragon on a Pedestal* (New York: Ballantine, 1983).

4. *Split Infinity* (New York: Ballantine, 1980); *Blue Adept* (New York: Ballantine, 1981); *Juxtaposition* (New York: Ballantine, 1982).

5. *On a Pale Horse* (New York: Ballantine, 1984); *Bearing an Hourglass* (New York: Ballantine, 1984). The remaining novels, beginning with *With a Tangled Skein*, will feature incarnations of Fate, Nature, and War as protagonists.

6. For a definition and discussion of "reading protocols," see Samuel R. Delany, "Some Reflections on SF Criticism," *Science-Fiction Studies* 8, No. 3 (Nov. 1981): 235–237.

7. For further discussion of Colin Wilson's treatment of the vampire theme, see my "Vampires in Space: Fantasy and Science Fiction in Colin Wilson's *The Mind Parasites* and *The Space Vampires*," submitted for *The Vampire in Literature*, ed. Leonard Heldrith, Greenwood Press, forthcoming.

8. Gagne, p. 21.

9. In *Warday* (New York: Holt, 1984), Strieber, as narrator of his pseudodocumentary, discusses his own earlier fiction, particularly *The Wolfen*, and notes that what generated fear in a pre-Warday society would be totally inadequate afterward.

10. Peter Straub, *Shadowland* (New York: Coward, McCann and Geohegan, 1980), 17.

11. Straub, p. 150.

12. See Stephen King, *Danse Macabre* (New York: Everest, 1981), 18ff; Gagne, 20; Charles Grant, "Introduction" to *Shadows* (New York: Berkley, 1980), 7–10.

13. Dorothy Scarborough, *The Supernatural in Modern English Fiction* (New York: Putnam, 1917), 82–83.

14. Jack Sullivan, "Green Tea: The Archetypal Ghost Story," in *Literature of the Occult*, ed. Peter B. Messent (Englewood Cliffs, NJ: 1981), 117. Citing Sullivan, *Elegant Nightmares: The English Ghost Story from Le Fanu to Blackwood* (Athens, OH: Ohio Univ. Pr., 1978).

15. Occasionally, of course, the vampire figure succeeds in re-creating its original sense of horror. Peter Straub suggests such an experience upon first reading King's *Salem's Lot*, in "Meeting Stevie," Straub's introduction to *Fear Itself: The Horror Fiction of Stephen King*, ed. Tim Underwood and Chuck Miller (San Francisco: Underwood-Miller, 1982), 7–14. For an almost perfect illustration of the unknown monster, coming from nowhere to inflict pain, suffering, and death, see King's short story "The Raft," the opening chapter of *Cujo* (New York: Viking, 1981), or the first chapter of *Cycle of the Werewolf* (New York: Signet, 1985).

16. Gagne, p. 20.

17. Strieber, *The Wolfen* (New York: Morrow, 1978), 252.

18. Tom Geddie, "Interview: Peter Straub," in *Fantasy Newsletter*, 46, no. 23 (March 1982) 19–20; Gagne, 26–28.

Konstantin Tsiolkovsky: Science Fiction and Philosophy in the History of Soviet Space Exploration

1. There should not have been, in fact, such widespread surprise in 1957: it is now often forgotten that Sputnik I was launched as a Soviet contribution to the International Geophysical Year. Two years before, at a meeting in Geneva of the nations planning to participate in this epochal scientific enterprise, the Americans made it clear they intended to send up a satellite. At the same meeting, Soviet representatives also publicly announced their nation would launch a satellite to monitor phenomena in the upper stratosphere. But as Bernard Lovell, the Director of the Jodrell Bank Observatory, remarked at the time, "The world believed the U.S., not the U.S.S.R."

2. N. N. Kibalchich, "Proekt vozdushnoplavetelnogo pribora, ("Project for an Aerial-navigational Device"), in: Akademija nauk SSSR, *Pionery raketnoj texniki* (Moscow: Nauka, 1964), 15.

3. For the latest account of his place in the development of world rocketry see Walter A. McDougall. . . . *The Heavens and the Earth* (New York: Basic Books, 1985), 20–40.

4. He is similar in many ways to his American contemporary, Thomas Edison, even in certain personal particulars: Tsiolkovsky, too, was deafened at an early age.

Victorian Urban Gothic: The First Modern Fantastic Literature

1. "Fantasy" here is defined not as the psychological activity from which all artistic creations derive, but in purely literary terms as that genre best represented by such works as Tolkien's *The Lord of the Rings* and Le Guin's *Earthsea Trilogy*, works set in another world in which the dominant functional power is magic rather than science.

2. For a detailed analysis of the better-known definitions of the genre— those by Tzvetan Todorov, Rosemary Jackson, and Eric Rabkin—and my reasons for rejecting them, please see chapter 1 of my dissertation, "The Urban Gothic in British Fiction 1880–1930," Ph.D. diss., Univ. of California at Los Angeles, 1986). For Zgorzelski's definition of the fantastic, see "Is Science Fiction a Genre of Fantastic Literature?" *Science-Fiction Studies* 6 (1979).

3. For a more detailed examination of this aspect of science fiction language, see Kathleen L. Spencer, " 'The Red Sun is High, the Blue Low': Toward a Poetics of Science Fiction," *Science-Fiction Studies* 10 (1983):35–49. See also Samuel R. Delany, *The Jewel-Hinged Jaw*, which has greatly influenced my thinking on this issue.

4. Jonathan Culler, *Structuralist Poetics: Structuralism, Linguistics, and the Study of Literature* (Ithaca: Cornell Univ. Pr., 1975), 193.

5. See Seymour Rudin, "The Urban Gothic: From Transylvania to the South Bronx," *Extrapolation* 25, no. 2 (Summer 1984):115–26. Rudin uses the term Urban Gothic to refer to fiction and film of the last ten years or so in which the terrible creatures of the old Gothic Stories—werewolves and vampires in particular—have reappeared in the decayed, blasted cities of our own time, metamorphosed into even more terrible forms in reaction to their surroundings. Thus, the creatures, he declares, are both old and new—new because "in a world partly destroyed by our greed and threatened by the ultimate inhumanity of nuclear destruction, we perceive them as inevitable products and beneficiaries of the blight we have wrought. They have always been our enemies; they may now be our heirs" (p. 116).

6. Although the Gothic novels of the late eighteenth century create an atmosphere which has much of the fantastic about it, the effect is diluted by settings which are distanced in time and place from the daily lives of the readers. However, for another and quite persuasive reading of the function of the Gothic, see William Patrick Day, *In the Circles of Fear and Desire: A Study of Gothic Fantasy* (Chicago and London: Univ. of Chicago Pr., 1985).

7. *The Country and the City* (New York: Oxford Univ. Pr., 1973), 217.

8. Jessie Douglas Kerruish, *The Undying Monster: A Tale of the Fifth Dimension* (London: Heath Cranton Ltd., 1922).

Jewels of Wonder, Instruments of Delight: Science Fiction, Fantasy, and Science Fantasy as Vision-Inducing Works

1. Aldous Huxley, *Heaven and Hell* (1956; reprint, New York: Harper-Colophon, 1963), 89.

2. J. R. R. Tolkien, *The Lord of the Rings*, 2d ed. (Boston: Houghton Mifflin, 1965), vol. 2: 197.

3. Roger Zelazny, *Doorways in the Sand* (New York: Avon, 1976), 119.

4. Arnold M. Ludwig, "Altered States of Consciousness," *Altered States of Consciousness*, Ed. Charles T. Tart, 2d ed. (New York: Anchor-Doubleday, 1974), 11–24. Reprint from *Archives of General Psychiatry* 15(1966):225–34.

5. Walter N. Pahnke and William A. Richards, "Implications of LSD and Experimental Mysticism," In *Altered States of Consciousness*, 409–39. Reprint from *Journal of Religion and Health* 5(1966):175–208.
6. Brian Aldiss, *Helliconia Spring* (New York: Berkeley, 1983), 185.

The Tooth That Gnaws

1. J. M. E. McTaggart, "Time," in *The Philosophy of Time*, ed. Richard M. Gale, (Clifton, New Jersey: Humanities Pr., 1968), 87–88.
2. From the editor's (Richard Gale's) introduction to McTaggart's Article, 65.
3. Gale, p. 66.
4. H. G. Wells, "The Inventor," in *Early Writings in Science and Science Fiction by H. G. Wells*, ed. Robert Philmus and David Y. Hughes (Berkeley: Univ. of California Pr., 1975), 93. In the standard version [the Heineman edition of *The Time Machine* (New York: Bantam, 1976)], Wells presents a fairly brief discussion of the nature of time near the beginning of the first chapter. The Time Traveller asserts that "there is no difference between Time and any of the three dimensions of Space except that our consciousnesses move along it" (p.3). A bit later in the discussion, he elaborates by claiming that "our mental existences, which are immaterial and have no dimensions, are passing along the Time-Dimension with a uniform velocity from the cradle to the grave" (p.5). Finally, in that same chapter, the Time Traveller prompts the psychologist to explain the disappearance of the small model of the time machine by explaining that the model accelerated in time, that the model "is travelling through time fifty times or a hundred times faster than we are . . . it gets through a minute while we get through a second." (p. 11). Although this discussion offers an interesting way of thinking of the nature of time, the *New Review* version provides a particularly graphic representation of the A-series and the B-series.
5. George N. Schlesinger, *Aspects of Time* (Indianapolis: Hackett Publishing Co., 1980), 31. Supertime is a name proposed for a superseries whose existence could help a philosopher explain the movement of the NOW in the standard time series.
6. H. G. Wells, *The Time Machine* (New York: Bantam, 1976), 5.
7. William Faulkner, *The Sound and the Fury* (New York: The Modern Library, 1929), 93–94.
8. Schlesinger, p. 33.
9. Jean-Paul Sartre, "On The Sound and the Fury: Time in The Works of Faulkner," in *Faulkner: A Collection of Critical Essays*, ed. Robert Penn Warren (Englewood Cliffs: Prentice Hall, 1966), 89.

10. Darko Suvin, *Metamorphoses of Science Fiction: On the Poetics and History of a Literary Genre* (New Haven: Yale Univ. Pr., 1979), 8.

11. Robert A. Heinlein, *The Menace from Earth* (New York: Signet, 1959), 39.

12. Wolfgang Iser, *The Implied Reader: Patterns of Communication in Prose Fiction from Bunyan to Beckett* (Baltimore: The Johns Hopkins Univ. Pr., 1974), 281.

13. Heinlein, p. 50.

14. Heinlein, p. 52.

The *And* In Fantasy and Science Fiction

1. Mark Rose, *Alien Encounters: Anatomy of Science Fiction* (Cambridge, MA: Harvard Univ. Pr., 1981), 19.

2. Rose, p. 4.

3. Paul Hernadi, *Beyond Genre: New Directions in Literary Classification* (Ithaca: Cornell Univ. Pr., 1972), 140.

4. Käte Hamburger, *Die Logik der Dichtung*, Zweite Auflage (Stuttgart: Ernst Klett Verlag, 1968), p. 9.

5. Robert Scholes, *Structural Fabulation: An Essay on Fiction of the Future* (Univ. of Notre Dame Pr., 1975), p. 7.

6. W. R. Irwin, *The Game of the Impossible: A Rhetoric of Fantasy* (Urbana: univ. of Illinois Pr., 1976), 8.

7. Hamburger, p. 55.

8. Emile Benveniste, *Problems in General Linguistics*, Miami Linguistic Series no. 8, trans. Mary Elizabeth Meeks (Coral Gables: Univ. of Miami Pr., 1971), 208. "It is sufficient and necessary that the author remain faithful to his historical purpose and that he proscribe everything that is *Alien* to the narration of events (discourse, reflections, comparisons). As a matter of fact, there is then no longer even a narrator. The events are set forth chronologically, as they occurred. No one speaks here; the events seem to narrate themselves."

9. Max Milner, *Le Romantisme: I, 1820–1843, Littérature française 12* (Paris: B. Arthaud, 1973), 155.

10. Samuel R. Delany, *The Einstein Intersection* (New York: Ace Books, 1967), 128.

11. James Gunn, *Isaac Asimov: The Foundations of Science Fiction* (New York: Oxford Univ. Pr., 1982), 157.

12. Brian Aldiss, *Cryptozoic!* (New York: Avon Books, 1969), 182.

13. Tzvetan Todorov, *Introduction à la littérature fantastique* (Paris: Editions du Seuil, 1970), 163.

14. Arthur C. Clarke, *2001: A Space Odyssey* (New York: Signet/New American Library, 1968), 215.

15. See Alexander Woodcock and Monte Davis, *Catastrophe Theory* (New York: E. P. Dutton, 1978), 11.

Science Fantasy and Myth

1. Ursula K. Le Guin, *The Language of the Night: Essays on Fantasy and Science Fiction*, ed. Susan Wood (New York: Putnam's, 1979), 134–35.

2. Maud Bodkin, *Archetypal Patterns in Poetry: Psychological Studies of Imagination*, 2d ed. (London: Oxford Univ. Pr., 1963), 76–77.

3. Owen Barfield, *Poetic Diction: A Study in Meaning*, 2d ed., intro. Howard Nemerov (New York and Toronto: McGraw-Hill, 1964), 85.

4. Verlyn Flieger, *Splintered Light: Logos and Language in Tolkien's World* (Grand Rapids, MI: 1983).

5. Samuel R. Delany, *The Einstein Intersection* (New York: Ace Books, 1967), 148.

6. Richard Cowper, *The Road to Corlay* (New York: Pocket Books, 1979), 55.

Gravity's Rainbow: Science Fiction, Fantasy, and Mythology

1. John Brunner, "Coming Events: An Assessment of Thomas Pynchon's *Gravity's Rainbow,*" *Foundation*, 10 (1976): 20–27, quotation p. 22; Geoffrey Cocks, "War, Man, and Gravity: Thomas Pynchon and Science Fiction," *Extrapolation*, 20 (1979): 368–77, p. 368. See also Richard Alan Schwartz, who considers *Gravity's Rainbow* a bridge between SF and mainstream fiction in "Thomas Pynchon and the Evolution of Fiction," *Science-Fiction Studies*, 8 (1981): 165–72. Others to discuss science-fictional elements include André Le Vot, "The Rocket and the Pig: Thomas Pynchon and science-fiction," *Caliban* (Annales publiées par l'Université de Toulouse-Le Mirail, nouvelle série, tome xi, 1975), 111–18; Speer Morgan, "*Gravity's Rainbow*: What's The Big Idea?" *Modern Fiction Studies*, 23 (Summer, 1977): 199–216; and Mark Siegel, "Thomas Pynchon and the Science Fiction Controversy," *Pynchon Notes*, 7 (October, 1981): 38–42.

2. For identification of the gothic elements, see Douglas Fowler, "Pynchon's Magic World," *SAQ*, 79 (1980): 51–60, and *A Reader's Guide to GRAVITY'S RAINBOW* (Ann Arbor: Ardis, 1980); for analysis as encyclopedic fiction, see Edward Mendelson, "Gravity's Encyclopedia," in *Mindful Pleasures: Essays on Thomas Pynchon*, ed. George Levine and David Leverenz (Boston: Little, Brown, 1976), 161–95; and for satiric readings, see Alfred MacAdam, "Pynchon as Satirist: To Write, To Mean," *Yale Review*,

67 (1978): 555–66; J. O. Tate, "*Gravity's Rainbow*: The Original Soundtrack," *Pynchon Notes*, 13 (1983): 3–24; and Speer Morgan (n. 1, above).

3. Rosemary Jackson, *Fantasy: The Literature of Subversion* (London: Methuen, 1981), 26.

4. Gary K. Wolfe, *The Known and the Unknown: The Iconography of Science Fiction* (Kent: Kent State Univ. Pr., 1979), 4–5.

5. Several critics seem almost to apply such scientific phenomena directly to the everyday level of Pynchon's story. See Schwartz (n. 1, above), and Richard Pearce, "Thomas Pynchon and the Novel of Motion," *Massachusetts Review* (Spring, 1980): 177–95. Others stipulate more clearly the metaphoric nature of the similarities. See Lance W. Ozier, "The Calculus of Transformation: More Mathematical Imagery in *Gravity's Rainbow*," *Twentieth Century Literature*, 21 (1975): 193–210; Robert L. Nadeau, "Readings from the New Book of Nature: Physics and Pynchon's *Gravity's Rainbow*," *Studies in the Novel*, 11 (1979): 454–71; and Alan J. Friedman and Manfred Puetz, "Science as Metaphor: Thomas Pynchon and *Gravity's Rainbow*," *Contemporary Literature*, 15 (1974): 345–59.

6. Brian McHale, "Modernist Reading, Post-Modern Text: The Case of *Gravity's Rainbow*," *Poetics Today*, 1 (1979): 85–110. "To destabilize novelistic ontology" is his phrase (p. 106).

7. Thomas Pynchon, *Gravity's Rainbow* (New York: Viking, 1973), 754.

8. For approaches of this kind, see Linda A. Westervelt, " 'A Place Dependent on Ourselves': The Reader as System-Builder in *Gravity's Rainbow*," *Texas Studies in Literature and Language*, 22 (Spring, 1980): 69–90; Carolyn S. Pyuen, "The Transmarginal Leap: Meaning and Process in *Gravity's Rainbow*," *Mosaic*, 15 (1982): 33–46; and Molly Hite, *Ideas of Order in the Novels of Thomas Pynchon* (Columbus: Ohio State Univ. Pr., 1983).

9. Northrop Frye, *The Secular Scripture: A Study of the Structure of Romance* (Cambridge, MA: Harvard Univ. Pr., 1976), 14.

10. Eric Gould discusses mythological writing as an attempt to fill the gap between event and meaning in his *Mythical Intentions in Modern Literature* (Princeton: Princeton Univ. Pr., 1981).

11. For a more detailed discussion of the complex orphic strains in this story, see Kathryn Hume and Thomas J. Knight, "Orpheus and the Orphic Voice in *Gravity's Rainbow*," *Philological Quarterly*, 64 (1985): 299–315.

12. I develop this method in depth in *Pynchon's Mythography: An Approach to GRAVITY'S RAINBOW* (Carbondale: Southern Illinois Univ. Pr. 1987). For Leach's method, see "Genesis as Myth," in *European Literary Theory and Practice: From Existential Phenomenology to Structuralism*, ed. Vernon W. Gras (New York: Delta, 1973), 317–30.

13. See Ludwig Wittgenstein, *Philosophical Investigations*, trans. G. E. M. Anscombe (Oxford: Basil Blackwell, 1953), nos. 65–77, pp. 31–36, for development of this concept of definition as a set of family resemblances.

Science Fiction: Going Around in Generic Circles

1. The present essay is a greatly revised and expanded version of the talk I gave at the 1985 Eaton Conference on Fantasy and Science Fiction. I have been aided in the task of revision by the helpful suggestions of Professors Michael Holquist, Robert Philmus, and Harry Polkinhorn, but I owe a special debt of gratitude to George Slusser for his endless patience and useful advice.

2. Boris Eichenbaum, "Auf der Suche nach der Gattung," *Aufsätze zur Theorie und Geschichte der Literatur*, ed. and trans. Alexander Kaempfe, Edition Suhrkamp, 114 (Frankfort on the Main: Suhrkamp, 1965), 80. All translations are my own unless otherwise indicated.

3. Rene Wellek, "Genre Theory, the Lyric, and *Erlebnis*," *Discriminations: Further Concepts of Criticism* (New Haven: Yale, 1970), 225.

4. Austin Warren, "Literary Genres," Rene Wellek and Austin Warren, *Theory of Literature*, 3d. ed., (1962, reprint, New York: HBJ, 1977), 234–235.

5. "The basis of generic criticism in any case is rhetorical, in the sense that the genre is determined by the conditions established between the poet and his public." Northrop Frye, *Anatomy of Criticism: Four Essays* (1957; reprint, Princeton: Princeton Univ. Pr., 1971), 247. But, as Claudio Guillén remarks, "The differences that exist between the various artistic vehicles—between poetry read, recited, and staged, or between a gouache and a pastel—do not coincide with the overall structural models we call genres." "On the Uses of Literary Genre," in *Literature as System: Essays toward the Theory of Literary History* (Princeton, Princeton Univ. Pr., 1971), 113.

6. Warren, p. 227.

7. Boris Tomachevskii, "Thématique: vie des procedes du sujet," *Théorie de la littérature. Textes des formalistes russes*, ed. and trans. Tzvetan Todorov, (Paris: Seuil, 1965), 306.

8. Mario Fubini, "Genesi e storia dei generi letterari," in *Critica e Poesia. Saggi e discorsi di teoria letteraria*, 2d ed., Biblioteca di cultura moderna, 513 (Bari delle Puglie: Laterza, 1966), 131.

9. Fubini, p. 132.

10. Darko Suvin, *Metamorphoses of Science Fiction: On the Poetics and History of a Literary Genre* (New Haven: Yale, 1979), 16.

11. Suvin, p. 17.

12. Suvin, p. 67.

13. Abraham Fraenkel, *Abstract Set Theory*, 4th ed., revised by Azriel Levy. (Amsterdam: North Holland Publishing Co., 1976), 11.

14. Suvin, p. 63.

15. For a critique of the anti-dialectical aspect of neo-positivism, see Adorno's reply to Karl Popper, "Einleitung zum >> Positivismustreit in der deutschen Soziologie <<," in: *Soziologische Schriften 1, Gesammelte Schriften*, ed. Rolf Tiedemann (Frankfort on the Main: Suhrkamp, 1972), Vol. 3: 280–353.

16. Suvin, p. 17.

17. Warren, p. 237.

18. Guillen, p. 116.

19. Karl Viëtor, "Die Geschichte literarischer Gattungen," *Geist und Form: Aufsätze zur deutschen Literaturgeschichte* (Bern: Francke, 1952), 305.

20. Theodor W. Adorno. *Aesthetische Theorie, Gesammelte Schriften* ed. Gretel Adorno and Rolf Tiedemann, (Frankfort on the Main: Suhrkamp, 1970) Vol. 7: 296–97.

21. Friedrich Schlegel, "Gespräch über Poesie," in *Schriften zur Literatur*, ed. Wolfdietrich Rasch (1970, reprint, Munich: DTV, 1972), 297.

22. Ibid.

23. Ibid.

24. Ibid.

25. Theodor W. Adorno, *Negative Dialektik* (1966, reprint, Frankfort on the Main: Suhrkamp, 1970), 21.

26. Peter Szondi, "Friedrich Schlegels Theorie der Dichtarten: Versuch einer Rekonstruktion auf Grund der Fragmente aus dem Nachlaß," *Euphorion*, 74, no. 2 (1970); 198

27. What the concept sets aside "appears divergent, dissonant, negative, as long as consciousness by its very formation must aim for unity: so long as it measures what is not identical with it by its own demand for totality." Adorno, *Dialektik*, p. 15.

28. Szondi, Ibid.

29. Warren, p. 232.

30. Yuri Tynyanov, "Das literarische Faktum," trans. Helene Imendörffer, *Russischer Formalismus: Texte zur allgemeinen Literaturtheorie und zur Theorie der Prosa*, ed. Jurij Striedter (1969 reprint, Munich: Fink-UTB, 1971), 399.

31. Leon Walras, *Elements of Pure Economics; or, the Theory of Social Wealth*, trans. William Jaffe (London: Richard D. Irwin, 1954), p. 84.

32. Tzvetan Todorov, *Introduction à la litterature fantastique* (1970 reprint, Paris: Seuil, 1976), 22.

33. A.-J. Greimas, *Sémantique structurale* (Paris: Larousse, 1966), p. 143.

34. Adorno, *Dialektik*, p. 15.

35. Adorno, *Dialektik*, p. 36.

36. Robert A. Heinlein, *Starship Troopers* (1959; reprint, New York: Berkeley Medallion, 1968), 82.

37. Heinlein, p. 83.

38. Heinlein, pp. 82–83.

39. Roland Barthes, "Introduction à l'analyse structurale des récits," *Communication*, no. 8 (1966):p. 8.

40. Barthes, pp. 8–9.

41. Heinlein, p. 81.

42. Heinlein, p. 147.

43. H. Bruce Franklin, *Robert Heinlein: America as Science Fiction* (New York: Oxford, 1980), 112.

44. See my essay "What Makes Hard Science Fiction 'Hard' ?" in *Hard Science Fiction*, ed. George Slusser and Eric Rabkin (Carbondale: Southern Illinois Univ. Pr., 1986), 58–69.

45. As Barthes notes, "indices [imply] metaphorical relata." "Introduction," p. 9.

46. Heinlein, pp. 77–80.

47. Barthes, p. 10.

48. Heinlein, p. 86.

49. Sigmund Freud, *Die Traumdeutung*, *Studienausgabe*, ed. Alexander Mitscherlich, Angela Richards, and James Strachey (Frankfort on the Main: Fischer, 1972), Vol. 2:314.

50. Greimas, pp. 154–57.

51. Max Horkheimer and Theodor Adorno, *Dialektik der Aufklärung* (1947 reprint, Frankfort on the Main: Fischer Taschenbuch, 1971), 94.

52. Greimas, p. 165.

53. Heinlein, p. 84.

54. Gilles Deleuze and Felix Guattari, *L' Anti-Oedipe: capitalisme et schizophrenie* (Paris: Minuit, 1972), 73.

55. Specifically in his classroom oration on pp. 92–93 of the novel.

56. Sigmund Freud, "Triebe und Triebschicksale," in *Psychologie des Unbewußten*, *Studienausgabe* (Frankfort on the Main: Fischer, 1975), Vol. 3: 94–95.

57. Heinlein, p. 86.

58. Deleuze and Guattari, pp. 223–24.

59. Deleuze and Guattari, p. 14.

60. Deleuze and Guattari, p. 16.

61. Deleuze and Guattari, p. 235.

62. Deleuze and Guattari, p. 16.
63. Deleuze and Guattari, p. 36.
64. Freud, "Triebe," p. 95.
65. Adorno, *Dialektik*, p. 149.
66. Adorno, *Dialektik*, p. 147.
67. Deleuze and Guattari, pp. 73–74.
68. Suvin, p. 22.
69. Horkheimer and Adorno, p. 35.
70. Guillen, p. 109.
71. Adorno, *Theorie*, pp. 350–51.
72. Deleuze and Guattari, p. 309.
73. Deleuze and Guattari, p. 280.
74. For a reproduction of Peterson's diagram as well as an excellent survey of modern genre theory, see Ursula Vogt's commentary to her translation of Fubini: *Entstehung und Geschichte der literarischen Gattungen*, Konzepte der Sprach- und Literaturwissenschaft, 7 (Tübingen: Niemeyer, 1971), 83–103.
75. *Encore*, Vol. XX of *Le séminaire*, ed. Jacques-Alain Miller (Paris: Seuil, 1975), 41–43.
76. H. R. Jauss, "Theorie der Gattungen und Literatur des Mittelalters," in *Alterität und Modernität der mittelalterlichen Literatur: Gesammelte Aufsätze 1956–1976* (Munich: Fink, 1977), 339.
77. Horkheimer and Adorno, p. 122.

Biographical Notes

BRIAN ATTEBERY teaches American literature at Idaho State University. He is the author of *The Fantasy Tradition in American Literature*.

J. TIMOTHY BAGWELL teaches humanities and German at Vanderbilt University and writes on semiotics and aesthetic theory.

DAVID CLAYTON has taught at the University of California, San Diego, and at the University of California, Santa Cruz. His specialty is literary theory. He is at work on a book on science fiction and modern fantastic literature.

MICHAEL CLIFTON is in the English Department at Fresno State University and is working on a study of the imagery of visionary states in literature.

MICHAEL R. COLLINGS teaches in the Humanities/Fine Arts Division of Pepperdine University and writes widely on modern fantasy and science fiction.

SAMUEL R. DELANY is the author of the essay collection *Starboard Wine*. His most recent fiction is *The Bridge of Last Desire*.

MICHAEL HOLQUIST is Professor of Comparative Literature at Yale University and a noted authority on Soviet literature and criticism.

KATHRYN HUME is Professor of English at Pennsylvania State University and is the author of *Fantasy and Mimesis*. She has just published a book on Pynchon.

DAVID A. LEIBY is completing his doctorate in English at the University of California, Los Angeles, with a dissertation on time travel literature.

MICHAEL McCLINTOCK is Professor of English at the University of Montana and has written widely of science fiction.

FRANK McCONNELL is Professor of English at the University of California, Santa Barbara, and is well known in the field of film criticism. He is also the author of several mystery novels.

JOSEPH D. MILLER teaches in the Department of Animal Physiology at the University of California, Davis, and works for the National Aeronautics and Space Administration.

CELESTE PERNICONE has completed her MA in English at the University of California, Santa Barbara, and now teaches at that institution.

ERIC S. RABKIN is Professor of English at the University of Michigan and is a noted authority on fantasy literature and theory of narrative.

ROBERT SCHOLES is Andrew W. Mellon Professor of Humanities at Brown University and is noted for his series of Yale University Press books on structuralism and semiotics.

GEORGE SLUSSER is Curator of the Eaton Collection at the University of California, Riverside. He writes on science fiction, science, and literature.

KATHLEEN SPENCER teaches in the English Department at the University of Nebraska. She has published widely on Victorian and early modern fantasy and on science fiction.

ROGER ZELAZNY is the Hugo and Nebula award winning author of *Lord of Light* and *The Dream Master*.

Index